Software Project Management

SOFTWARE PROJECT MANAGEMENT

(For B.Tech, M.Tech, BCA, MCA, B.Sc (Comp. Science) and IT Professionals)

By

BHARAT BHUSHAN AGARWAL
B. Tech. (CS & IT) (Honours), M.Tech
Assistant Professor
Deptt. of Computer Science & Engineering
College of Engineering & Technology (I.F.T.M)
Moradabad, Uttar Pradesh

SHIVANGI DHALL
B.Tech. (CS), MBA (IT & Finance)
Assistant Professor
Deptt. of Computer Science & Information Technology Moradabad Institute of Technology (M.I.T)
Moradabad, Uttar Pradesh

SUMIT PRAKASH TAYAL
B. Tech. (Electronic & Communications), MCAD
Solutions Developer, Tata Technologies.
Michigan, USA

UNIVERSITY SCIENCE PRESS

(An Imprint of Laxmi Publications Pvt. Ltd.)

BANGALORE • CHENNAI • COCHIN • GUWAHATI • HYDERABAD
JALANDHAR • KOLKATA • LUCKNOW • MUMBAI • PATNA
RANCHI • NEW DELHI

Published by :

UNIVERSITY SCIENCE PRESS

(*An Imprint of Laxmi Publications Pvt. Ltd.*)

113, Golden House, Daryaganj,

New Delhi-110002

Phone : 011-43 53 25 00

Fax : 011-43 53 25 28

www.laxmipublications.com

info@laxmipublications.com

First Edition : 2011

OFFICES

✆ **Bangalore**	080-26 75 69 30	✆ **Chennai**	044-24 34 47 26
✆ **Cochin**	0484-237 70 04, 405 13 03	✆ **Guwahati**	0361-251 36 69, 251 38 81
✆ **Hyderabad**	040-24 65 23 33	✆ **Jalandhar**	0181-222 12 72
✆ **Kolkata**	033-22 27 43 84	✆ **Lucknow**	0522-220 99 16
✆ **Mumbai**	022-24 91 54 15, 24 92 78 69	✆ **Patna**	0612-2300097
✆ **Ranchi**	0651-221 47 64		

USP-9616-150-SOFTWARE PROJECT MGMT-AGA **C—**

Typesetted at : Shubham Composer, New Delhi.

Contents

PREFACE

Even though software engineering is formalized into a discipline not quite fifty years ago, software applications today are pervasive and critically important in many areas of society. Although there are many good books about project management and software management, the focus of existing books seem to be either on detail mechanics and tools of project monitoring and task tracking, or about high level ideas and approaches on how organization's capabilities might be improved. This book focuses on the concepts as demanded by the syllabus of Uttar Pradesh Technical University (U.P.T.U).

This book blazes the way toward the next generation of software management practice. Many organizations still cling to the waterfall model because, even with its shortfalls, it provides the most fully elaborated management guidelines on how to proceed in a given software situation.

The B.Tech students in U.P.T.U, Lucknow, are offered a course titled Software Project Management. In order that the students understand the subject thoroughly and do not miss any important concepts, this book has been developed with extreme care. The book is specifically aimed at the students and teachers of this course. The chapters are developed according to the sequence demanded by the Syllabus and also according to the project management life cycle. However, the students/professors should note that due to logical groupings, some chapters contain portions from other areas within the syllabus as they fit better there.

The salient features of book are:

1. Coverage of all the topics in the syllabus of the course
2. Inclusion of many diagrams to facilitate quick understanding to the students
3. Use of simple language
4. Detailed coverage of all important topics.

The book has been divided into thirteen chapters. *Chapter 1* deals with the fundamentals of Software Project Management, including the various problems faced by project managers including project characteristics, constraints, benefits, life cycles etc., have been discussed.

Chapter 2 discusses the various models used in the software development life cycle.

Chapter 3 deals with the various issues and steps involved in software project planning.

Chapters 4 and 5 deals with a very important stage of SPM *i.e.*, Project Scheduling. It includes the detailed discussion on Work Breakdown Structure (WBS), its types, characteristics etc., these chapters also deal with various Project Scheduling Techniques *viz,* Network Diagrams and Bar Charts.

The next three *Chapters 6, 7 and 8* are about the various measures taken for Project Monitoring and Control. These chapters include the fundamentals of Project Monitoring and Control. It also includes the various techniques used for Project Monitoring and Control *viz.*, Earned Value Analysis (EVA) and Software Reviews are discussed in detail.

Chapters 9 and 10 are about the Software Testing and Software Quality. This includes the detailed concepts of Software Testing and how the Software Quality is maintained and achieved including the formal approaches of Software Quality Assurance.

Chapter 11 deals with the Software Configuration Management activity. Various tasks and activities, change control, change request management, version control management are discussed as part of SCM activity.

Chapter 12 deals with Software Project Risk Management. It includes what is risk, its types, sources, process of risk management are covered in details.

Chapter 13 deals with CASE Tools, the important tool used for Software Project Management.

Software project management could be very challenging at times, but can also be very much fun and rewarding. I anticipate that the book serves its intended purpose, and that the students benefit from it in the maximum possible manner and I hope this book can help future software project managers not only to be successful in their projects but also to enjoy the assignment as well.

—Anthors

ACKNOWLEDGEMENT

The authors feel privileged and fortunate enough to retain the affection of following distinguished personalities, Dr. R. M. Dubey, the Managing Director, IFTM Moradabad, and Mr. Prakash M. Telang, Managing Director India Operations, Tata Motors Limited, for providing an environment where one can use their intellect and creativity to develop something fruitful and where one is allowed to get in touch with new up-surging technologies.

We are extremely indebted to Prof. Anupam Srivastava (Director), CET, IFTM Moradabad, Prof. (Dr.) R. Yadav (Director), M.I.T. Moradabad to inspire and motivate us without whose valuable suggestion it would have been difficult to complete the book.

We express our special gratitude, very heartly, to Prof. B.N. Kaul Dean Administration CET, IFTM Moradabad, and Dr. V. Singh Dean Administration M.I.T. Moradabad for their time-to-time suggestions and guidance.

Special thanks are also due to Mr. G.S. Singh, Practice Head, Tata Technologies Ltd. Pune, Mr.Rahul Shandilya, Associate Vice President, Tata Technologies Ltd. Pune, Mr. David Viola, Manager, Chrysler, USA, Mr. Bruce Pendock, Manager, Chrysler, USA, Mr. Simon H Wu, Project Leader, Chrylser, USA, Mr. Christopher Prost, Project Leader, Chrysler, USA, Mr. SG Kulkarni, Project Manager, Tata Technologies Ltd. Pune, Mr. Saurabh Sharma, Delivery Manager, Tata Technologies, USA, Mr. Ramraj Pandey, Consultant, Chrysler , U.S.A., and Mr. R Pandian, Project Manager who have guided, encouraged and advised us throughout the process of writing the book.

We wish to put on record our sincere thanks, honor, and gratitude to our close family members Shri. Akhilesh Kothiwal, Shri K.B. Agarwal, Shri Sandeep Agarwal (brother), consecutive four times elected as MLA of Moradabad (U.P.) and Mr. Ashendra Kumar Agarwal (brother), U.P. Bureau chief of (Rastriya Vishwas and Commissionary, and Dainik Uttaranchal Deep) and Shri. Anil Agarwal, (Manager, Danik Jagran Moradabad) for their soft words, continuous encouragement and necessary help whenever required.

The authors would also like to offer their warm thanks to Dr. S.H.H. Mufti (Director) Ahsan paramedical College and Hospital Moradabad for their intense support and co-operation.

Sincere thanks are also due to Mr. Ashish Gupta (HOD), Department of Computer Science, Mr. Suneet Shukla (HOD), Department of Information Technology, CET, IFTM Moradabad & Mr. Vikas Mittal (HOD), C.S. and IT Department, M.I.T. Moradabad, Dr. S. S. Bedi (HOD), CS and IT Engineering and Technology Rohilkhand Bareilly, Mr L.S Maurya (HOD), Department of Information Technology, SRMS Bareilly, Mr. Yogesh Sharma (HOD), S.D. College of Engineering and Technology for then-encouragement and critical suggestions.

Also we are thankful to Prof. B.K Singh (Chief Proctor), Prof. Intezar Mahdi, Prof. Nikhil Rastogi, Prof. Vikas Gupta, Prof. Rahul Mishra-CET, IFTM, Moradabad who have helped and motivated us for writing this book.

We would like to acknowledge our special thanks to our well-wishers (Dr. Manish Saxena, Dr. Animesh Agarwal, and Mr. Kshitij Shinghal, Mr. Anurag Malik-MIT, Moradabad) for valuable suggestions.

We are indebted to all the colleagues of Tata Technologies Ltd., CS and IT Department, GET, IFTM Moradabad and CS. and IT Department of M.I.T. Moradabad during the whole process of writing the book.

We through our indebtedness to our parents Shri. Ravi Prakash Agarwal and Smt. Bindu Agarwal for their perpetual love and concern which cannot be summed up in words. Our acknowledgement would be incomplete without recognizing Shivangi Dhall's parents Mr. Suresh Kumar Dhall and Mrs. Sushma Dhall for their support and love, is the rock upon which everything else is built.

We are also grateful to Bharat's wife Aparna Agarwal for her words of cheer and encouragement and special thanks to Bharat's little son Dhruv and Gauri (niece) and Shivangi Dhall's brother Mr. Dhiraj Dhall for bearing with us at odd hours.

At last, our sincere heart felt thanks to each and every one, who significantly involved in accomplishing this job.

Finally, I thank God for giving us life and this precious opportunity to be an author for a book and achieve my objective in the provided period. I'd like to end my acknowledgements with the motto, "With God, everything is possible!"

—Authors

1

Introduction to Software Project Management

1.1 FUNDAMENTALS OF SOFTWARE PROJECT MANAGEMENT (SPM)

A software project has two main activity dimensions: engineering and project management. The engineering dimension deals with building the system and focuses on issues such as how to design, test, code, and so on. The project management dimension deals with properly planning and controlling the engineering activities to meet project goals for cost, schedule, and quality.

Software project management is an umbrella activity within software engineering. It begins before any technical activity is initiated and continues throughout the definition, development, and support of computer software. Software project management encompasses the knowledge, techniques, and tools necessary to manage the development of software products.

1.1.1 Software

Software is described by its capabilities. The capabilities relate to the functions it executes, the features it provides and the facilities it offers. Software written for sales-order processing would have different functions to process different types of sales orders from different market segments. The features, for example, would be to handle multi-currency computing, updating of product, sales and tax status in MIS reports and books of accounts. The facilities could be printing of sales orders, e-mail to customers, reports and advice to the stores department to dispatch the goods. The facilities and features could be optional and based on customer choice.

The software is developed keeping in mind certain hardware and operating system considerations, known as platform. Hence, software is described along with its capabilities and the platform specifications that are required to run it.

1.1.1.1 Definition of Software

Software is a set of instructions to acquire inputs and to manipulate them to produce the desired output in terms of functions and performance as determined by the user of the software. It also includes a set of documents, such as the software manual, meant for users to understand the software system. Today's software comprises the Source Code, Executables, Design Documents, Operations and System Manuals and Installation and Implementation Manuals.

Software is:

(*i*) Instructions (computer programs) that when executed provide desired function and performance.

(*ii*) Data structures that enable the programs to adequately manipulate information.

(*iii*) Documents that describe the operation and use of the programs.

OR

The term software refers to the set of computer programs, procedures, and associated documents (flowcharts, manuals, etc.) that describe the programs and how they are to be used. To be precise, software means a collection of programs whose objective is to enhance the capabilities of the hardware.

OR

Definition of Software given by IEEE

"Software is the collection of computer programs, procedure rules and associated documentation and data."

1.1.1.2 Importance of Software

Computer software has become a driving force:

- It is engine that drives business decision-making.
- It serves as the basis for modern scientific investigation and engineering problem solving.
- It is embedded in all kinds of systems like transportation, medical, telecommunications, military, industrial processes, entertainment, office products etc.

It is important as it affects nearly every aspect of our lives and has become pervasive in our commerce, our culture and our everyday activities software impact on our society and culture is significant. As software importance grows, the software community continually attempts to develop technologies that will make it easier, faster and less expensive to build high-quality computer programs.

1.1.2 Project

The word "project" was first used in or around the sixteenth century and derives from the Latin *projicere* (= throw forward). The Latin root thus suggests movement, a trajectory, a certain relationship with space and time.

A project is a unique venture with specific start and end dates. This is different from an ongoing task that doesn't have an end date. Projects are run by people and often involve different parts of an organization. Constraints on project include cost, schedule, resources, and quality. There's a give and taken between these items *i.e.*, you can't have it all. Usually projects are divisible into stages or phases each with their own set of priorities and goals.

1.1.2.1 Definitions

A project is a temporary activity characterized by having a start date, specific objectives and constraints, established responsibilities, a budget and schedule, and a completion date.

OR

A project is a set of related tasks that are coordinated to achieve specific objectives in a given time limit.

OR

"A project is a series of activities or tasks that have a specific objective to be completed within certain specifications, have defined start and end dates, have funding limits (if applicable), and consume resources (*i.e.*, money, people, equipment)." **Harold Kerzner**

OR

James Lewis views a project

"as a one-time job that has definite starting and ending points, clearly defined objectives, scope and a budget; differentiated from repetitive activities such as production, order processing and so on; a special activity with very tactical goals."

OR

The Oxford English Dictionary defines "project" as

"An individual or collaborative enterprise that is carefully planned and designed to achieve a particular aim: [*e.g.*,] *a research project/a nationwide project to encourage business development*".

OR

A project is a unique, temporary endeavor with defined start and end dates to achieve one or more objectives within the constraints of cost, schedule and quality performance.

OR

A temporary endeavor undertaken to create a unique product, service, or result.

OR

Project is a process in which all aspects of a proposed project are explored to examine the relationship between activities, events, durations, and costs. Areas of uncertainty or conflict are identified, and possible alternatives or trade-offs are developed to strike a satisfactory balance.

OR

A project, by definition, is a temporary activity with a starting date, specific goals and conditions, defined responsibilities, a budget, a planning, a fixed end date and multiple parties involved.

1.1.2.2 Characteristics of a Project

The various characteristics of a project are as follows:

1. *Projects have a purpose*: Projects have clearly-defined aims and set out to produce clearly-defined results. Their purpose is to solve a "problem", and this involves analyzing needs beforehand. Suggesting one or more solutions, it aims at lasting social change.
2. *Projects are realistic*: Their aims must be achievable, and this means taking account both of requirements and of the financial and human resources available.
3. *Projects are limited in time and space*: They have a beginning and an end, and are implemented in a specific place and context.
4. *Projects are complex*: Projects call on various planning and implementation skills, and involve various partners and players.
5. *Projects are collective*: Projects are the product of collective endeavour. They are run by teams, involve various partners and cater for the needs of others.

6. *Projects are unique*: All projects stem from new ideas. They provide a specific response to a need (problem) in a specific context. They are innovative.
7. *Projects are an adventure*: Every project is different and ground-breaking; they always involve some uncertainty and risk.
8. *Projects can be assessed*: Projects are planned and broken down into measurable aims, which must be open to evaluation.
9. *Projects are made up of stages*: Projects have distinct, identifiable stages.

1.1.2.3 Prerequisites of a Project

According to an American thinker **John Dewey**, a project has four prerequisites:

- a communal reflection process, which shapes its growth and development;
- observation of the conditions in the environment where it is devised;
- knowledge of what has happened in similar situations in the past;
- an approach which synthesizes observation of the present and knowledge of the past and so identifies their meaning.

Thus, a project:

- is a method which enables us to move from idea to action, structuring the various stages in that process.
- sets out to alter the environment in which it is to take place.
- has an educational dimension and enables people to learn by experiment.
- is the product of collective activity.

1.1.2.4 Examples of Notable Projects

- Human Genome Project which mapped the human genome
- Manhattan Project, which developed the first nuclear weapon
- Polaris missile project: an ICBM control-system
- Project Apollo, which landed humans on the moon
- Soviet atomic bomb project
- Soviet manned lunar projects and programs.

1.1.2.5 Problems with Software Projects

A survey of managers is done, which identified the following commonly experienced problems during a project the following problems of software projects are from the manager's point of view:

- Poor estimates and plans;
- Lack of quality standards and measures;
- Lack of guidance about making organizational decisions;
- Lack of techniques to make progress visible;
- Poor role definition—who does what?
- Incorrect success criteria.

Below is a list of the problems identified by a number of Computing and Information System degree students who had just completed a year's industrial placement:

- Inadequate specification of work;
- Management ignorance of ICT;

- Lack of knowledge of application area;
- Lack of standards;
- Lack of up-to-date documentation;
- Preceding activities not completed on time—including late delivery of equipment;
- Lack of communication between users and technicians;
- Lack of communication leading to duplication of work;
- Lack of commitment—especially when a project is tied to one person who then moves;
- Narrow scope of technical expertise;
- Changing statutory requirements;
- Deadline pressure;
- Lack of quality control;
- Remote management;
- Lack of training.

The various problems which are faced by the customers of the product of computer projects. Some reported problematic projects have swallowed up huge amounts of money:

- The United States Internal Revenue System abandoned a tax system modernization programme after having spent $4 billion.
- The state of California spent $1 billion on its non-functional welfare database system.

1.1.2.6 Reasons why Project Fails or Succeeds

There are eight reasons why projects succeed:

1. The organizational structure is suited to the project team.
2. The project team participates in planning.
3. The project team is committed to establishing schedules.
4. The project team is committed to establishing realistic budgets.
5. The project makes proper use of network planning techniques and does not let the plan become an end at itself.
6. The project team works with bureaucracy, politics and procedures and not against them.
7. The project team agrees on specific and realistic project goals.
8. The target public is involved from the start of the project.

There are eight reasons why some projects fail:

1. Inadequate authority.
2. Lack of project team participation and planning.
3. Lack of project team participation in problem solving.
4. Inadequate communication skills.
5. Inadequate technical skills.
6. Inadequate administrative skills.
7. Unrealistic project schedules.
8. Unclear project goals.

1.1.3 Management

Management is defined, in simple terms as the skill or practice of controlling, directing or planning something; "The act of directing, or managing for a purpose". In other words, it is the effort of planning, organizing and mobilizing people and resources for a given purpose. It involves the activities and tasks undertaken by one or more persons for the purpose of planning and controlling the activities of others in order to achieve objectives that could not be achieved by the others acting alone.

1.1.3.1 Management Activities

Management involves the following activities:

1. *Planning*: Deciding what is to be done
2. *Organizing*: Making arrangement
3. *Staffing*: Selecting the right people for the job etc
4. *Directing*: Giving instructions
5. *Monitoring*: Checking on progress
6. *Controlling*: Taking action to remedy hold-ups
7. *Innovating*: Coming up with new solutions
8. *Representing*: Liasing with clients, users, developers, suppliers, and other stake-holders.

1.1.3.2 Key Objectives of Effective Management

A software development manager must keep in mind quality, productivity, and risk reduction throughout the planning and execution of product development.

1. *Quality*: Quality is best achieved by careful adherence to standards, effective development techniques, and periodic technical review throughout the process. Management must cooperate and coordinate with quality assurance organizations, if they exist. The Japanese emphasis on continuous quality improvement and its remarkable results offer important lessons for software developers.
2. *Productivity*: Increased productivity lowers costs. In the current state of development technology, the most important productivity factors are the ability of the individual software engineers, the tools they work with, and the work environment
3. *Risk reduction*: Managers should identify the most difficult parts of a particular development and systematically come to grips with efficient solutions. Requirements that can become "show-stoppers" later must be dealt with early in the process.

1.2 SOFTWARE PROJECT MANAGEMENT

Software project management is the art and science of planning and leading software projects. It is a sub-discipline of project management in which software projects are planned, monitored and controlled.

1.2.1 Definitions

Software Project Management is the process of planning, organizing, staffing, monitoring, controlling and leading a software project' **(ANSI/IEEE Std 1058.1-1987).**

OR

Software Project management is a discipline of project in which software projects are planned, monitored and controlled.

OR

Project management is the application of knowledge, skills, tools and techniques to project activities to meet project requirements.

OR

Project management methodology:" the planning, monitoring and control of all aspects of the project and the motivation of all those involved in it to achieve the project objectives on time and to the specified cost, quality, and performance.

OR

Project management is the complete set of tasks, techniques, tools applied during project execution."

1.2.2 Objectives of SPM

The project objectives define the target status at the end of the project. The abbreviation S.M.A.R.T. is sometimes used to describe well defined objectives:

1. **Specific:** Effective objectives are concrete and well defined. Vague aspirations such as "to improve customer relations" are unsatisfactory. Objectives should be defined in such a way that it is obvious to all whether the project has been successful or not.
2. **Measurable:** Ideally there should be measures of effectiveness which tell us how successful the project has been. For example, 'to reduce customer complaints' would be more satisfactory as an objective than 'to improve customer relations'. The measure can, in some cases, be an answer to simple yes/no question, *e.g.* 'did we install the new software by 9 May?'
3. **Achievable:** It must be within the power of the individual or group to achieve the objective. Agreement with all the stakeholders what the goal should be. Is there a realistic path to achievement?
4. **Relevant:** The objective must be relevant to the true purpose of the project.
5. **Time constrained:** There should be a defined point in time by which the objective should have been achieved.

1.2.3 Activities of SPM

Software project management encompasses the following activities: measurement, project estimating, risk analysis, scheduling, tracking, and control.

1. **Measurement and metrics:** To be most effective, software metrics should be collected for both the process and the product. Process oriented metrics can be collected during the process and after it has been completed. Process metrics collected during the process focus on the efficacy of quality assurance activities change management, and project management. Process metrics collected after a projected has been completed examine quality and productivity. Process measures are normalized using either lines of code or function points so that data collected from many different projects can be compared and analyzed in a consistent manner. Product metrics measure technical characteristics of the software that provide an indication of software quality measure can be applied to models created during analysis and design activities, the source code and testing data .

2. **Project estimating:** Scheduling and budgets are often dictated by business issues. The role of estimating within the software process often serves as a "sanity check" on the predefined deadlines and budgets that have been established by management. (Ideally, the software engineering organization should be intimately involved in establishing deadlines and budgets, but this is not a perfect or fair world)

   All software project estimation techniques require that the project have a bounded scope, and all rely on a high level functional decomposition of the project and an assessment of project difficulty and complexity. There are three broad classes of estimation techniques for software projects:

   (*a*) *Effort estimation techniques*: The project manager creates a matrix in which the left hand column contains a list of major system functions derived using functional decomposition applied to project scope. The top row contains a list of major software engineering tasks derived from the common process framework. The manager (with the assistance of technical staff) estimates the effort required to accomplish each task for each function.

   (*b*) *Size-oriented estimation*: A list of major system functions derived using functional decomposition applied to project scope. The "size" of each function is estimated using either Lines of Code (LOC) or Function Points (FP). Average productivity data (for instance, function points per person month) for similar functions or projects are used to generate an estimate of effort required for each function.

   (*c*) *Empirical models*: Using the results of a large population of past projects, an empirical model that relates product size (in LOC or FP) to effort is developed using a statistical technique such as regression analysis. The product size for the work to be done is estimated and the empirical model is used to generate projected effort.

   In addition to the above techniques, a software project manager can develop estimate by analogy. That is, by examining similar past projects and projecting effort and duration recorded for these projects to the current situation.

3. **Risk assessment, risk prioritization and risk management:** The goals of these activities are:

   (*a*) to identify those risks that have a high likelihood of occurrence

   (*b*) to assess the consequence (impact) of each risk should it occur, and

   (*c*) to develop a plan for mitigating the risks when possible, monitoring factors that may indicate, their arrival, and developing a set of contingency plans should they occur.

4. **Scheduling:** The process definition and project management activities that have been discussed above feed the scheduling activity. The common process framework provides a work breakdown structure for scheduling. Available human resources, coupled with effort estimates and risk analysis provide the task interdependencies, parallelism, and time lines that are used in constructing a project schedule.

5. **Tracking and control:** Project tracking and control is most effective when it becomes an integral part of software engineering work. A well defined process framework should provide a set of milestones that can be used for project tracking. Control focuses on two major issues: quality and change.

   To control quality, a software project team must establish effective techniques for software quality assurance, and to control change, the team should establish a software configuration management framework.

1.2.4 Importance of SPM

A project must successfully pass through each of the project phases in order to continue to the next. Because the organization usually commits more money as a project continues, a management review should occur after each phase to evaluate progress, likely success, and continued compatibility with organization goals. These management reviews, called phase exit or kill points, are very important for keeping project on track and determining if they should be continued, redirected, or terminated. Recall that projects are just one part of entire system of an organization. Changes in other parts of the organization might affect what is happening on projects, and what happens on projects might likewise affect what is happening in other parts of the organization. By breaking projects into phases, senior management can make sure that the projects are still compatible with needs of the rest of company.

Let's take another look at the opening case. Suppose Tom Walters' college did a study on increasing the use of technology. At the end of the concept phase, the project team could have presented information to the faculty and administration that described different options for increasing the use of technology, an analysis of what competing colleges were doing, and result of a survey of local stakeholders opinions on the subject. This presentation at the end of the concept phase represents a management review. Suppose the study reported that 90 percent of students, faculty, and staff surveyed strongly opposed the idea of requiring all students to have laptops and that many adult students said they would attend other colleges if they were required to pay for the additional technology. The college would probably decide not to pursue this idea any further. Had Tom taken a phased approach, he and his staff would not have wasted the time and money it took to develop more detailed plans.

1.2.5 SPM Framework

According to the Software Engineering Institute (SEI), a methodology must possess certain attributes in order to meet the requirements of being called a methodology another framework for methodologies is the software engineering body of knowledge that contains other knowledge development methods to be used by any professional software engineer.

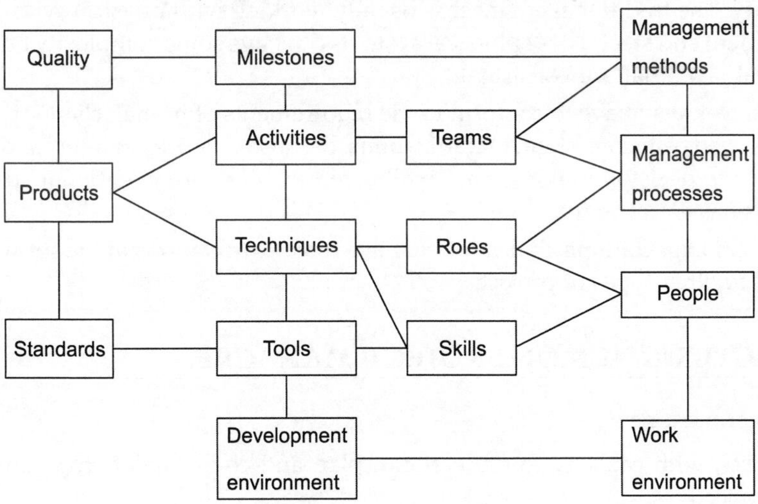

Fig. 1.1 SPM framework

SPM framework is a process pattern view of project activities. This approach focuses on the communication and people centric aspects of project management. Software project management can be built on this framework.

1.3 SOFTWARE PROJECTS V/S OTHER TYPES OF PROJECTS

Software projects have several properties that make them very different to other kinds of engineering project:

1. **Invisibility/the Product is Intangible:** It's hard to claim a bridge is 90% complete if there is not 90% of the bridge there. It is easy to claim that a software project is 90% complete, even if there are no visible outcomes.
2. **We don't have Much Experience:** Software engineering is a new discipline, and so we simply don't have much understanding of how to engineer large scale software projects.
3. **Complexity:** Software products contain more complexity than other engineered artifacts (such as bridge or road). We can't measure the complexity of a software project until we actually work on it.
4. **Large Software Projects are Often "Bespoke":** Most large software systems are one-off, with experience gained in one project being of little help in another.
5. **The Technology Changes Very Quickly:** Most large software projects employ new technology; for many projects, this is the raison d'etre (means the purpose that justify a things existence).
6. **Working:** Software projects are based on logical work while others are based on physical work
7. **Flexibility:** The ease with which software can be changed is usually seen as one of its strength. Software projects are flexible. Customer only wants final results, so rest of things are in control of the programmer he can modify software at any stage while this thing is not in other projects, as everything is in front of customers, he is aware about progress, he can view what work is being done by project manager and team, so it is not in the hands of project team to make changes at any stage of the project.
8. **Conformity:** The traditional engineer is usually working with physical systems and materials like cement and steel. These physical systems can have some complexity but are governed by physical laws that are consistent.
   Software developers have to conform to the requirements of human clients; it is not just that individuals can be inconsistent. Organizations, because of lapses in internal communication or in effective decision-making, can exhibit remarkable 'organizational stupidity' which developers have to cater for.
9. **Stakeholders Expectations:** Stakeholders have more expectations in the software projects as compared to other types of project.

1.4 CHARACTERISTICS OF PROJECT MANAGER

A project manager must be:

1. *An **organiser**,* with capacity to understand, plan and co-ordinate efforts and resources to meet the objectives.
2. *A **strategist**,* able to set clear long and short-term objectives, keeping these in mind together with the reasons for the project's existence.

3. *A* ***motivator,*** with skills and attitudes enabling him/her to motivate and commit people to the project or to participate in it (workers, volunteers, young people).
4. *A* ***fund-raiser,*** with knowledge and confidence to apply for funds to administer and account for them with integrity and competence.
5. *An* ***activist,*** in the meaning of someone able to spot initiatives and to organise ideas into meaningful social actions with clear values evolving over time.
6. A ***visionary,*** someone able to imagine social innovation and change.
7. *A* ***community worker*** with particular concern for the affairs of the community or/and organization he/she are involved in.
8. *A* ***social worker,*** capable of caring for people without replacing them, *i.e.*, instilling in them the motivation and confidence to take part in shaping their own future and realizing their projects.
9. ***A teacher and a learner*** capable of empowering people while at the same time being able to learn from the experiences and use that for the organization, project or community—monitoring and evaluating a process in relation to the objectives, changing plans and ultimately objectives in relation to the circumstances.

1.5 PROJECT MANAGERS ROLES & RESPONSIBILITIES

When they are appointed, project managers should be given terms of reference that define their:

- objectives;
- responsibilities;
- limits of authority.

The objective of every project manager is to deliver the product on time, within budget and with the required quality. Although the precise responsibilities of a project manager will vary from company to company and from project to project, they should always include planning and forecasting. Three additional areas of management responsibility defined by Mintzberg [Ref. 17] are:

1. ***Interpersonal responsibilities,*** which include:
   - leading the project team;
   - liaising with initiators, senior management and suppliers;
   - being the 'figurehead', *i.e.*, setting the example to the project team and representing the project on formal occasions.
2. ***Informational responsibilities,*** which include:
   - monitoring the performance of staff and the implementation of the project plan;
   - disseminating information about tasks to the project team;
   - disseminating information about project status to initiators and
   - senior management;
   - acting as the spokesman for the project team.
3. ***Decisional responsibilities,*** which include:
   - allocating resources according to the project plan, and adjusting those allocations when circumstances dictate (*i.e.*, the project manager has responsibility for the budget);
   - negotiating with the initiator about the optimum interpretation of contractual obligations, with the company management for resources, and with project staff about their tasks;

- handling disturbances to the smooth progress of the project such as equipment failures and personnel problems.

1.6 SOME TERMINOLOGIES

Some terminologies are discussed in these sections which are frequently used in the field of Software Project Management.

1. **Deliverables:** Deliverable is any unique and verifiable product, result, or capability to perform a service that must be produced to complete a process, phase, or project. A deliverable is an output of the project that can meaningfully be assessed. In other words, *Deliverables* are project results delivered to customers. Different *deliverables* are generated during software development. The examples are source code, user manuals, operating procedure manuals etc.

   Deliverables are results the project must deliver so the client can achieve their objectives. Deliverables include: Facilities, systems, equipment, product designs, hardware, software, services, documentation, training, support, new methods and procedures. Projects deliverables are produced by the project and may be defined in a Statement of Work attached to the contract. Phases and activities may produce intermediate deliverables such as specifications, documents and components required to complete the project. Deliverables are indicators (but only indicators) of progress.
2. **Milestone:** A milestone is a scheduled event signifying the completion of a major deliverable or a set of related deliverables. In other words, *Milestones* are the end-point of a process activity. A milestone has zero duration and no effort—there is no work associated with a milestone. It is a flag in the work plan to signify some other work has completed.

   The *milestones* are the events that are used to ascertain the status of the project. Finalization of specification is a milestone. Completion of design documentation is another milestone. Thus, a milestone is a point at which progress on the project may be assessed. It is typically a major turning point in the project. The milestones are essential for project planning and management.

   Usually a milestone is used as a project checkpoint to validate how the project is progressing and revalidate work. Milestones are also used as high-level snapshots for management to validate the progress of the project. In many cases there is a decision to be made at a milestone. The examples are:
   - delivery of requirements spec;
   - delivery of alpha tested code.

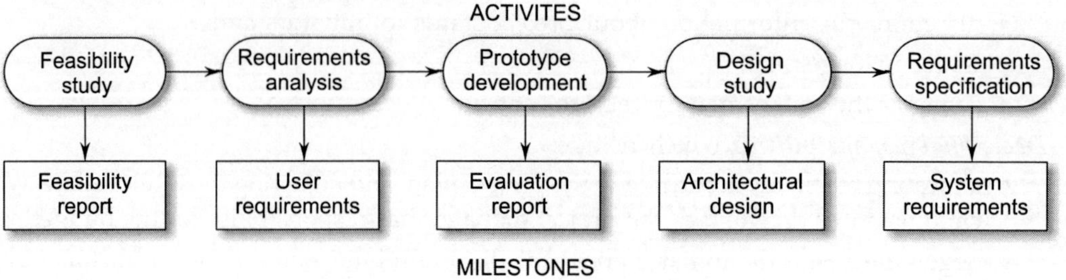

Fig. 1.2 Example showing milestones

3. **Product and Process:** What is delivered to the customer is called a ***product***? It may include source code specification document, manuals, documentation etc. Basically, it is nothing but a set of deliverables only.

   Process is the way in which we produce software. It is the collection of activity that leads to (a part of) a product. An efficient process is required to produce good quality products.

   If the process is weak, the ends product will undoubtedly suffer, but an obsessive over reliance on process is also dangerous.

4. **Measures, Metrics and Indicators:** In software engineering ***measures*** provides a quantitative indication of amount, dimension, capacity or size of given attribute of a product.

   The ***metrics*** is a quantitative measures of the degree to which a system, component, or process possesses a given attribute of a product. An ***indicator*** is a combination of metrics.

   Measurement occurs as the result of the collection of one or more data points (*e.g.*, a number of module reviews are investigated to collect measures of the number of errors in each module.

1.7 STAKEHOLDERS

"Anyone with an interest (stake) in the projects successful completion".

Stakeholders are an integral part of a project. They are the end-users or clients, the people from whom requirements will be drawn, the people who will influence the design and, ultimately, the people who will reap the benefits of your completed project.

It is extremely important to involve stakeholders in all phases of the project for two reasons: *Firstly*, experience shows that their involvement in the project significantly increases the chances of success by building in a self-correcting feedback loop. *Secondly*, involving them in the project builds confidence in a product and will greatly ease its acceptance in the target audience.

Stakeholders are anyone who has an interest in the project. They may also exert influence over the project's objectives and outcomes. The project management team must identify the stakeholders, determine their requirements and expectations, and, to the extent possible, manage their influence in relation to the requirements to ensure a successful project. The various activities in a project that add value to a stakeholder include:

- improved productivity
- reduced rework
- cost savings
- streamlined business processes
- automation of previously manual tasks
- ability to perform entirely new tasks or functions
- conformance to current standards or regulations
- improved usability or reduced frustration level compared to current applications.

1.7.1 Definitions

Project stakeholders are individuals and organizations that are actively involved in the project, or whose interests may be affected as a result of project execution or project completion.

OR

Stakeholder is any individual, group or organization, community, with an interest in the outcome of a programme/project.

OR

"Any person or organization that is actively involved in a project, or whose interests may be positively or negatively affected by execution or completion of the project".

OR

Stakeholders are the specific people or groups who have a stake, or an interest, in the outcome of the project. Normally stakeholders are from within the company, and could include internal clients, management, employees, administrators... etc.

OR

Stakeholders are individuals, groups, or organizations that are actively involved in a project, are affected by its outcome, or can influence its outcome.

OR

Project stakeholders are those entities within or outside an organization which:

(*a*) Sponsor a project or,

(*b*) Have an interest or a gain upon a successful completion of a project.

(*c*) May have a positive or negative influence in the Project Completion.

1.7.2 Examples of Project Stakeholders

The example of project stakeholders includes the following:

- Project leader
- Project team members
- Upper management
- Project customer
- Resource Managers
- Line Managers
- Product user group
- Project testers.

There are narrower views of the term stakeholder, focusing on the influencers and decision-makers of a business or technological change. In this context, stakeholders are managers who have the organizational authority to allocate resources (people, money, services) and set priorities for their own organizations in support of a change. They are the people who make or break a change.

1.8 VISION AND SCOPE OF A PROJECT

A project's scope defines the broad parameters of the project, be it an eco-regional programme, an effort to conserve a priority area, an initiative to combat a particular threat, or actions to protect a species. Efforts to conserve or effectively manage eco-regions, priority areas, or protected areas typically have a geographic scope or project area. Efforts to address threats, enabling conditions, or species have a thematic scope.

A project's vision is the desired state or ultimate condition that the project is working to achieve. It is typically expressed in a vision statement which is a clear and brief summary of what the project team members and their partners would like to achieve.

1.8.1 Why is Defining a Scope and Vision Important?

A project's scope and vision define the broad parameters of the project and provide the foundation for all subsequent steps in project or programme cycle. A clear scope sets the rough boundaries for what the project will attempt to do. For example, in a project with a geographic scope that encompasses a specific protected area, while some actions may be directed outside of the project area, the project scope makes it clear what the team is focusing on and where the final outcomes will be measured.

Likewise, defining a vision enables the core project team members to discuss and agree on what the broad purpose of their project will be. Although this should be a relatively easy task in many conservation projects, it becomes particularly important in multi-stakeholder efforts in which the different partners may have radically different ideas of what they would like to accomplish. If some of the stakeholders are interested in conservation and others are primarily interested in using natural resources to promote rapid economic development, then at the very least, you need to negotiate how you will work together. Without clear boundaries, there may be considerable confusion among staff and stakeholders as to where the project ends, and there is a risk of being drawn into an ever-widening circle of interventions. A well crafted vision statement grabs and directs the project team's attention, sets their agenda, and energizes their work. This statement becomes the common starting point for discussion about more specific activities and outcomes.

1.8.2 Vision & Scope Document

The vision and scope document is one of the most important tools that a project manager has; it is also one of the easiest to implement. A good vision and scope document will help a project avoid some of the costliest problems that a project can face. By writing the document and circulating it among everyone involved in the project, the project manager can ensure that each of the stakeholders and engineers share a common understanding of the needs being addressed—and that the software must address them.

Table 1.1 Vision and scope document outline

1. **Problem Statement**
(*a*) Project background
(*b*) Stakeholders
(*c*) Users
(*d*) Risks
(*e*) Assumptions
2. **Vision of the Solution**
(*a*) Vision statement
(*b*) List of features
(*c*) Scope of phased release (optional)
(*d*) Features that will not be developed

1. **Problem Statement**
   (*a*) *Project background*: This section contains a summary of the problem that the project will solve. It should provide a brief history of the problem and an explanation of how the organization justified the decision to build software to address it. This section should cover the reasons that the problem exists, the organization's history with this problem,

any previous projects which were undertaken to try to address it, and the way that the decision to begin this project was reached.

(b) *Stakeholders*: This is a bulleted list of the stakeholders. Each stakeholder may be referred to by name or by title or role ("support group manager", "CTO", "senior manager"). The needs of each stakeholder are described in a few sentences.

(c) *Users*: This is a bulleted list of the users. As with the stakeholders, each user can either be referred to by name or role ("support rep", "call quality auditor", "home website user")—however, if there are many users, it is usually inefficient to try to name each one. The needs of each user are described.

(d) *Risks*: This section lists any potential risks to the project. It should be generated by a project team's brainstorming session. It could include external factors that could impact the project, issues or problems that could potentially cause project delays or raise issues. (The process for assessing and mitigating risk can be used to generate the risks for this section.)

(e) *Assumptions*: This is the list of assumptions that the stakeholders, users or project team have made. Often, these assumptions are generated during a Wideband Delphi estimation session. If Wideband Delphi is being used, the rest of the vision and scope document should be ready before the Delphi meeting and used as the basis for estimation. The assumptions generated during the estimation kickoff meeting should then be reviewed, and any non-technical assumptions should be copied into this section. (Technical assumptions—meaning assumptions that affect the design and development but not the scope of the project—should not be included in this document. The estimate results will still contain a record of these assumptions, but they are not useful for this particular audience.)

If Wideband Delphi is not being used to generate the assumptions, the project manager should hold a brainstorming session with the team to come up with a list of assumptions instead.

2. **Vision of the Solution**

(a) *Vision statement*: The goal of the vision statement is to describe what the project is expected to accomplish. It should explain what the purpose of the project is. This should be a compelling reason, a solid justification for spending time, money and resources on the project. The best time to write the vision statement is after talking to the stakeholders and users and writing down their needs; by this time, a concrete understanding of the project should be starting to jell.

(b) *List of features*: This section contains a list of features. A feature is as a cohesive area of the software that fulfills a specific need by providing a set of services or capabilities. Any software package—in fact, any engineered product—can be broken down into features. The project manager can choose the number of features in the vision and scope document by changing the level of detail or granularity of each feature, and by combining multiple features into a single one. Sometimes those features are small ("screw-top cap", "holds one liter of liquid"); sometimes they are big ("four wheel drive", "seats seven passengers"). It is useful to describe a product in about ten features in the vision and scope document, because this usually yields a level of complexity that most people reading it are comfortable with. Adding too many features will overwhelm most readers, and each extra feature adds time and effort to the project and makes it difficult or unrealistic to accomplish.

Each feature should be listed in a separate paragraph or bullet point. It should be given a name, followed by a description of the functionality that it provides. This description does not need to be detailed; it can simply be a few sentences that give a general explanation of the feature. However, if there is more information that a stakeholder or project team member feels should be included, it is important to include that information. For example, it is sometimes useful to include a use case in a specific feature (see Chapter 6), as long as it is written in such a way that all of the stakeholders can read and understand it.

(c) *Scope of phased release (optional)*: Sometimes software projects are released in phases: a version of the software with some subset of the features is released first, and a newer, more complete version is released later. This section describes the plan for a phased release, if that approach is to be taken.

This is useful when there is an important deadline for the software, but developing the entire software project by that deadline would be unrealistic. The most common way to compromise on this release date is to divide the features into two or more releases. In that case, this section should identify specifically when those versions will be released, and which features will be included in each version. It's reasonable to divide one feature up between two releases, as long as it is made clear exactly how that will happen. If a project manager needs to release a project in phases, it is critical that the project team be consulted. Some features are much more difficult to divide than others, and the engineers might see dependencies between features that are not clear to the stakeholders and project manager. After the phased release plan is written down and agreed upon, the project team should always be asked to re-estimate the effort and a new project plan should be generated. This will ensure that the phased release is feasible and compatible with the company's priorities.

(d) *Features that will not be developed*: Features are often left out of a project on purpose. When a feature is explicitly left out of the software, it should be added to this section to tell the reader that a decision was made to exclude it. For example, one way to handle an unrealistic deadline is by removing one or more features from the software, in which case the removed features should be moved into this section. The reason these features should be moved rather than deleted from the document is that otherwise readers might assume that they were overlooked and bring the up in a review. This is especially important during the review of the document because it allows everyone to agree on the exclusion of the feature (or object to it).

1.9 PROJECT MANAGEMENT CYCLE

Project management is the application of knowledge, skills, tools and techniques to project activities to meet project requirements. Project management is accomplished through the application and integration of the project management processes of initiating, planning, executing, monitoring and controlling, and closing.

OR

Project management is a combination of techniques, procedures, people, and systems focused on the successful completion of a project. It is also a discipline that will support the planning, implementation, tracking, and control of projects.

OR

Project management is a set of principles, practices, techniques, and facilitation of the planning, scheduling, and control of all activities that must be done to meet project objectives. It is a disciplined way of organizing a job and leading a team to help control costs, manage scope, performance, and outcomes and also to mitigate risks.

"The project life cycle consists of four phases as shown in Fig. 1.4. A detailed description of the project management methodology and life cycle is as follows:

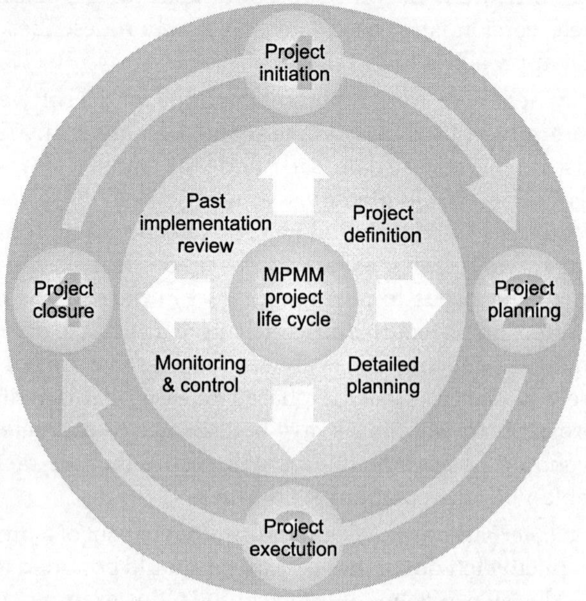

Fig. 1.3 The four phases of the project life cycle

1. **Project Initiation:** Project Initiation is the first phase in the Project Life Cycle and essentially involves starting up the project. We initiate a project by defining its purpose and scope, the justification for initiating it, documenting a business case, feasibility study, terms of reference and the solution to be implemented. Also we need to recruit a suitably skilled project team, set up a Project Office and perform an end of Phase Review. The Project Initiation phase involves the following six key steps:

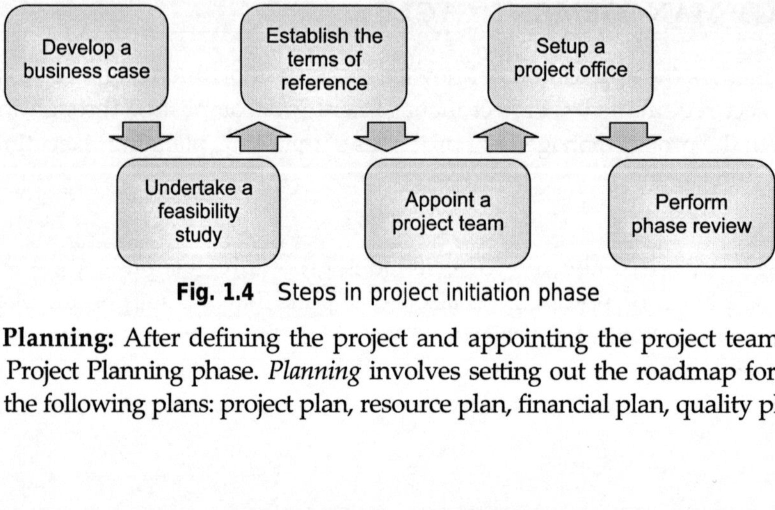

Fig. 1.4 Steps in project initiation phase

2. **Project Planning:** After defining the project and appointing the project team, we enter the detailed Project Planning phase. *Planning* involves setting out the roadmap for the project by creating the following plans: project plan, resource plan, financial plan, quality plan, acceptance

plan and communications plan *i.e.,* creating a suite of planning documents to help guide the team throughout the project delivery. The Planning Phase involves completing the following 10 key steps:

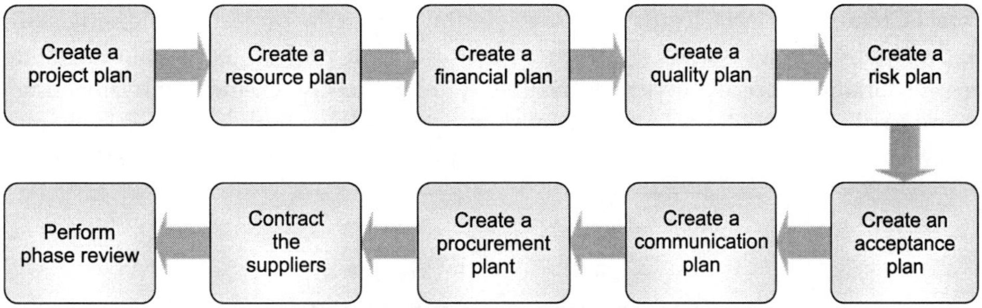

Fig. 1.5 Steps in project planning phase

3. **Project Execution:** With a clear definition of the project and a suite of detailed project plans, we are now ready to enter the execution phase of the project. This is the phase in which the deliverables are physically built and presented to the customer for acceptance. While each deliverable is being constructed, a suite of management *processes* are undertaken to monitor and control the deliverables being output by the project.

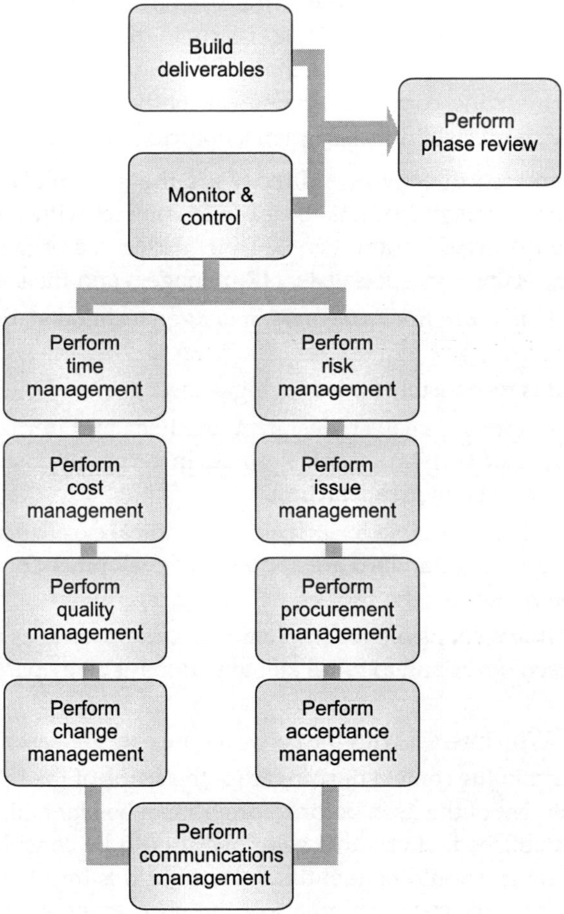

Fig. 1.6 Steps in project execution phase

These processes include managing time, cost, quality, change, risks, issues, suppliers, customers and communication. Once all the deliverables have been produced and the customer has accepted the final solution, the project is ready for closure.

4. **Project Closure:** Project Closure involves winding-down the project by releasing staff, handing the final deliverables to the customer, handing over project documentation to the business, terminating supplier contracts, releasing project resources and communicating project closure to all stakeholders. The last remaining step is to undertake a Post Implementation Review to identify the level of project success and note any lessons learned for future projects.

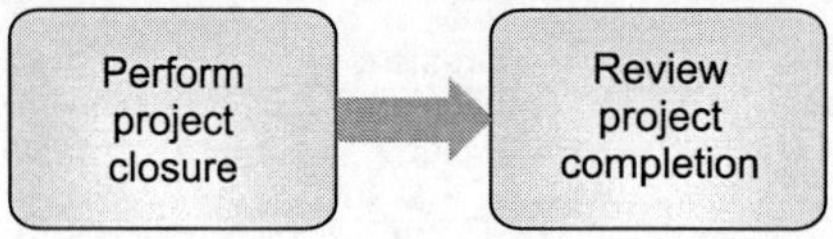

Fig. 1.7 Steps in project closure phase

1.10 MANAGEMENT SPECTRUM

Effective software project management focuses on the four P's: people, product, process, and project. The order is not arbitrary. The manager who forgets that software engineering work is an intensely human endeavor will never have success in project management. A manager who fails to encourage comprehensive customer communication early in the evolution of a project risks building an elegant solution for the wrong problem. Finally, the manager who pays little attention to the process runs the risk of inserting competent technical methods and tools into a vacuum. The manager who embarks without a solid project plan jeopardizes the success of the product.

1. **People:** People connected directly or indirectly are the dynamic and live factor in project management. Project management has to deal and interact with different levels of people within and outside the organization. People from within the organization are developers, analysts, designers, technology specialists, HR managers and the senior management.

   The ***people resource falls into five categories:*** manager, technocrat, developer, customer and end user.

   - *The manager*: It is responsible for achieving project goal and business goal.
   - *Technocrats*: Comprising analyst, designer, architect, and implementer are responsible for achievement of software goal, defined in terms of cost, quality, productivity, deliverables and customer satisfaction.
   - *The developer*: It is responsible for achieving technical excellence and ensuring that the policies and stipulated standard are applied in development of the software in order to achieve the larger goal of the project.
   - *The customer*: It is responsible for implementing the project as per SP implementation guideline agreed upon, and to fulfill all obligations as a key participant in the SP development.
   - *The end-users*: Who interact with the software once it is released for production use.

2. **Product:** The product in the context of software is the scope of the software that is proposed to solve the requirement of the user. Before a project can be planned, product objectives and scope should be established, alternative solutions should be considered and technical and management constraints should be identified. Without this information, it is impossible to define reasonable (and accurate) estimates of the cost, an effective assessment of risk, a

realistic breakdown of project tasks, or a manageable project schedule that provides a meaningful indication of progress. The software and its scope is a product that is defined and described by four factors namely:

- *Context*: The scenario or situation in business which has problems and which need solutions with in the given domain, and with due regard to constraints and limitations prevailing in the environment.
- *Objective*: Software system objective in terms of information, analysis, report etc. as output for the benefit of users to solve business problems.
- *Functions*: Software system processes and function such as data sourcing and processing such as ease of use, adaptability, interoperability, achieving certain measurable objectives such as cost reduction, reduction in cycle time, improving management effectiveness and so on.
- *Performance*: This stipulates non-functional requirements of speed, quality and features such as ease of use, adaptability, interoperability, achieving certain measurable objectives such as cost reduction, reduction in cycle time, improving management effectiveness and so on.

3. **Process:** The generic phases of development, namely define: analyze, design, develop, test and implement are common to all products. The issue is how these phases will be executed to develop the software product. The execution of these phases is through a process. There are several process models to select from, as the need be. Thus, a software process provides the framework from which a comprehensive plan for software development can be established. Each process model has its strength in a given development scenario. The process models are:
   - Linear sequential when the requirements are stable.
   - Prototyping when the requirement is unclear to all.
   - Rapid application development when the requirement is stable and clear, and can be split into modules for parallel development.
   - Incremental development when the requirement can be split for development purposes and can be delivered in increments.
   - Spiral model (Boehm's model) when the requirement is not clear and stable hence can develop in stages.
   - Components—based developments model when the requirement can be mapped to existing components.
   - Concurrent development where the requirements are fairly clear and can be split into development components, whose development can be concurrently.

   It is very important to select the appropriate process model for development. Incorrect choice of the model will affect have an adverse effect, affecting cost, quality and performance. The choice of model also automatically decides the planning, development and implementation strategies. It decides software development critical success factor in software development.
4. **Project:** A project is defined as an activity that has a definite start and a definite end require multiple resources and is full uncertainties on a number of counts. Project management is "the application of knowledge, skills, tools and techniques to manage resources to deliver customer needs within agreed terms of cost time, and scope of delivery".

An effective project management process requires that the project team members have knowledge in nine areas in order to manage the operating and support functions. The operating management's functions are scope, time, cost, and quality. The support management functions are human resource, communication, risk, and procurement and outsourcing.

So when we define a project, we define it in terms of the scope of delivery, the time take for delivery, the costs to be incurred and the quality that must be achieved. We further describe formally the resource requirements; communication protocols and artifacts that have to be generated; the collection, distribution and storage of project information; the cost targets by function activity and task and the quality specifications in terms of requirements, function, features, integration and performance.

The project is managed through tools and techniques of analysis, design, testing, assessment and improvements and prior to this, it needs tools to estimate effort, cost, resources and risk in the project and product.

Modern software projects have characteristic profiles in different areas. In the modern software development projects, integration is a continuous process and does not take place only at the end as in conventional developments projects.

Table 1.2 Factors of effective SP management

Factor	*Elaboration*	*Focus*
People	Users, developers, stakeholders, vendors and partners	Environment, communication, productivity, skills, motivation, PM-CMM
Product	Deliverables, scope, form and format objectives, key functions and objecttives often as a solution in one–off case	Cost, feasibility, quality, risk
Process	The method through which product will be delivered-process models choice of technology, processes of development	Plan of SP development catering for SPM framework made of common umbrella activities like scope definition, analysis, estimation, feasibility, risk management, and quality assurance and task such as WBS milestones, monitoring and tracking correcting and reporting
Project	Definition scope, business goal, economics, resource, budget, configuretion, clear start and closure	Key deliverables, cost control, time management, meeting deadline and fulfilling commitments to customer satisfaction.

2

Software Development Life Cycle Models

2.1 SOFTWARE DEVELOPMENT LIFE CYCLE

The software development life cycle is used to facilitate the development of a large software product in a systematic, well-defined and cost effective way.

An information system goes through a series of phases from conception to implementation. This process is called the **Software Development Life Cycle**. Various purposes of using a life cycle model are:

- Helps understand the entire process
- Enforces a structured approach to development
- Enables planning of resources in advance
- Enables subsequent controls of them
- Aids management to track progress of the system.

Software development life cycle consists of several phases and these phases need to be identified along with defining the entry and exit criteria for every phase. A phase can begin only when the corresponding phase entry criteria are satisfied. Similarly, a phase can be considered to be complete only when the corresponding exit criteria are satisfied. If there is no clear indication of the entry and exit for every phase, it becomes very difficult to track the progress of the project.

The software development life cycle can be divided into 5–9 phases *i.e.*, it must have minimum of five phases and maximum of nine phases it may have. On an average it has seven or eight phases. These are:

(*i*) Project initiation and planning / Recognition of need / Preliminary investigation
(*ii*) Project identification and selection/ Feasibility study
(*iii*) Project analysis
(*iv*) System design
(*v*) Coding
(*vi*) Testing

(*vii*) Implementation
(*viii*) Maintenance.

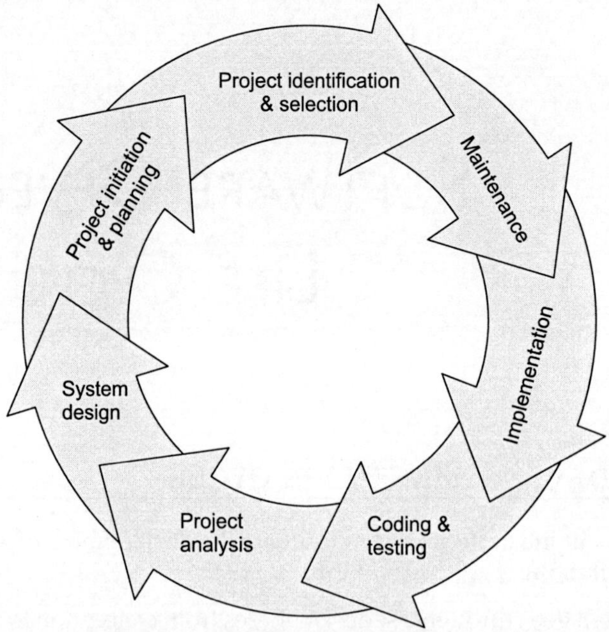

Fig. 2.1 Software development life cycle

1. **Recognition of Need:** ***Recognition of need is nothing but problem definition. It is decision about problems in the existing system and impetus for system change.*** First stage of any project or system development life cycle is called the **preliminary investigation**. It is a brief investigation of the system under consideration. This investigation provides the organization's computer steering committee and any project team, a set of terms of references for more detailed work. This is carried out by some senior manager and will result in a study proposal. At this stage the needs of change in the existing system are identified, shortcomings of the existing system are detected. These are stated clearly providing the basis for the initial or feasibility study.
2. **Feasibility Study:** A feasibility study is a preliminary study which investigates the information needs of prospective users and determines the resource requirements, costs, benefits, and feasibility of a proposed project.

   The goal of feasibility studies is to evaluate alternative systems and to propose the most feasible and desirable systems for development. The feasibility of a proposed system can be evaluated in terms of four major categories, as illustrated in Table 2.1.

   (*i*) **Organizational feasibility:** Organizational feasibility is on how well a proposed information system supports the objectives of the organization and is strategic plan for information system. For example, projects that do not directly contribute to meeting an organization's strategic objectives are typically not funded.

   (*ii*) **Economic feasibility:** Economic feasibility is concerned with whether expected cost savings, increased revenue, increased profits, reductions in required investment, and other types of benefits will exceed the costs of developing and operating a proposed system. For example if a project can't cover its development costs, it won't be approved, unless mandated by government regulations or other considerations.

(*iii*) **Technical feasibility:** Technical feasibility can be demonstrated if reliable hardware and software capable of meeting the needs of a proposed system can be acquired or developed by the business in the required time.

(*iv*) **Operational feasibility:** Operational feasibility is the willingness and ability of the management, employees, customers, suppliers, and others to operate, use, and support a proposed system. For example, if the software for a new system is too difficult to use, employees may make too many errors and avoid using it . Thus it would fail to show operational feasibility.

Table 2.1 Key features of categories of feasibility

Organizational Feasibility	*Economic Feasibility*
• How well the proposed system supports the strategic objectives of the organization	• Cost savings • Increased revenue • Decreased investment • Increased profits
Technical Feasibility	*Operational Feasibility*
• Hardware, software, and network-capability, reliability and availability	• End user acceptance • Management support • Customer, supplier, and government requirements

3. **Project Analysis:** ***Analysis is a detailed study of the various operations performed by a system and their relationships with in and outside of the system.*** Detailed investigation should be conducted with personnel closely involved with the area under investigation, according to the precise terms of reference arising out of the initial study reports. The tasks to be carried out should be clearly defined like:
   - Examine and document the relevant aspects of the existing system, its shortcomings and problems.
   - Analyze the findings and record the results.
   - Define and document in outline a proposed system.
   - Test the proposed design against the known facts.
   - Produce a detailed report to support the proposals.
   - Estimate the resources required to design and implement the system.

   The objectives at this stage are to provide solutions to stated problems, usually in form of specifications to meet the users requirements and to make recommendations for a new computer-based system. Analysis is an iterative and progressive process, examining information flows and evaluating various alternative design solutions until a preferred solution is available. This is documented as system proposal.
4. **System Design:** ***Design is the most creative and challenging phase of the system development life cycle. The term design describes the final system and process by which it is developed.*** Different stages of design phase are shown in Fig. 2.2. This phase is very important phase of life cycle. This is a creative as well as a technical activity including the following tasks:

- Appraising the terms of reference
- Appraising the analysis of the existing system, particularly regarding problem areas
- Defining precisely the required system output
- Determining data required to produce the output
- Deciding the medium and open the files
- Devising processing methods and use of software to handle files and to produce output
- Determining methods of data capture and data input
- Designing the output forms
- Defining detailed critical procedures
- Calculating timings of processing and data movements
- Documenting all aspects of design.

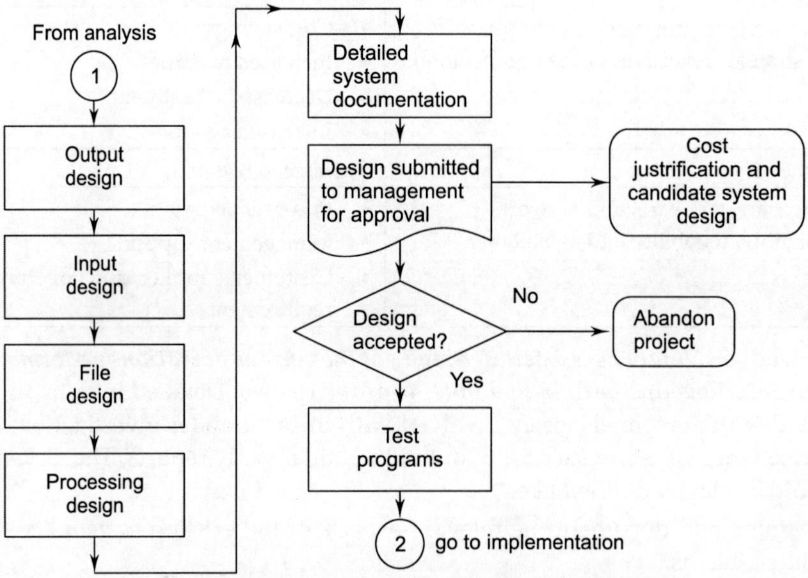

Fig. 2.2 Cycle of design phase

5. **Coding:** The goal of the coding phase is to translate the design of the system into code in a given programming language. In this phase the aim is to implement the design in the best possible manner. This phase affects both testing and maintenance phases. Well-written code can reduce the testing and maintenance effort. Hence, during coding the focus is on developing programs that are easy to read and understand and not simply on developing programs that are simple to write.

   Coding can be subject to company wide standards that may define the entire layout of programs such as headers for comments in every unit, naming conventions for variables, classes and functions, the maximum number of lines in each component and other aspects that the company deems of standardization.

   Structured programming helps in understandability of programs. The goal of structured programming is to linearize the control flow in the program. A single entry—single exit constructs should be used. The constructs include selection (if-then-else) and iteration (while, repeat-unit).

6. **Testing:** Testing is the major quality control measure used during software development. Its basic function is to detect errors in the software. Thus, the goal of testing is to uncover requirement, design and coding errors in the programs.

   Testing is an extremely critical and time-consuming activity. It requires proper planning of the overall testing process. During the testing of the unit, the specified test cases are executed and the actual result compared with the expected output. The final output of the testing phase is the ***test report*** and the ***error report***, or a set of such reports (one for each unit tested). Each test report contains the set of test cases and the result of executing the code with these test cases. The error report describes the errors encountered and the action taken to remove the errors.

   Testing cannot show the absence of defects it can show only software errors are present. During testing phase emphasis on following:

   - Test should be planned long before testing begins.
   - All tests should be traceable to customer requirements.
   - Tracing should began "in the small" and the progress towards testing "in the large".
   - For most effective, independent third party should conduct testing.

7. **Implementation:** ***Implementation phase is less creative than system design. It is mainly concerned with user training, site selection and preparation and file conversion.*** Once the system has been designed, it is ready for implementation. Implementation is concerned with those tasks leading immediately to a fully operational system. It involves programmers, users and operations management, but it's planning and timing is a prime function of system's analyst. It includes the final testing of complete system to user satisfaction, and supervision of initial operation of the system. Implementation of the system includes providing security to the system, also so that some person may not misuse it.

   Types of Implementation:

   There are three types of implementation:

   - Implementation of a computer system to replace a manual system
   - Implementation of a new computer system to replace an existing one
   - Implementation of a modified application (software) to replace an existing one using the same computer.

8. **Maintenance:** ***Maintenance is an important part of SDLC. If there is any error to correct or change needed by the system then it is done in the maintenance phase.*** Maintenance of software is also a very necessary aspect related to software development. Many times the maintenance may consumer more time than the time consumed in the development. Also cost of maintenance varies from 50%-80% of the total development cost.

   Maintenance is not as rewarding or exciting as developing the systems. It may have problems like.

   - Availability of only few tools of maintenance
   - User may not accept the cost of maintenance
   - Standards and guidelines of project are poorly defined
   - Minimal standards for maintenance
   - A good test plan is lacking
   - Maintenance is viewed as a necessary evil often delegated to junior programmer
   - Most programmers view maintenance as low level drudgery.

Types of Maintenance:

Maintenance may be ***classified*** as:

1. **Corrective Maintenance:** Corrective maintenance means repairing processing or performance failures or making changes because of previously uncorrected problems.
2. **Adaptive Maintenance:** Adaptive maintenance means changing the program function. This is done to adapt to the external environment change. For example, the current system was designed so that it calculates taxes on profits after deducting the dividend on equity shares. The government has issued orders now to include the dividend in the 4company profit for tax calculation. This function needs to be changed to adapt to the new system.
3. **Perfective Maintenance:** Perfective maintenance means enhancing the performance or modifying the programs to respond to the user's additional or changing needs. For example, earlier data was sent from stores to headquarters on magnetic media but after stores were electronically linked via leased lines, the software was enhanced to send data via leased lines.

   As maintenance is very costly and very essential, efforts have been done to reduce its costs. One way to reduce the costs is through maintenance management and software modification audit. Software modification consists of programs rewriting, system level up gradation.
4. **Preventive Maintenance:** Preventive maintenance is the process by which we prevent our system from being obsolete. Preventive maintenance involves the concept of re-engineering and reverse engineering in which an old system with an old technology is re-engineered using new technology. This maintenance prevents the system from dying out.

2.2 WATERFALL MODEL

It is a very common software development process model. The waterfall model was popularized in the 1970s and permeates most current software engineering textbooks and standard industrial practices. Its first appearance in the literature dates back to the late 1950s. As the result of experience gained in the development of a large air-defense software system called SAGE (Semi-Automated Ground Environment).

The waterfall model, Illustrated in Fig. 2.3. Because of the cascade from one phase to another, this model is known as the 'waterfall model' or software life cycle.

As the figure shows, the process is structured as a cascade of phases, where the output of one phase constitutes the input to the next one. Each phase, in turn, is structured as a set of activities that might be executed by different people concurrently.

The phases shown in the figure are the following:

- Feasibility study
- Requirements analysis and specification
- Design and specification
- Coding and module testing
- Integration and system testing
- Delivery
- Maintenance.

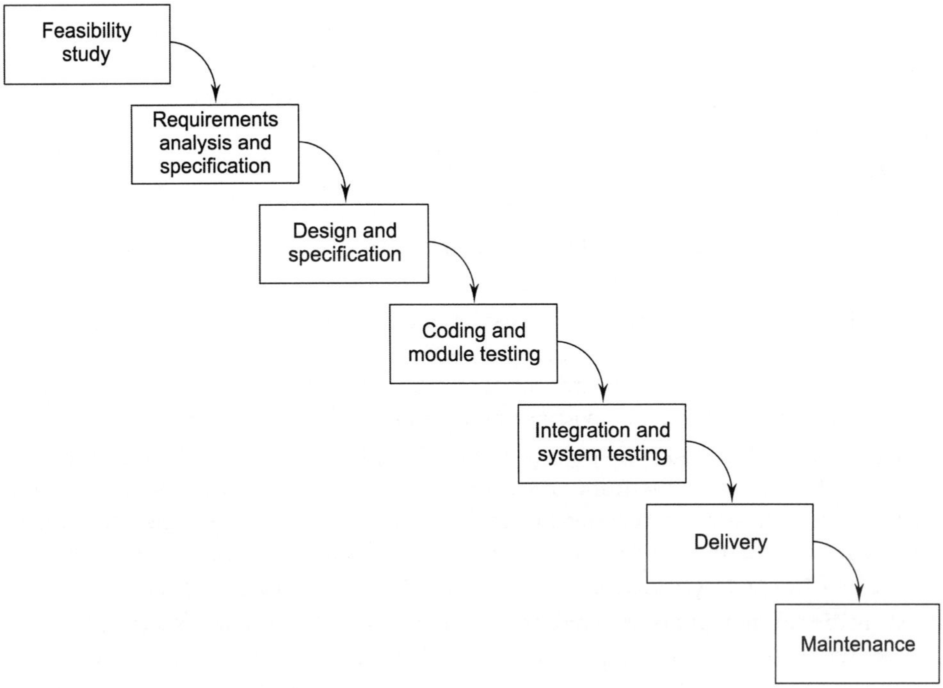

Fig. 2.3 Waterfall model

1. **Feasibility Study:** The first phase is known as feasibility study. The purpose of this phase is to produce a feasibility study document that evaluates the costs and benefits of the proposed application. To do so, it is first necessary to analyze the problem, at least at a global level. Obviously, the more we understand the problem, the better we can identify alternative solutions, their costs, and their potential benefits to the user. Therefore ideally, one should perform as much analysis of the problem as is needed to do a well-founded feasibility study. The feasibility study is usually done within limited time bounds and under pressure. Often, its result is an offer to the potential customer. Since we cannot be sure that the offer will be accepted, economic reasons prevent us from investing too many resources into analyzing the problem.

   In sum, the feasibility study tries to anticipate future scenarios of software development. Its result is a document that should contain at least following items:

   - A definition of the problem
   - Determination of technical and economic viability
   - Alternative solutions and their expected benefits
   - Required resources, costs, and delivery dates in each proposed alternative solution.

   At the end of this phase, a report called feasibility study is prepared by a group of software engineers. The client or the customer is also consulted through a questionnaire. This report determines whether the project is feasible or not. After being successful in the feasibility study, the requirement analysis is carried out.

2. **Requirement Analysis and Specification:** This phase exactly tells the requirement and needs of the project. This is very important and critical phase in waterfall model.

   The purpose of a requirements analysis is to identify the qualities required of the application, in terms of functionality, performance, ease of use, portability, and so on.

The requirements describe the "what" of a system, not the "how". This phase produces a large document, contains a description of what the system will do without describing how it will be done. The resultant document is known as software requirement specification (SRS) document. An SRS document must contain following:

- Detailed statement of problem
- Possible alternative solution to problem
- Functional requirement of the software system
- Constraints on the software system.

The SRS document must be precise, consistent and complete. There is no scope for any ambiguity or contradiction in the SRS document. A SRS document may be organized as problem statement, introduction to problem, functional requirement of the system, non-functional requirement of the system, behavioral description and validation criteria.

3. **Design and Specification:** The goal of the design phase is to transform the requirements specified in the SRS document into a structure that is suitable for implementation in some programming language. In technical terms, during the design phase the software architecture is derived from the SRS document. Two distinctly different design approaches are available: the ***traditional design approach*** and the ***object-oriented design approach.***

   (*i*) **Traditional design approach:** The traditional design approach is currently being used by many software development houses. Traditional design consists of two different activities; first a structured analysis of the requirements specification is carried out where the detailed structure of the problem is examined. This is followed by a structured design activity. During structured design, the results of structured analysis are transformed into the software design.

   Structured design is undertaken once the structured analysis activity is complete. Structured design consists of two main activities: architectural design (also called high level design) and detailed design (also called low-level design). High-level design involves decomposing the system into modules, and representing the interfaces and the invocation relationships among the modules. During detailed design, internals of the individual modules are designed in greater detail, *e.g.*, the data structures and algorithms of the modules are designed and documented.

   (*ii*) **Object-oriented design approach:** This is a new paradigm. Various objects in the system are identified. After the identification of objects, the relationships among them are also explored. The OOD approach has several benefits such as lower development time and effort, and better maintainability.

4. **Coding and Module Testing:** Coding and module testing is the phase in which we actually write programs using a programming language. It was the only recognized development phase in early development processes, but it is just one of several phases in a waterfall process. The output of this phase is an implemented and tested collection of modules.

   Coding can be subject to company wide standards, which may define the entire layout of programs, such as the headers for comments in every unit, naming conventions for variables and subprograms, the maximum number of lines in each component, and other aspects that the company deems worthy of standardization.

   Module testing is also often subject to company standards, including a precise definition of a test plan, the definition of testing criteria to be followed (*e.g.*, black-box versus white-box, or a mixture of the two), the definition of completion criteria (when to stop testing), and the management of test cases. Debugging is related activity performed in this phase.

Module testing is the main quality control activity that is carried out in this phase. Other such activities may include code inspections to check adherence to coding standards and, more generally, to check for a disciplined programming style, as well as checking of software qualities other than functional correctness (*e.g.*, performance), although this is often better done at a later stage coding.

5. **Integration and System Testing:** During the integration and system testing phase, the modules are integrated in a planned manner. The different modules making up a software product are almost never integrated in one shot (can you guess the reason for this?). Integration is normally carried out incrementally over a number of steps. During each integration step, the partially integrated system is tested and a set of previously planned modules are added to it. Finally, when all the modules have been successfully integrated and tested, system testing is carried out.

   The objective of system testing is to determine whether the software system performs as per the requirements mentioned in SRS document. This testing is known as system testing. A fully developed software product is system tested. The system testing is done in three phase called Alpha, Beta and Acceptance Testing.

   - ***Alpha Testing*** is conducted by the software development team at the developer's site.
   - ***Beta Testing*** is performed by a group of friendly customers in the presence of the software development team.
   - ***Acceptance Testing*** is performed by the customers themselves. If the software is successful in acceptance testing, the product is installed at the customer's site.

6. **Delivery and Maintenance:** The delivery of software is often done in two stages. In the first stage, the application is distributed among a selected group of customers prior to its official release. The purpose of this procedure is to perform a kind of controlled experiment to determine, on the basis of feedback from users, whether any changes are necessary prior to the official release. In the second stage, the product is distributed to the customers.

   We defined maintenance as the set of activities that are performed after the system is delivered to the customer. Basically, maintenance consists of correcting any remaining errors in the systems (corrective maintenance), adapting the application to changes in the environment (adaptive maintenance), and improving, changing, or adding features and qualities to the application (perfective maintenance). Recall that the cost of maintenance is often more than 60% of the total cost of software and that about 20% of maintenance costs may be attributed to each of corrective and adaptive maintenance, while over 50% is attributable to perfective maintenance. Based on this breakdown, we observed that evolution is probably a better term than maintenance, although the latter is used more widely.

2.2.1 Advantages of Waterfall Model

1. It is a linear model.
2. It is a segmental model.
3. It is systematic and sequential.
4. It is simple one.
5. It has proper documentations.

2.2.2 Disadvantages of Waterfall Model

1. It is difficult to define all requirements at the beginning of a project.
2. This model is not suitable for accommodating any change.

3. A working version of the system is not seen until late in the project's life.
4. It does not scale up well to large project.
5. It involves heavy documentation.
6. We cannot go in the backward direction while SDLC performs.
7. There is no sample model for clearly in realization the customers needs.
8. There is no risk analysis.
9. If there is any mistake or error in any phase then we cannot make good software.
10. It is a document driven process that requires formal documents at the end of each phase.

2.3 PROTOTYPING MODEL

It always happens that a customer defines a set of general objectives for software but does not identify detailed input, processing, or output requirements. In other cases, the developer may be unsure of the efficiency of an algorithm, the adaptability of an operating system or the form that human/machine interaction should take. In these and many other situations, a prototyping paradigm may offer the best approach.

The prototyping begins with communication. Developer and customer meet and define the overall objectives for the software, identify whatever requirements are known, and outline areas where further definition is mandatory. A quick design then occurs. The quick design focuses on the representation of those aspects of the software that will be visible to the customer/user (*e.g.*, input approaches and output formats). The quick design leads to the construction of a prototype. The prototype is evaluated by the customer/user and user to refine requirements for the software to be developed. Iteration occurs as the prototype is tuned to satisfy the needs of the customer, while at the same time enabling the developer to better understand what needs to be done.

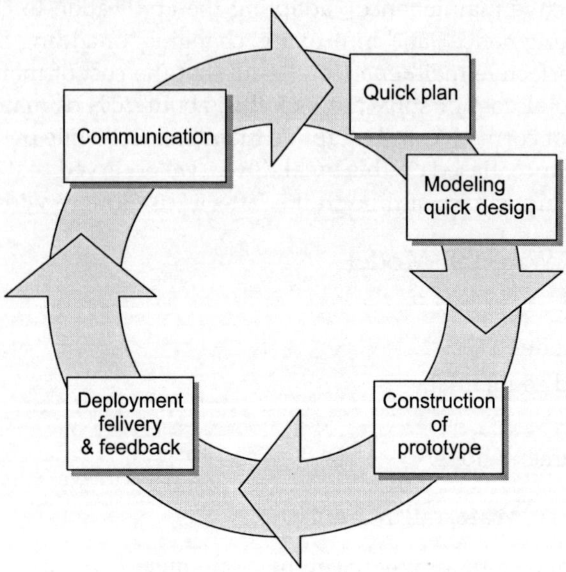

Fig. 2.4 The prototyping model

Ideally, the prototype serves as a mechanism for identifying software requirements. If a working prototype is built, the developer attempts to use existing program fragments or applies tools that enable working programs to be generated quickly.

2.3.1 Reasons for Using Prototyping Model

There are several uses of a prototype. An important purpose is to illustrate the input data formats, messages, reports, and the interactive dialogues to the customer. This is valuable for gaining better understanding of the customer's needs. The prototype model is very useful in developing the Graphical User Interface (GUI) part of a system.

The prototyping model can be used when the technical solutions are unclear to the development team. Often, major design decisions depend on issues like the response time of a hardware controller, or the efficiency of a sorting algorithm, etc. In such circumstances, a prototype may be the best or the only way to resolve the technical issues. The third reason for developing a prototype is that it is impossible to "get in right" the first time and one must plant to throw away the first product in order to develop a good product later, as advocated.

2.3.2 Controlling Changes During Prototyping

A major problem with prototyping is controlling changes to the prototype following suggestions by the users. One approach has been to categorize changes as belonging to one of three types:

- **Cosmetic (about 35% of changes):** These are simply changes to the layout of the screen. They are:
  (*a*) Implemented.
  (*b*) Recorded.
- **Local (about 60% of changes):** These involve changes to the way that the screen is processed but do not affect other parts of the system. They are:
  (*a*) Implemented;
  (*b*) Recorded;
  (*c*) Backed-up so that they can be removed at a later stage is necessary;
  (*d*) Inspected retrospectively.
- **Global (about 5% of changes):** These are changes that affect more than one part of the processing. All changes here have to be the subject of a design review before they can be implemented.

2.3.3 Advantages of Prototyping Models

1. Suitable for large system for which there is no manual process to define the requirements.
2. User training to use the system.
3. User services determination.
4. System training.
5. Quality of software is good.
6. Prototyping makes requirements more clear and system more transparent.
7. Flexibility in design and development is also supported by the model.

2.3.4 Limitations of Prototyping Model

1. It was difficult to find all the requirements of the software initially.
2. It was very difficult to predict how the system will be after development.

These two limitations will be removed in the prototyping model.

First limitation is removing by unfreezing the requirements before any design or coding can proceed.

Second limitation is remove by making a throw away prototype to understand the requirements.

2.3.5 Disadvantage of Prototyping Models

The developer often compromises in order to get working prototype quickly. Thus in appropriate operating system language may be used simply because it's available and known. Thus anefficient algorithm may be implemented.

The other disadvantages are:

1. End users may not like to know the difference between a prototype and a well engineered fully developed system.
2. If not managed properly, the interactive process of prototype demonstration and refinement can continue for long duration.
3. If end user is not satisfied with initial prototype, he may loose interest in the project.

2.4 SPIRAL MODEL

The spiral model was originally proposed by Boehm is an evolutionary software model that couples the iterative nature of prototyping with the controlled and systematic aspects of the linear segmental model.

The goal of the spiral model of the software production process is to provide a framework for designing such processes, guided by the risk levels in the projects at hand. As opposed to the previously presented models, the spiral model may be viewed as a meta-model, because it can accommodate any process development model. By using it as a reference, one may choose the most appropriate development model (*e.g.*, evolutionary versus waterfall). The guiding principle behind such choice is the level of risk; accordingly, the spiral model provides a view of the production process that supports risk management.

Let us present a few definitions. Risks are potentially adverse circumstances that may impair the development process and the quality of products. Boehm [1989] defines risk management as a "discipline whose objectives are to identify, address, and eliminate software risk items before they become either threats to successful software operation or a major source of expensive software rework". The spiral model focuses on identifying and eliminating high-risk problems by careful process design, rather than treating both trivial and severe problems uniformly.

The spiral model is recommended where the requirements and solutions call for developing full-fledged, large, complex systems with a lot of features and facilities from scratch. It is used when experimenting on technology, trying out new skills, and when the user is not able to offer requirement in clear terms. When the requirement is not clear and when the solution intended has multi-user, multi-functions, multi-features, multi-location applications to be used on multiple platforms, where seamless integration, interfacing, data migration and replication are the issues. The radial dimension of a cycle represents the cumulative cost, and the angular dimension represents the progress made in completing each cycle of the spiral.

Each phase in this model is split into four sectors (or quadrants) as shown in Fig. 2.5.

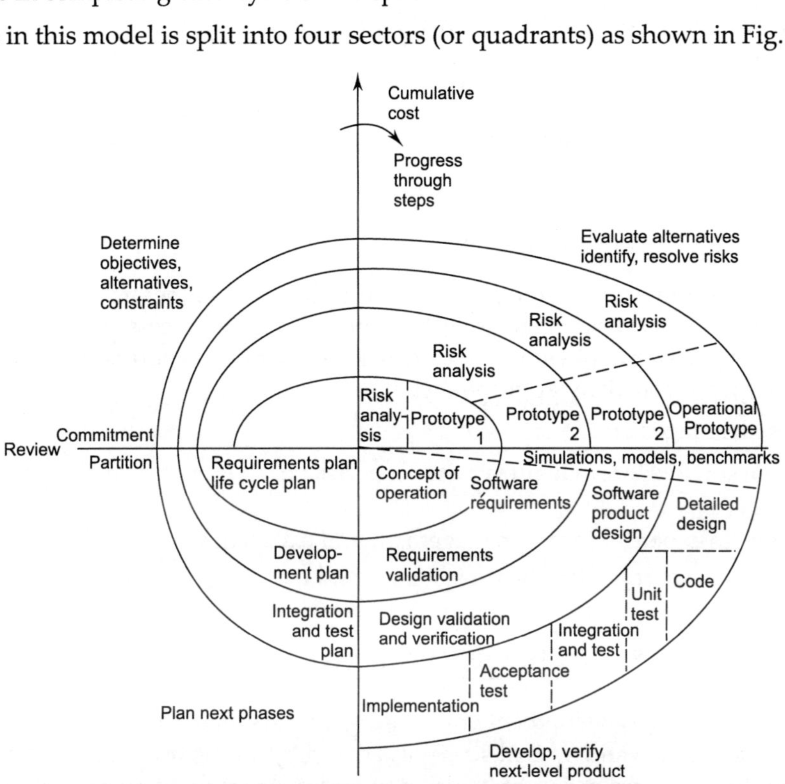

Fig. 2.5 The spiral model (from boehm [1988])

The ***first quadrant*** identifies the objectives of the phase and the alternative solutions possible for the phase under consideration.

In the ***second quadrant*** we evaluate different alternatives based on the objectives and constraints. The evaluation is based on the risk perceptions for the project.

The ***third quadrant*** is the next step that emphasizes development of strategies that resolve the uncertainties and risks. This may involve activities like benchmarking, simulation and prototyping.

In the last or ***fourth quadrant*** we determine the objective that should be fulfilled in next cycle of our software development in order to build the complete system.

2.4.1 Characteristics of Spiral Model

The main characteristic of the spiral model is that it is cyclic and not linear like the waterfall model (See Fig. 2.5). Each cycle of the spiral consists of four stages, and each stage is represented by one quadrant of the Cartesian diagram. The radius of the spiral represents the cost accumulated so far in the process; the angular dimension represents the progress in the process.

2.4.2 Limitations of Spiral Model

1. No strict standards for software development.
2. No particular beginning or end of particular phase.

2.4.3 Advantages of Spiral Model

There are some advantages of spiral model which are as follows:

1. It is risk driven model.
2. It is very flexible.
3. Less documentation is needed.
4. It uses prototyping.

2.4.4 Disadvantages of Spiral Model

The spiral model has some disadvantages that need to be resolved before it can be a universally applied life cycle model. The disadvantages include lack of explicit process guidance in determining objectives, constraints, alternatives, relying on risk assessment expertise and providing more flexibility than required for many applications.

The other disadvantages are:

1. Model is not suitable for small project as cost of risk analysis may exceed the actual cost of the project.
2. Model requires expertise in risk management and excellent management skills.
3. Different persons involved in the project may find it complex to use.

2.5 EVOLUTIONARY DEVELOPMENT MODEL

In the Evolutionary Model, development engineering effort is made first to establish correct, precise requirement definitions and system scope, as agreed by all the users across the organization. This is achieved through application of iterative processes to evolve a system most suited to the given circumstances. The process is 'iterative' as the software engineer goes through a repetitive process of requirement Analysis-Design-Testing through prototype-Implementation-Assessment-Evaluation, till all users and stakeholders are satisfied.

This model differs from iterative enhancement model in the sense that this does not require a useable product at the end of each cycle. In evolutionary development, requirements are implemented by category rather than by priority.

2.5.1 Need of an Evolutionary Model

Various reasons why there exists a need of an evolutionary model are as follows:

1. Business and product requirements often change as development proceeds.
2. Tight market deadlines make completion of a comprehensive software product impossible but a limited version must be introduced to meet competitive and business pressure.
3. A set of core product or system requirements is well understood, but the details of product or system extensions have yet to be defined.

2.5.2 Uses of Evolutionary Model

This model is useful for projects using new technology that is not well understood. This is also used for complex projects where all functionality must be delivered at one time, but the requirements are unstable or not well understood at the beginning.

2.5.3 Advantages of Evolutionary Model

1. Early delivery of portions of the system even though some of the requirements are not yet decided.
2. The core modules get tested thoroughly thereby reducing chances of errors in the final product.
3. Use of early releases as tool for requirements elicitation.
4. For most practical problems, it is difficult to subdivide the problem into several functional units that can be incrementally implemented and delivered.
5. Model can be used only for very large problems, where it is easier to identify modules for incremental implementation.

2.6 ITERATIVE ENHANCEMENT MODEL

The Iterative enhancement model combines elements of the linear sequential model (applied repetitively) with the iterative philosophy of prototyping. In this model, the software is broken down into several modules, which are incrementally developed and delivered. First, the development team develops the core module of the system and then it is later refined into increasing levels of capability of adding new functionalities in successive version.

Each linear sequence produces a deliverable "increment" of the software. For example, word processing software developed using the iterative paradigm might deliver basis file management, editing, and document production functions in the first increment; more sophisticated editing, and document production capabilities in the second increment; spelling and grammar checking in the third increment; and advanced page layout capability in the fourth increment. It should be noted that the process flow for any increment could incorporate the prototyping paradigm.

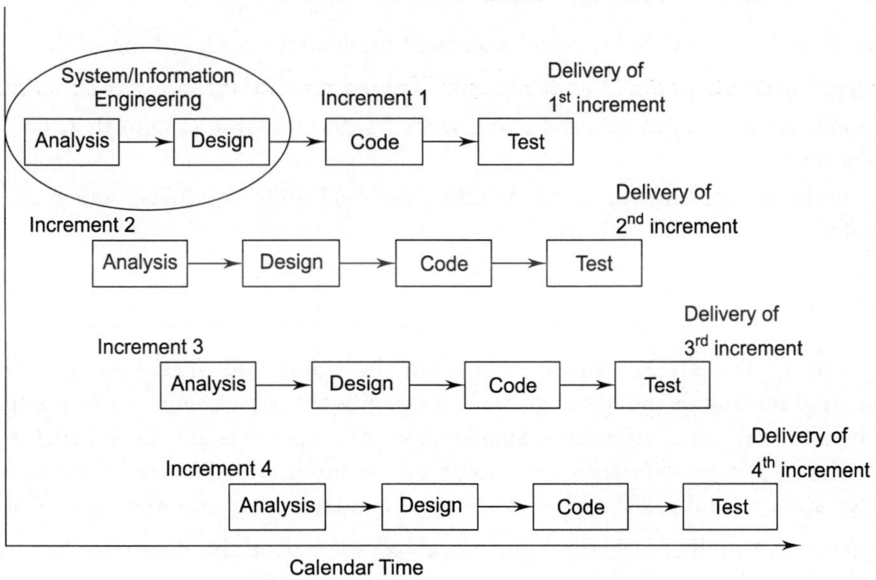

Fig. 2.6 Iterative enhancement model

When an iterative enhancement model is used, the first increment is often a core product. That is, basic requirements are addressed, but many supplementary features (some known, other unknown) remain undelivered. The core product is used by the customer (or undergoes detailed review). As a result of use and/or evaluation, a plan is developed for the next increment. The plan addresses the modification of the core product to better meet the needs of the customer and the delivery of additional features and functionality. This process is repeated following the delivery of each increment, until the complete product is produced.

2.6.1 Advantages of Iterative Enhancement Model

The various advantages of following the approach of the iterative enhancement are as follows:

1. The feedbacks from early increments improve the later stages.
2. The possibility of changes in requirement is reduced because of the shorter time span between the design of a component and its delivery.
3. Users get benefits earlier than with a conventional approach.
4. Early delivery of some useful components improves cash flow, because you get some return on investment early on.
5. Smaller sub-projects are easier to control and manage.
6. 'Gold-plating', that is the requesting of features that are unnecessary and not in fact used, is less as users will know that they get more than one bite of the cherry if a feature is not in the current increment then it can be included in the next.
7. The project can be temporarily abandoned if more urgent work crops up.
8. Job satisfaction is increased for developers who see their labours bearing fruit at regular, short, intervals.

2.6.2 Disadvantages of Iterative Enhancement Model

The various disadvantages of iterative enhancement model have been put forward:

1. Software breakage, that is, later increments may require modifications to earlier increments.
2. Programmers may be more productive working on one large system than on a series of smaller ones.
3. Some problems are difficult to divide into functional units (modules), which can be incrementally developed and delivered.

2.7 RAD MODEL

The RAD (Rapid Application Development Model) model is proposed when requirements and solutions can be modularized as independent system or software components, each of which can be developed by different teams. After these smaller system components are developed, they are integrated to produce the large software system solution. The modularization could be on a functional, technology or architectural basis, such as front-end-back-end, client side-server side and so on.

RAD becomes faster if the software engineer uses components technology such that the components are really available for reuse. Since the development is distributed into component development teams, the teams work in tandem and total development is completed in a short period (*i.e.*, 60 to 90 days) Fig. 2.7 shows the RAD model.

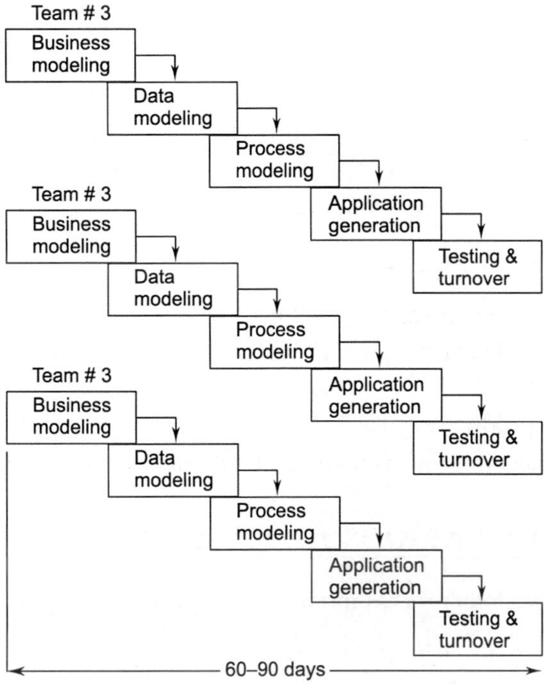

Fig. 2.7 The RAD model

1. **Business Modelling:** It covers the following functions:
   (*i*) Where does information come from and go?
   (*ii*) Who processes it?
   (*iii*) What information driven the business process?
   (*iv*) What information is generated?
2. **Data Modelling:** The information flow defined as part of the business-modelling phase is refined into a set of data objects that are needed to support the business. The characteristics of each object are identified and the relationships between these objects are defined.
3. **Process Modelling:** In this model information is flow from object to object to implement a business function. To add, modify, delete or retain a data object, there is a need of description which is done in this phase.
4. **Application Generation:** RAD assumes the use of fourth generation techniques, the RAD process works to reuse existing program components or create reusable components. To facilitate the construction of the software using above cases, automated tools are used.
5. **Testing & Turnover:** In this we have test the programs, but we use some already existing programs which are already tested, so the time involve in testing is less. Only the new program or components must be tested.

2.7.1 Drawbacks of RAD Model

The various drawbacks of RAD model are discussed as follows:

1. For large, but scalable projects, RAD requires sufficient human resources to create the right number of RAD teams.
2. If developers and customers are not committed to the, rapid-fire activities necessary to complete the system in a much abbreviated time frame, RAD projects will fail.

3. If a system cannot be properly modularized, building the components necessary for RAD will be problematic.
4. If high performance is an issue, and performance is to be achieved through tuning the interfaces to system components, the RAD approach may be work.
5. RAD may not be appropriate when technical risks are high (for example, when a new application makes heavy use of new technology).

2.7.2 Advantages of RAD Model

1. Using RAD model a product can be developed with in a short time duration.
2. As customer is involved at all stages of development it leads to a product achieving customer satisfaction.
3. In order to increase productivity case tools and frameworks are used.
4. Feedback from the customer is available at the initial stages.

2.8 COMPARISON OF VARIOUS PROCESS MODEL

The comparison between various process models are depicted in the Table 2.2 below:

Table 2.2 Comparison of process models

Type of Model	*Strength*	*Weaknesses*	*Types of Projects*
Waterfall	• Simple • Easy to execute • Intuitive and logical	• All or nothing approach • Requirements frozen early • Disallows changes • Cycle time too long • May choose outdated hardware technology • User feedback not allowed • Encourages req. bloating	• For well understood problems • Short duration project • Automation of existing manual systems
Prototyping	• Helps in requirements elicitation • Reduces risk • Leads to a better system	• Front heavy process • Possibly higher cost • Disallows later changes	• Systems with novice users • When uncertainties in requirements • When UI very important
Iterative Enhancement	• Regular/quick deliveries • Reduces risk • Accommodates changes • Allows user feedback • Allows reasonable exit points • Avoids req. bloating • Prioritizes requirements	• Each iteration can have planning overhead • Cost may increase as work done in one iteration may have to be undone later • System architecture and structure may suffer as frequent changes are made	• For businesses where time is of essence • Where risk of a long project cannot be taken • Where requirements are not known and will be known only with time
Spiral	• Controls project risks • Very flexible • Less documentation needed	• No strict standards for software development • No particular beginning or end of particular phase.	• Projects built on untested assumptions

3

SOFTWARE PROJECT PLANNING

3.1 SOFTWARE PROJECT PLANNING

Software project management begins with a set of activities that are collectively called *project planning*. Before the project can begin, the manager and the software team must estimate the work to be done, the resources that will be required, and the time that will elapse from start to finish.

Project planning is part of project management, which relates to the use of schedules such as Gantt charts to plan and subsequently report progress within the project environment.

The purpose of software project planning is to establish reasonable plans for performing all activities that are the part of software Engineering. The Software Project Management Plan (SPMP) is the controlling document for a software project. It specifies the technical and managerial approaches to be used to develop software components. For example, SPMP may include configuration management, quality assurance, verification and validation.

An SPMP is the project manager's statement of understanding with the development organization and the project team members.

Also, the Software Project Planning Metrics Plan (SPPMP) is intended to develop estimate for the work to be performed, establish the necessary commitments and define the plan to perform the work.

Projects begin with project planning. Project complexity can affect this process. Software project planning can be done in stages also. For example, sliding window approach to planning is followed in which the project is planned more accurately in each of the development phases.

Project planning is important because project tend to be large, complex and time consuming. Note that the goal of project planning is to establish a pragmatic strategy for controlling, tracking and monitoring a complex project.

Whatever the size of the project, good planning is essential if it is to succeed. The software project planning process is shown in Fig. 3.1. The five major planning activities are:

- Define products;
- Define activities;

- Estimate resources and duration;
- Define activity network;
- Define schedule and total cost.

This process can be applied to a whole project or to a phase of a project. Each activity may be repeated several times to make a feasible plan. In principle, every activity in Fig. 3.1 can be linked to the other activities by 'feedback' loops, in which information gained at a later stage in planning is used to revise earlier planning decisions. These loops have been omitted from the figure for simplicity. Iteration is essential for optimizing the plan.

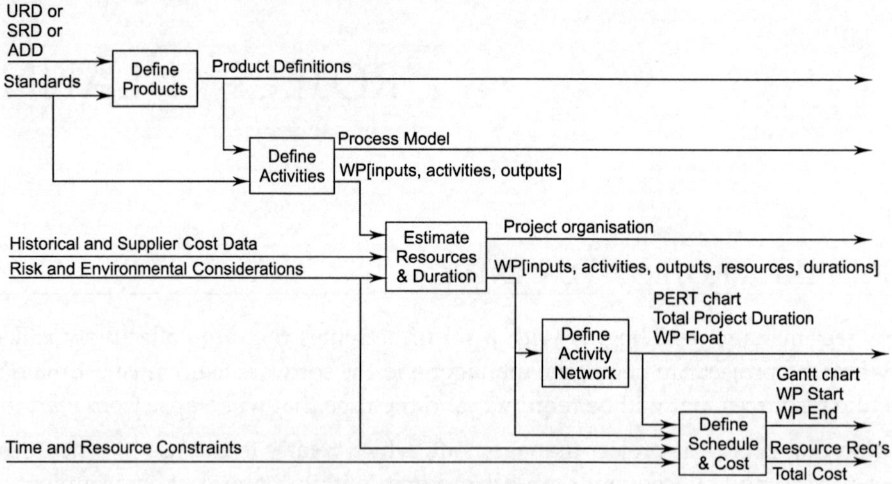

Fig. 3.1 Planning process

The ***inputs*** to software project planning are:

- User Requirements Document (URD), Software Requirements Document (SRD) or Architectural Design Document (ADD), according to the project phase;
- Software standards for products and procedures;
- Historical data for estimating resources and duration;
- Supplier cost data;
- Risks to be considered;
- Environmental factors, such as new technology;
- Time constraints, such as delivery dates;
- Resource constraints, such as the availability of staff.

The primary ***output*** of project planning is the Software Project Management Plan. This should contain:

- Definitions of the deliverable products;
- A process model defining the life cycle approach and the methods and tools to be used;
- The work breakdown structure, *i.e.*, a hierarchically structured set of work packages defining the work;
- The project organization, which defines the roles and reporting relationships in the project;
- An activity network defining the dependencies between work packages, the total time for completion of the project, and the float times of each work package;

- A schedule of the project, defining the start and end times of each work package;
- A list of the resources required to implement the project;
- A total cost estimate.

3.1.1 Planning Objectives

The objective of software project planning is to provide a framework that enables the manager to make reasonable estimates of resources, cost, and schedule. These estimates are made within a limited time frame at the beginning of a software project and should be updated regularly as the project progresses. In addition, estimates should attempt to define best case and worst case scenarios so that project outcomes can be bounded.

The planning objective is achieved through a process of information discovery that leads to reasonable estimates. We should keep in mind certain objectives during planning. Some of these objectives are given below:

1. **The project definition, it's a scope must be bounded, accurate and unambiguous:** This is must, as initially the requirements understand are very less. The Knowledge Base (KB) widens only when the project proceeds. A software project manager is confronted with a dilemma at the very beginning of a software engineering project. Quantitative estimate are required but solid information is unavailable. The project starts by mapping unclear, ambiguous and incomplete requirements to accurate and precise requirements.
2. **Develop a conceptual design:** A conceptual design acts as a basis for planning. This is design provides an organizational framework for planning. It breakdown the product into units, allocates functions to these units and identifies the relationship among them.
3. **Refinement is done:** During requirements refinement, we must also refine resource projections, size estimates and time schedules.
4. **Details design is developed:** When all requirements have been clearly defined, a detailed design and the implementation strategy is developed and introduced with in the plan.
5. **Documentation is done:** As various parts of the project are well understood, the implementation details are established and documented in future plan refinements.

So, the plan provides and framework to ensure that there are no cost overruns, no time slippages and no poor quality software.

3.2 PROJECT PLAN

A project plan is "a formal, approved document used to guide both project execution and project control. The primary uses of the project plan are to document planning assumptions and decisions, facilitate communication among stakeholders, and document approved scope, cost and schedule baselines. Thus,

- Projects plan also document project planning assumptions and decisions regarding choices, facilitate communication among stakeholders, define the contents, extent, and timing of key management reviews, and provide a baseline for progress measurement and project control.
- Plans should be dynamic, flexible and subject to change when the environment or project changes.
- Plans should greatly assist the project manager in leading the project team and assessing project status.

- A typical project plan consists of: statement of work, a resource list, work breakdown structure, a project schedule and a risk plan.
- Developing a realistic project plan is essential to gain an understanding of the resources required, and how these should be applied.
- Specifies the order of work to be carried out, resources, responsibilities, and so on.

3.2.1 Definitions

A project plan is a document used to coordinate all project planning documents and help guide a project's execution and control.

OR

In some industries, particularly information technology, the term "project plan" can refer to a Gantt chart or other document that shows project activities along a time line.

OR

Project plan defines all work in a project and who will do it.

OR

Project plan is "a statement of how and when a project's objectives are to be achieved, by showing the major products, milestones, activities and resources required on the project."

OR

A project plan is a plan for an activity must be based on some idea of a method of work.

3.2.2 Types of Project Plan

The various types of project plans are discussed as follows:

1. **Scope management plan:** This plan must contain the plan for managing the scope of the project. The project scope specifies the project work processes that shall be completed in order to deliver a product. This plan shall specify the methods by which the project scope will be measured against the management plans. The plan should include:
   (*a*) The assessment of probability of changes to the project scope.
   (*b*) The factors that may result in project scope change.
   (*c*) The assessment of probable occurrences, frequency, duration and the degree to which factors are likely to affect the scope.
   (*d*) The consideration on low changes to project scope may affect the product scope and vice-versa. So, we can say that the project scope and product scope are interrelated.

   Note that: This plan will indicate low causative factors and resulting changes should be identified and also the method, by which the changes will be documented, communicated and controlled.
2. **Schedule management plan:** This plan shall consist up of a plan for ensuring that the project is completed on time. The plan should specify the documents that serve as inputs or that places constraints on the schedule, it should also include.
   (*a*) The tools or methodology that will be used to manage the schedule.
   (*b*) The delineation of factors that shall result in schedule changes.

(c) The extent (or degree) to which these known factors will potentially affect the schedule.

(d) The extent to which causative factors affect and resulting changes should be identified.

(e) The method by which the changes will be documented, communicated and controlled.

3. **Cost management plan:** This plan shall consist up of a plan that ensures that the project is completed with in the established budget. The plan should specify the documents that serve as inputs or that places some constraints on the budget. The plan shall include.

   (a) The tools that will be used to manage the budget (cost).

   (b) The factors that will result in budget changes.

   (c) The extent to which these factors would affect the budget.

   (d) The extent to which causative factors affect and the resulting changes should be identified.

   (e) The method by which the changes will be documented, communicated and controlled.

4. **Quality management plan:** This plan must include the plan for both process and project quality. It should specify the standards that are integral to the project and the methods and resources required to implement and ensure compliance with those standard. The plan shall include:

   (a) A description of the factors likely to result in changes to project quality.

   (b) A description of the degree to which changes to project quality will affect the project.

   (c) How changes to project quality will be identified?

   (d) The method by which identified changes will be documented, communicated and controlled.

5. **Staffing management plan:** This plan shall specify the plan for resource management. It should specify the methods used to estimate staff /personnel/human requirements. The plan should include:

   (a) Estimates of required skill levels of personnel(in terms of numbers)

   (b) Required quality attributes of resources.

   (c) Training requirements must be specified.

   (d) The description of the point in the project when each resource will be required.

   (e) Restrictions on resource procurement.

   (f) Potential conflicts that may result from shared resources.

6. **Risk management plan:** This plan should specify the plans for managing the risk factors associated with the project. It shall describe the methods that will be used to identify risk factors as well as its impact. It should also include.

   (a) A description of contingency planning and methods for implementing these plans

   (b) The mechanisms for tracking various risk factors like contractual risks, technological risks, risks due to size and complexity of the product, risks in personal acquisition and retention and risks in achieving customer acceptance of the product.

   (c) The degree to which the identified risks will affect the project should be described

   (d) To indicate how changes resulting from identified risks will be identified.

   (e) The methods by which those changes will be documented, communicated and controlled.

7. **Communication management plan:** Specifies the plan for managing communications related to the project. This plan will define the reporting mechanisms; report formats, information

flow, review and audit mechanisms and other tools and techniques to be used in monitoring and controlling. Project monitoring should occur at the activity level. The frequency and detail of communications related to project planning and monitoring should be consistent with the project scope, critically, risks and visibility. It must include:

(*a*) The degree to which specific communication failures can affect the project should be described.

(*b*) How changes resulting from communication failures will be identified.

(*c*) The method by which changes will be documented, communicated and controlled.

8. **Procurement management plan:** It specifies the plan for managing the project procurement process. This plan should include a description of the procurement process. It should include the process for obtaining tangible and intangible resources. It should specify the procurement process for both expendable and nonexpendable materials. It should include:

(*a*) Estimates of computer time, computer hardware and software, service contracts, facilities, transportation and training.

(*b*) A description of the point in the project when each procurement effort will be required.

(*c*) A description of factors most likely to result in the need for procurement changes.

(*d*) How changes in procurement needs will be identified?

(*e*) The method by which the changes will be documented, communicated and controlled.

3.2.3 Characteristics of a Project Plan

A project plan can be considered to have five key characteristics that have to be managed:

- **Scope:** defines what will be covered in a project.
- **Resource:** what can be used to meet the scope.
- **Time:** what tasks are to be undertaken and when.
- **Quality:** the spread or deviation allowed from a desired standard.
- **Risk:** defines in advance what may happen to drive the plan off course, and what will be done to recover the situation.

3.2.4 Project Plan Template

The introduction or overview of the project should include, as a minimum, the following information:

- **The project name:** Every project should have a unique name. Unique names help distinguish each project and avoid confusion among related projects.
- **A brief description of the project and need it addresses:** This description should clearly outline the goals of the project and why it is being done. It should be written in layman's terms, avoid technical jargon, and include a rough time and cost estimate.
- **The sponsor's name: Every** project needs a sponsor. Include the name, title, and contact information of the sponsor in the introduction.
- **The names of the project manager and key team members:** The project manager should always be the contact for project information. Depending on the size and nature of the project, names of key team members may also be included.
- **Deliverables of the project:** This section should briefly list and describe the products that will be produced as part of the project. Software packages, pieces of hardware, technical reports, and training materials are examples of deliverables.

- **A list of important reference materials:** Many projects have a history preceding them. Listing important documents or meetings related to a project helps project stakeholders understand that history. This section should reference the plans produced for other knowledge areas. For example, the overall project plan should reference and summarize important parts of the scope management, schedule management, cost management, quality management, staffing management, communications management, risk management, and procurement management plans.
- **A list of definitions and acronyms, if appropriate:** Many projects, especially information technology projects, involve terminology unique to a particular industry or technology. Providing a list of definitions and acronyms helps to avoid confusion.

The description of how the project is organized should include the following information:

- **Organizational charts:** In addition to an organizational chart for the company sponsoring the project and for the customer's company (if it is an external customer), there should be a project organizational chart to show the lines of authority, responsibilities, and communication for the project.
- **Project responsibilities:** This section of the project plan should describe the major project functions and activities and identify those individuals who are responsible for them. A responsibility assignment chart is a tool often used for displaying this information.
- **Other organizational or process related information:** Depending on the nature of the project, there may be a need to document major processes followed on the project. For example, if the project involves releasing a major software upgrade, it might help everyone involved in the project to see a diagram or timeline of the major steps involved in this process.

The section of the project plan describing management and technical approaches should include the following information:-

- **Management objectives:** It is important to understand senior management's view of the project, what the priorities are for the project, and any major assumptions or constraints.
- **Project controls:** This section describes how to monitor project progress and handle changes. Will there be monthly status reviews and quarterly progress reviews? Will specific forms or charts be used to monitor progress? Will the project use earned value analysis to assess and track performance? What is the process for change control? What level of management is required to approve different types of changes?
- **Risk management:** This section briefly addresses how risks will be identified, managed and controlled. It should refer to the risk management plan, if one is required for the project.
- **Project staffing:** This section describes the number and types of people required for the project. It should refer to the staffing management plan, if one is required for the project.
- **Technical processes:** This section describes specific methodologies a project might use and how information is to be documented. For example, information technology projects follow specific software development methodologies or use particular Computer Aided Software Engineering (CASE) tools. Many companies or customers also have specific formats for technical documentation. It is important to clarify these technical processes in the project plan.

The section of the overall project plan describing the work to be done should reference the scope management plan and summarize the following:

- **Major work packages:** Project work is usually organized into several work packages using a Work Breakdown Structure (WBS), and a Statement Of Work (SOW) is often produced to describe the work in more detail. The section should briefly summarize the main work packages for the project and refer to appropriate sections of the scope management plan.

- **Key deliverables:** This section lists and describes the key products produced as part of the project. It should also describe the quality expectations for the deliverables.
- **Other work related information:** This section highlights key information related to the work done on the project. For example, it might list specific hardware or software that must be used on the project or certain specifications that must be followed. It should document major assumptions made in defining the project work.

The project schedule information section should include the following:

- **Summary schedule:** It is helpful to see a one-page summary of the overall project schedule. Depending on the size and complexity of the project, the summary schedule might list only key deliverables and their planned completion dates. For smaller projects, it might include all of the work and associated dates for the entire project in a Gantt chart.
- **Detailed schedule:** This section provides more detailed information on the project schedule. It should reference the schedule management plan and discuss dependencies among project activities that could affect the project schedule. For example, it might explain that a major part of the work cannot be started until funding is provided by an external agency. A project network diagram or PERT chart can be used to show these dependencies.
- **Other schedule related information:** Many assumptions are often made in preparing project schedules. This section should document major assumptions and highlight other important information related to the project schedule.

The budget section of the overall project plan should include the following:

- **Summary budget :** The summary budget includes the total estimate of the overall projects budget. It could also include the budget estimate each month or year by certain budget categories. It is important to provide some explanations of what these numbers mean. For example, is the total budget estimate a firm number than cannot change, or is it a rough estimate based on projected costs over the next three years?
- **Detailed budget:** This section summarizes what is in the cost management plan and includes more detailed budget information. For example, what are the fixed and recurring cost estimates for the project each year? What are the projected financial benefits of the project? What types of peoples are needed to do the work, and how are the labour cost calculated?
- **Other budget related information:** This section document major assumptions and highlights other important information related to financial aspects of the project.

3.2.5 Project and Organizational Systems

- Project processes need to be integrated with organizational processes like TQM, change management, risk management, etc.

  Note: some processes may get integrated in future, *e.g.*, supply chain management, cost benefit analysis, capital budgeting, etc.
- Organization normally have their own management system in place *e.g.*, finance system for simultaneously executing all their projects:
- It is essential that the project team knows exactly how:
  - The organizational management system operate
  - These systems will affect their project.

- Compliance with regulation may be required at different levels :
  - Regulatory agencies
  - Political framework
  - Style and culture
  - Project organization
  - Socioeconomic environment
  - Sponsor organization
  - Symbolic framework
  - Hr framework
  - Interests of stakeholders.

3.3 SOFTWARE PROJECT MANAGEMENT PLAN

The Software Project Management Plan (SPMP) is the controlling document for a software project. It specifies the technical and managerial approaches to be used in developing a software product or the software components of a larger product.

The format of the SPMP is presented in Table 3.1. The various clauses and sub-clauses of an SPMP should be ordered in the prescribed sequence; however, initial development and subsequent updating to the SPMP need not proceed in the indicated sequences as indicated in table, the essential elements of an SPMP are:

1. **Front Matter:** This material includes the title page, a revision sheet that contains the history of updates to the SPMP, a preface that summarizes the scope and purpose of the SPMP, a table of contents, and lists of figures and tables.
2. **Overview:** A clause of the SPMP that specifies the scope of the SPMP, the purpose of the SPMP, the deliverables and the mechanism for managing the evolution of the SPMP. The first clause of an SPMP shall always be "overview".
3. **Reference:** A clause of the SPMP that specifies all documents and other sources of information referenced in the SPMP.
4. **Definition:** A clause of the SPMP that specifies all definition acronyms and abbreviation needed to properly interpret the SPMP.
5. **Project Organization:** a clause of the SPMP that specifies the process model for the project describes the project organizational structure identifies organizational boundaries and interfaces: and defines key responsibilities for the project.
6. **Managerial Process:** A clause of the SPMP that specifies the project management process for the project. Items include with in this clause shall be consistent with the statement of scope and shall include management objectives and priorities; project assumption, dependencies, and constraints; the plans for project — integral processes; and the monitoring and controlling plans to be used.
7. **Technical Process:** A clause of the SPMP that specifies plans for managing the scope of the product; the technical method, tools and techniques used to deliver the specified product; and software documentation plans.
8. **Work Activity Plan:** A clause of the SPMP that specifies the project activities and their scope; identifies the dependency relationship among the activities, establishes schedules; provides

the allocation of budget; states the resource requirements; and states quality assurance and risk considerations.

9. **Additional Components:** A clause of the SPMP that specifies certain other components that may be in this clause of the SPMP as annexes. Additional areas of importance on a particular project might include a training plan for product users, a system installation plan, or a product maintenance plan.

Annexes can be used to provide supporting details that would detract from the SPMP if included in the body. An index of key terms and acronyms may include in the SPMP when it is necessary or helpful to the reader.

3.3.1 Outline/Structure of a Software Project Management Plan

The outline of a software project management plan is shown in the Table 3.1

Table 3.1 Outline of SPMP

Title page

Revision

Preface

Table of content

List of figures

List of tables.

1. Overview
   - Scope
   - Purpose
   - Project deliverables
   - Evolution of the SPMP.
2. References
3. Definitions
4. Project organization.
   - Process model
   - Organizational structure
   - Organizational boundaries and interface
   - Project responsibilities.
5. Managerial process
   - Management objective or priorities
   - Assumptions, dependencies, and constraints
   - Integral processes
   - Scope management
   - Schedule management plan
   - Budget management plan
   - Resource management plan

- Quality assurance management plan
- Risk management plan
- Resource procurement plan
- Communications management plan

6. Technical process
    - Product scope
    - Methods, tools, and techniques
    - Software documentation
7. Work activities plan
    - Activity definitions and scope
    - Activity dependencies
    - Activity scheduling
    - Activity budget
    - Activity resource requirements
8. Additional components
    - Annexes
    - Index.

3.4 SOFTWARE PROJECT ESTIMATION

Software project estimation is the process of estimating various resources required for the completion of a project. Effective software project estimation is an important activity in any software development project. Underestimating software project and under staffing it often leads to low quality deliverables, and the project misses the target deadline leading to customer dissatisfaction and loss of credibility to the company. On the other hand, overstaffing a project without proper control will increase the cost of the project and reduce the competitiveness of the company.

Software project estimation mainly encompasses the following steps:

1. **Estimating the Size of Project:** There are many procedures available for estimating the size of a project, which are based on quantitative approaches like estimating ***Lines of Code*** or estimating the functionality requirements of the project called ***Function point***.
2. **Estimating Efforts Based on Person-Month or Person-Hour:** Person-month is an estimate of personal resources required for the project.
3. **Estimating Schedule in Calendar Days/Month/Year Based on Total Person-Month Required and Manpower Allocated to the Project:** Duration in calendar month = Total person-months/ Total manpower allocated.
4. **Estimating Total Cost of the Project Depending on the Above and Other Resources:** In a commercial and competitive environment, Software project estimation is crucial for managerial decision-making. The following Table 3.2 gives the relationship between various management functions and software metrics/indicators. Project estimation and tracking help to plan and predict future projects and provide baseline support for project management and supports decision-making.

Consider the following Table 3.2:

Table 3.2 Depicts the software project estimation

Activity	*Tasks Involved*
Planning	Cost estimation, planning for training of manpower, project scheduling and budgeting the project
Controlling	Size metrics and schedule metrics help the manager to keep control of the project during execution
Monitoring/improving	Metrics are used to monitor progress of the project and wherever possible sufficient resources are allocated to improve.

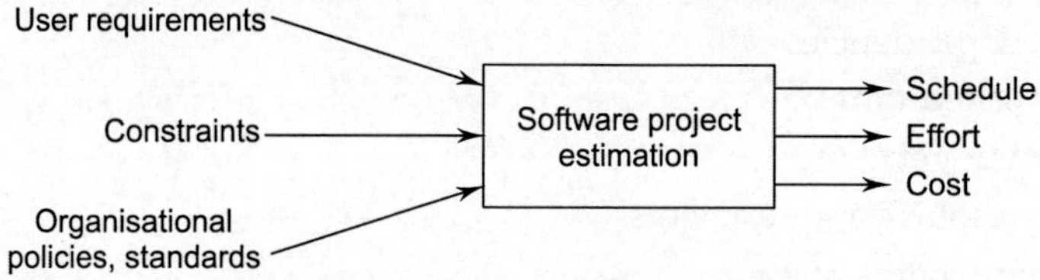

Fig. 3.2 Software project estimation

3.4.1 Estimating the Size

Estimating the size of the software to be developed is the very first step to make an effective estimation of the project. Customer's requirements and system specification forms a baseline for estimating the size of a software. At a later stage of the project, system design document can provide additional details for estimating the overall size of software.

- The ways to estimate project size can be through past data from an earlier developed system. This is called ***estimation by analogy***.
- The other way of estimation is through product feature/ functionality. The system is divided into several subsystems depending on functionality, and size of each subsystem is calculated.

3.4.2 Estimating Effort

Once the size of software is estimated, the next step is to estimate the effort based on the size. The estimation of effort can be made from the organizational specifies of software development life cycle. The development of any application software system is more than just coding of the system. Depending on deliverable requirements, the estimation of effort for project will vary.

Efforts are estimated in number of person months:

- The best way to estimate effort is based on the organization's own historical data of development process. Organizations follow similar development life cycle for developing various application.
- If the project is of a different nature, which requires the organization to adopt a different strategy for development, then different models based on algorithmic approach can be devised to estimate effort.

3.4.3 Estimating Schedule

The next step in estimation process is estimating the project schedule from the effort estimated. The schedule for a project will generally depend on human resources involved in a process. Efforts in person-months are translated to calendar months.

Schedule estimation in calendar month can be calculated using the following model [McConnell]:

$$\textbf{Schedule in calendar months} = \textbf{3.0*(person-months)}^{1/3}$$

The parameter 3.0 is variable, used depending on the situation which works best for the organization.

3.4.4 Estimating Cost

Cost estimation is the next step for projects. The cost of project is derived not only from the estimates of effort and size but from other parameters such as hardware, travel expenses, telecommunication costs, training cost etc, should also be taken into account. Figure 3.3 depicts the cost estimation process.

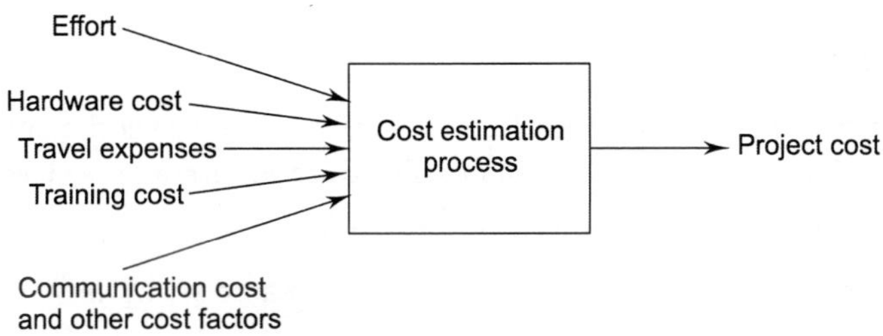

Fig. 3.3 Cost estimation process

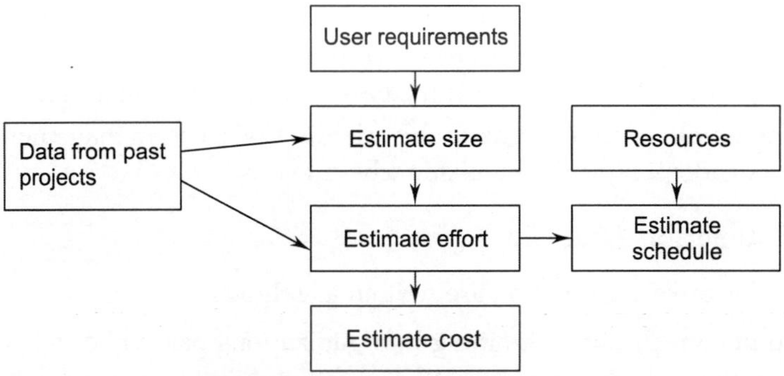

Fig. 3.4. Project estimation process

Now, once the estimation is complete, we may be interested to know how accurate the estimates are to reality. The answer to this is "we do not know until the project is complete." There is always some uncertainty associated with all estimation techniques. The accuracy of project estimation will depend on the following.

- Accuracy of historical data used to project the estimation
- Accuracy of input data to various estimates
- Maturity of organization's software development process.

The following are some of the reasons, which make the task of cost estimation difficult:

- Software cost estimation requires a significant amount of effort. Sufficient time is not allocated for planning.
- Software cost estimation is often done hurriedly, without an appreciation for the actual effort required and is far from real issues.

- Lack of experience for developing estimates, especially for large projects.
- An estimator uses the extrapolation technique to estimate, ignoring the non-linear aspects of software development process.

3.4.5 Reasons for Poor/Inaccurate Estimation

The following are some of the reasons for poor and inaccurate estimation:

- Requirements are imprecise. Also, requirements change frequently.
- The project is new and is different from past projects handled.
- Non-availability of enough information about past projects.
- Estimates are forced to the based on available resources.

Cost and time tradeoffs

If we elongate the project, we can reduce overall cost. Usually, customers and managements do not like long project durations. There is always shortest possible duration for a project, but it comes at a cost.

The following are some of the problems with estimates:

- Estimating size is often skipped and a schedule is estimated which is of more relevance to the management.
- Estimating size is perhaps the most difficult step, which has a bearing on all other estimates.
- Let us not forget that even good estimates are only projections and subject to various risks.
- Organizations often give less importance to collection and analysis of historical data of past development project. Historical data is the best input to estimate a new project.
- Project managers often underestimate the schedule because management and customers often hesitate to accept a prudent realistic schedule.

3.4.6 Project Estimation Guidelines

Some guidelines for project estimation are written as follows:

- Preserve and document data pertaining to organizations past projects.
- Allow sufficient time for project estimation especially for bigger projects.
- Prepare realistic developer-based estimate. Associate people who will work on the project to reach at a realistic and more accurate estimate.
- Use software estimation tools.
- Re-estimate the project during the life cycle of development process.
- Analyze past mistakes in the estimation of projects.

3.4.7 Where are Estimates Done?

Estimates are carried out at various stages of a software project. At each stage the reasons for the estimate and the methods used will vary.

1. **Strategic planning:** At this stage, the costs of computerizing potential applications and the benefits of doing so may need to be estimated to help decide what priority to give to each project. Such estimates may also influence the numbers of various types of development staff to be recruited by the organizations.
2. **Feasibility study:** This ascertains that the benefits of the potential system will justify the costs.

3. **System specification:** Most system development methodologies usefully distinguish between the definition of the user's requirements and the design which documents how those requirements are to be fulfilled. The effort needed to implement different design proposals will need to be estimated. Estimates at the design stage will also confirm that the feasibility study is still valid taking into account all that has been learnt during detailed requirements analysis.
4. **Evaluation of suppliers' proposals:** In the case of the IOE maintenance group accounts subsystem, for example, IOE might consider putting the actual system building out to tender. potential contractors considering a bid would need to scrutinize the system specification and produce estimates on which to base proposals. Amanda might still be required to carry out her own estimate to help judge the bids received. IOE may wish to questions a proposal which seems too low: they might wonder for example whether the proposer had properly understood the requirement. If on the other hand the bids seem too high they might reconsider in—house development.
5. **Project planning:** As the planning and implementation of the project progresses to greater levels of details, more detailed estimate of smaller work components will be made. As well as confirming the earlier and broader brush estimate, these will help answer questions about, for example when staff will have completed particular tasks and be available for new activities.

Two general points can be made here:

- as the project proceeds so the accuracy of the estimates should improves as knowledge about the nature of the project increase;
- a conventional wisdom is that at the beginning of the project the user requirement (that is a logical model of the required system) is of paramount importance and that premature consideration of the physical implementation is to be avoided. in order to produce an estimate, however the estimator will have to speculate about this physical implementation (for instance, about the number of software components to be written)

3.4.8 Problems with Over and Under-Estimates

An over-estimate may cause the project to take longer than it would otherwise. This can be explained by the application of two 'laws'.

1. **Parkinson's law:** In 1958, English author and historian C Northcote Parkinson (1909–1993) wrote a satirical book describing human behavior, Parkinson's Law: The Pursuit of Progress. This was the source of the quote "Work expands to fill the time available."

   Parkinsons Law (sometimes called Parkinson's Principle) has been found startlingly accurate, enough to merit its adoption into mainstream thinking. Even if the law is only partially valid, there are major implications for the efficiency of organizations, management efficiency, and motivation of the workforce.

   Application

   The simple definition: **"work expands to fill the time available"** *i.e.,* given an easy target staff will work less hard. For example, is provided two people writing a postcard. An elderly retired person may consume an entire day for this task: carefully choosing the card, contemplating the word choice, followed by a long, leisurely walk to the post office. A busy person will pick the first appropriate card, write it and mail it on the way home.

   Many other examples were given by Parkinson. One of his most alarming relates to bureaucracies. For example, most of the population assumes that a growing civil service reflects a growing workload. Parkinson believes otherwise and provides this argument:

Civil servant A is overworked (this may be illusory or the result of reaching their *level of incompetence*). The worker has only a few options; he may leave, share his work with colleagues at the same level or appoint two juniors. It is important to note that he has to appoint two juniors. A single subordinate would very quickly assume almost equal status with A in their own minds as well as others and would therefore be a rival. This is also the reason against sharing the work with someone on the same level. So now, assuming A didn't leave, we have A and two subordinates B and C. Very soon either B or C will complain about being overworked and two more subordinates to them will be appointed. Another two will have to be appointed to keep the other original subordinate happy.

Seven are now doing the work of one. All will be busy shuffling paperwork, holding meetings, and passing e-mails amongst themselves, correcting grammar, passing decisions down the line and back up again, and plotting or defending themselves from coworker backstabbing. Person A is now reduced to management, something he may not be happy with; in fact he may have had his level of incompetence enforced on him.

2. **Brook's law:** The effort required to implement a project will go up disproportionately with the number of staff assigned to the project. As the project team grows in size, so will the effort that has to go into management, coordination and communication. This has given rise in extreme cases to the notion of brook's law putting more people on a late job makes is later. If there is an over estimate of the effort required then this could lead to more staff being allocated than are needed and managerial overheads being increased. This is more likely to be of significance with large projects.

   Some have suggested that while the under estimated project might not be completed on time or to cost, it might still be implemented in a shorter time than a project with a more generous estimate. There must however be limits to this phenomenon where all the slack in the project has been taken up.

   The danger with the under—estimate is the effect on quality. Staff particularly those with less experience could respond to pressing deadline by producing work which is substandard. Since we are into laws, this may be seen as a manifestation of weinberg's zeroth law of reliability. "If a system does not have to be reliable it can meet any other objective. In other words, if there is no need for the program to actually work you can meet any programming deadline that may be set substandard work might only become visible at the later testing phase of a project which are particularly difficult to control and where extensive rework can have catastrophic consequences for the project completion data. Because of the possible effects on the behavior of development staff, the size of estimates might be artificially reduced by their managers to increase pressure on staff. This will only work where staff is unaware that this has been done. Research has found that motivation and morale are enhanced where targets are achievable. If over a period of time staff become aware that the targets set are unattainable and that project are routinely not meeting their published targets then this will help to destroy motivation. Furthermore people like to think of themselves as winners and there is a general tendency to put success down to our own efforts while failure is blamed on the organization.

   In the end an estimate is not really a prediction, it is a management goal. Barry Boehm has suggested that if a software development cost is within 20% of the estimated cost for the job then a good manager can turn it into a self—fulfilling prophecy. A project leader like amanda will work hard to make the actual performance conform of the estimate.

3.5 CONSTRUCTIVE COST MODEL (COCOMO)

COCOMO stands for Constructive Cost Model. It was introduced by Barry Boehm in 1981. It is perhaps the best known and most thoroughly documented of all software cost estimation models. It provides the following three levels of models:

- **Basic COCOMO:** A single-value model that computes software development cost as a function of estimate of LOC.
- **Intermediate COCOMO:** This model computes development cost and effort as a function of program size (LOC) and a set of cost drivers.
- **Complete COCOMO:** This model computes development effort and cost which incorporates all characteristics of intermediate level with assessment of cost implication on each step of development (analysis, design, testing etc).

This model may be applied to three classes of software project as given below:

- **Organic:** Small size project. A simple software project where the development team has good experience of the application.
- **Semi-detached:** An intermediate size project and project is based on rigid and semi-rigid requirements.
- **Embedded:** The project developed under hardware, software and operational constraints. Examples are embedded software, flight control software.

3.5.1 Basic COCOMO Model

The basic COCOMO model gives an approximate estimate of the project parameters. The basic COCOMO estimation model is given by the following expressions:

$$\text{Effort} = a_1 \times (\text{KLOC})^{a_2} \text{ PM}$$

$$\text{T}_{\text{dev}} = b_1 \times (\text{Effort})^{b_2} \text{ Months}$$

Where,

KLOC is the estimated size of the software product expressed in Kilo Lines, Code a_1, a_2, b_1, b_2 are constants of software products

T_{dev} is the estimated time to develop the software, expressed in months

Effort is the total effort required to develop the software product, expressed in Person-Month (PM)

Person months curve is shown in Fig. 3.5.

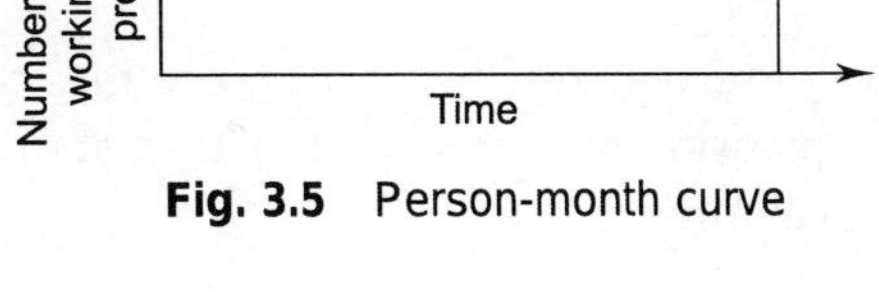

Fig. 3.5 Person-month curve

Estimation of Development Effort

Organic : Effort = 2.4 $(KLOC)^{1.05}$ PM

Semidetached : Effort = 3.0 $(KLOC)^{1.12}$ PM

Embedded : Effort = 3.6 $(KLOC)^{1.20}$ PM

Figure 3.6 (*a*) shows a plot of estimated effort versus size for various product sizes

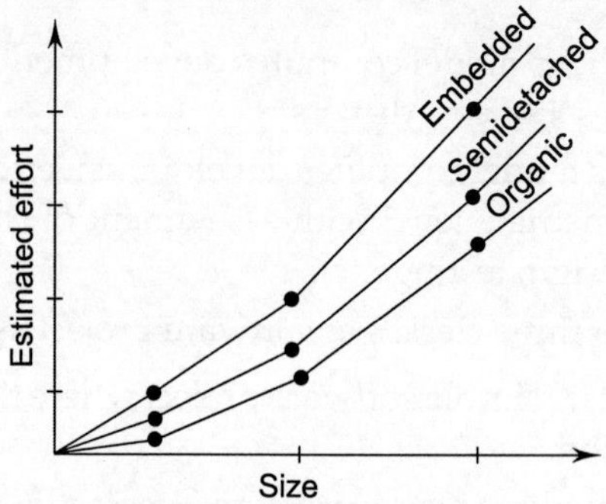

Fig 3.6.(a) Effort vs size

From Fig. 3.6 (*a*), we can observe that the effort is almost linearly proportional to the size of the software product

Estimation of Development time

Organic : T_{dev} = 2.5 $(Effort)^{0.38}$ Months

Semidetached : T_{dev} = 2.5 $(Effort)^{0.35}$ Months

Embedded : T_{dev} = 2.5$(Effort)^{0.32}$ Months

Figure 3.6 (*b*) shows the plot is development size versus product size.

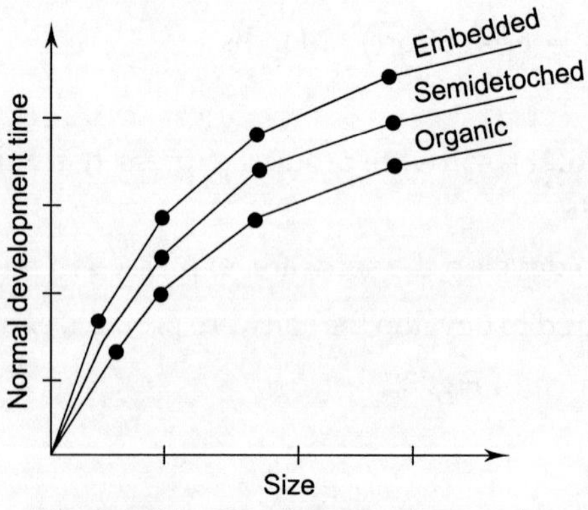

Fig. 3.6.(b) Development time vs size

From Fig. 3.6 (*b*), we can observe that the development time is a sub-linear function of the size of the product.

3.5.2 Intermediate COCOMO Model

The intermediate COCOMO model recognizes this fact and refines the initial estimate obtained through the BASIC COCOMO expression by using a set of 15 cost drivers (multipliers) based on various attributes of software development.

Table 3.3 COCOMO intermediate cost drivers

Driver Type	*Code*	*Cost Driver*
Product attributes	RELY	Required software reliability
	DATA	Database size
	CPLX	Product complexity
Computer attributes	TIME	Execution time constraints
	STOR	Main storage constraints
	VIRT	Virtual machine volatility-degree to which the operating system changes
	TURN	Computer turn around time
Personnel attributes	ACAP	Analyst capability
	AEXP	Application experience
	PCAP	Programmer capability
	VEXP	Virtual machine (*i.e.*, operation system) experience
	LEXP	Programming language experience
Project attributes	MODP	Use of modern programming practices
	TOOL	Use of software tools
	SCED	Required development schedule.

3.5.3 Complete COCOMO Model

The short-comings of both basic and intermediate COCOMO models are that they: -

(*i*) Consider a software product as a single homogenous entity.

(*ii*) However, most large systems are made up of several smaller sub-systems. Some sub-systems may be considered as organic type, some embedded, etc. For some the reliability requirements may be high, and so on.

(*iii*) Cost of each sub-system is estimated separately.

(*iv*) Costs of the sub-systems are added to obtain total cost.

(*v*) Reduces the margin or error in the final estimate.

A large amount of work has been done by Boehm to capture all significant aspects of a software development. It offers a means for processing all the project characteristics to construct a software estimate. The complete model introduces two more capabilities:

1. **Phase sensitive effort multipliers:** Some phases (design, programming, and integration/test) are more affected than others by factors defined by the cost drivers. The complete model provides a set of phase sensitive effort multipliers for each cost driver. This helps in determining the manpower allocation for each phase of the project.
2. **Three level product hierarchy:** Three product levels are defined. These are module, subsystem and system levels. The ratings of the cost drivers are done at appropriate level; that is, the level at which it is most susceptible to variation.

3.6 FUNCTION POINT ANALYSIS

3.6.1 Function Point

Function points and feature points are methods of estimating the "amount of functionality" required for a program, and are thus used to estimate project completion time. The basic idea involves counting inputs, outputs, and other features of a description of functionality.

3.6.2 Function Point Metric

Function point metric was proposed by Allan ***Albrecht*** (1983), when he worked for IBM. Function oriented software metrics use a measure of the functionality delivered by the application as a normalization value. Since functionality cannot be measured directly, it must be derived indirectly using other direct measures. Function points are derived using an empirical relationship based on direct measures of software's information domain and assessments of software complexity.

Function points are computed by completing the following Table 3.4.

Table 3.4 Function point contribution of an element

Function Type	*Simple*	*Average*	*Complex*
External input	3	4	6
External output	4	5	7
Logical internal file	7	10	15
External interface file	5	7	10
External inquiry	3	4	6

The different function types mentioned in the Table 3.4 are discussed as under:

1. **External types:** The are input transactions that update internal computer files.
2. **External output types:** The are transactions where data is output to user. Typically theses would be printed reports.
3. **Logical internal file types:** The are the standing files used by the system. The term 'file' does not sit easily with modern information systems. It refers to a group of data that is usually accessed together. It might be made up of one or more record types.
4. **External interface file types:** Allow for output and input that might pass to and from other computer applications.
5. **External inquiry types:** Note the US spelling of inquiry—are transactions initiated by the user that provide information but do not update the internal files. The user inputs some information that directs the system to the details required.

3.6.3 Special Features

1. Function point approach is independent of the language, tools or methodologies used for implementation; *i.e.*, they do not take into consideration programming languages, database management systems, processing hardware or any other database technology.
2. Function points can be estimated from requirement specification or design specifications, thus making it possible to estimate development effort in early phases of development.
3. Function points are directly linked to the statement of requirements; any change of requirements can easily be followed by are-estimate.
4. Function points are based on the system user's external view of the system; non-technical users of the software system have a better understanding of what function points are measuring.

3.6.4 Advantages of Function Points

1. It is not restricted to code.
2. It is language independent.

3. The necessary data is available early in a project and thus only a detailed specification is needed.
4. More accurate than estimated LOC
5. It can be used to easily estimate the size of a software product directly from the problem specification.

3.6.5 Drawbacks of Function Point

1. Subjective counting-different people can come up with different estimates for the same problem.
2. Hard to automate and difficult to compute
3. Ignores quality of output
4. Oriented to traditional data processing applications

3.6.6 Feature Point Metrics

A function point extension called feature points is a superset of the function point measure that can be applied to systems and engineering software applications. Therefore its size should be larger compared to simpler functions.

Proponents of function point and feature point metrics claim that these metrics are language-independent and can be easily computed from the SRS document during project planning, whereas opponents claim that these metrics are subjective and require a sleight of hand. An example of the subjective nature of the function point metric can be that the way one would group logically related data items could be very subjective. For example if a data employee—details consists of the employee name and his address, one person can consider it a single unit of data while someone else can consider the address as one unit and name as another. Therefore, different engineers can arrive at different function point measures for the same problem.

Example 3.1. *Compute the function point value for a project with the following information domain characteristics.*
Number of user Inputs: 32
Number of User output: 60
Number of User Inquiries: 24
Number of files: 8
Number of external interface: 2
Assume that all complexity adjustment values are average.

Solution.

Measurement parameter	**Count**	**Weighting factor (Average)**		
Number of user inputs	32	4	=	128
Number of User outputs	60	5	=	300
Number of user Inquires	24	84	=	96
Number of files	8	10	=	80
Number of external interfaces	2	7	=	14
Count total				**618**

$$\text{Function point (FP)} = \text{Count Total X } (0.65 + 0.01 \times \Sigma\,(f_i)$$

$$\text{FP} = 618 \times (0.65 + 0.01 \times 30)$$

$$= 618 \times (0.65 + 0.3)$$
$$= 618 \times (0.95)$$
$$= 587.10$$

3.7 MAKE-OR-BUY TECHNIQUE/DECISION PROCESS

Make or Buy technique, is a general management technique, which is a part of the scope definition process.

- It can be used for determining if the performing organization can produce a product in a cost effective manner.

  Note: This includes policy issues in respect of procurement, *e.g.*, some organizations always outsource coding services
- It considers both the direct and indirect costs, *e.g.*, the "buy" side of analysis should include both the direct cost of procurement and the cost of managing the procurement process
- Make-or-buy analysis must also reflect:
  - The perspective of performing organization, and
  - The immediate needs of the project, *e.g.*, purchasing or hiring /leasing hardware.

  Note: If the performing organization has an ongoing need for an item then, the project may benefit due to a lower apportioned cost.

3.7.1 Principle of Software Project Decision Process

The decision process is a framework that helps project managers solve a variety of decision-making problems. There is no exact method for how decision analysis should be structured. The process can be different for different companies, type of projects, and the types of decisions that must be made.

Any decision process is based on three main rules, which can be called 3C principle (See Fig. 3.7):

1. **Consistency:** It is important to standardize the decision process for similar kinds of problems and opportunities to enable consistent decision making over time.
2. **Comprehensiveness:** Decision processes should include a comprehensive assessment and analysis of the business situation. Missing or incomplete information can lead to incorrect decisions.
3. **Continuity:** The value of decision process will significantly diminish if it is done only in discrete situations during the course of a project. Decision process is a continuous process of making and refining decisions during a course of a project.

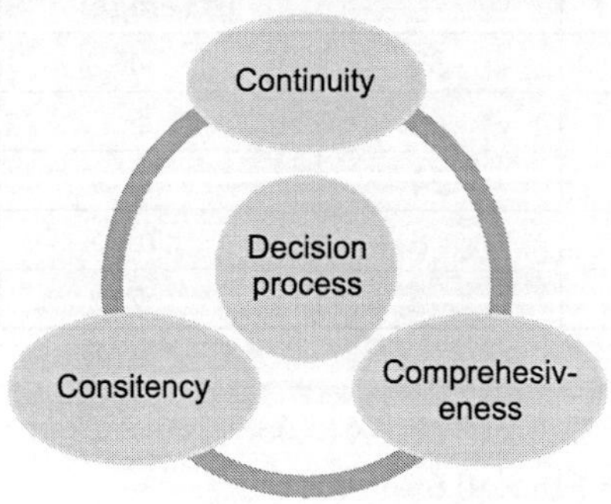

Fig. 3.7 Decision process of 3C principle

For example, decision process helps oil and gas companies to determine optimal exploration and production strategies with uncertainties in cost, prices, and exploration prospects. Lawyers are using decision analysis for assessment of complex litigations (synonyms: disputations, quarrelsome) with the uncertain outcomes. Decision analysis helps medical professionals to make a correct diagnosis and prescribe a most effective treatment.

4

WORK BREAKDOWN STRUCTURE

4.1 INTRODUCTION TO WORK BREAKDOWN STRUCTURE

The Work Breakdown Structure provides a common framework for the natural development of the overall planning and control of a contract and is the basis for dividing work through the process of Decomposition into definable increments from which the statement of work can be developed and technical, schedule, cost, and labor hour reporting can be established.

A work breakdown structure permits summing of subordinate costs for deliverables, materials, etc.; into their successively higher level "parent" deliverables, materials, etc. For each element of the work breakdown structure, a description of the task to be performed is generated. This technique (sometimes called a System Breakdown Structure) is used to define and organize the total scope of a project.

A Work Breakdown Structure (WBS) is a chart in which the critical work elements, called tasks, of a project are illustrated to portray their relationships to each other and to the project as a whole. The graphical nature of the WBS can help a project manager predict outcomes based on various scenarios, which can ensure that optimum decisions are made about whether or not to adopt suggested procedures or changes.

When creating a WBS, the project manager defines the key objectives first and then identifies the tasks required to reach those goals. A WBS takes the form of a tree diagram with the "trunk" at the top and the "branches" below. The primary requirement or objective is shown at the top, with increasingly specific details shown as the observer reads down.

When completed, a well-structured WBS resembles a flowchart in which all elements are logically connected, redundancy is avoided and no critical elements are left out. Elements can be rendered as plain text or as text within boxes. The elements at the bottom of the diagram represent tasks small enough to be easily understood and carried out. Interactions are shown as lines connecting the elements. A change in one of the critical elements may affect one or more of the others. If necessary, these lines can include arrowheads to indicate time progression or cause-and-effect.

A well-organized, detailed WBS can assist key personnel in the effective allocation of resources, project budgeting, procurement management, scheduling, quality assurance, quality control, risk management, product delivery and service oriented management. Thus WBS is:

- A key strategy of effective planning is to partition the project into manageable chunks that can be individually planned estimated and controlled.
- A graphical tool that displays the project's statement of work making it easier to understand and communicate. It is employed from the earliest stages of project planning.
- A chart or a type of diagram that displays a project in a Top-Down fashion.
- A chart that shows the structure of a project and how the project breaks down into various phases (summary) and task (detail) levels.
- A chart that generally, uses a tree diagram/structure diagram to show the resolution of overall requirements into increasing levels of detail.
- WBS allows a team to accomplish its general requirements by partitioning a large task into smaller components and focusing on work that can be more easily accomplished.

4.1.1 Definitions

WBS is a hierarchical structure used to organize tasks for planning, scheduling, reporting and measuring cost and effort.

OR

WBS is the process of breaking the goal driven task into components in such a way that when they are executed together, accomplish a measurable goal of the task.

OR

WBS is a hierarchy of elements that decomposes the software development plan, based on RDD (Requirement Definition & Description), into discrete work tasks.

OR

WBS is used to break the RDD into smaller units or components for planning and budgeting and for controlling costs, resources and efforts.

OR

The Work Breakdown Structure (WBS) is a powerful tool for expressing the scope or extent of a project in simple graphic terms. It represents the project in terms of the hierarchy of deliverables and services it will produce.

OR

A Work Breakdown Structure (WBS) in project management and systems engineering, is a tool used to define and group a project's discrete work elements in a way that helps organize and define the total work scope of the project.

OR

The Work Breakdown Structure (WBS) is a tool that defines a project and groups the project's discrete work elements in a way that helps organize and define the total work scope of the project.

OR

A Work Breakdown Structure (WBS) is a process for defining the final and intermediate products of a project and their relationships.

OR

The Work Breakdown Structure is a tree structure, which shows a subdivision of effort required to achieve an objective; for example a program, project, and contract. In a project or contract, the WBS is developed by starting with:

- The end objective and
- Successively subdividing it into manageable components
- In terms of size, duration, and responsibility (*e.g.*, systems, subsystems, components, and work packages)
- Which include all steps necessary to achieve the objective.

4.1.2 Representation of WBS

A complex project is made manageable by first breaking it down into individual components in a hierarchical structure, known as the work breakdown structure, or the WBS. Such a structure defines tasks that can be completed independently of other tasks, facilitating resource allocation, assignment of responsibilities, and measurement and control of the project.

The work breakdown structure can be illustrated in a block diagram:

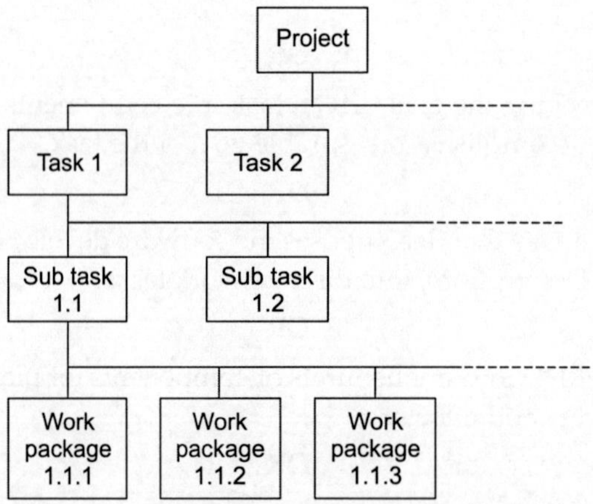

Fig. 4.1 Hierarchical Representation of WBS

Because the WBS is a hierarchical structure, it may be conveyed in outline form:

Table 4.1 Representation of WBS in outline form

Level 1	*Level 2*	*Level 3*
Task 1		
	Subtask 1.1	
		Work Package 1.1.1
		Work Package 1.1.2
		Work Package 1.1.3
	Subtask 1.2	
		Work Package 1.2.1
		Work Package 1.2.2

		Work Package 1.2.3
Task 2		
	Subtask 2.1	
		Work Package 2.1.1
		Work Package 2.1.2
		Work Package 2.1.3

4.1.3 Example of WBS

A WBS chart or Work Breakdown Structure chart is a type of diagram that displays a project in a Top-Down fashion. It shows the structure of a project and how the project breaks down into various phases (summary) and task (detail) levels. A WBS chart can also show the rollup of information to each level of the project depending on the view selected.

In other words, the WBS starts with a single box at the top which represents the whole project. The project is then partitioned into its components with lower level boxes. Here is an example (See Fig. 4.2) of a WBS chart:

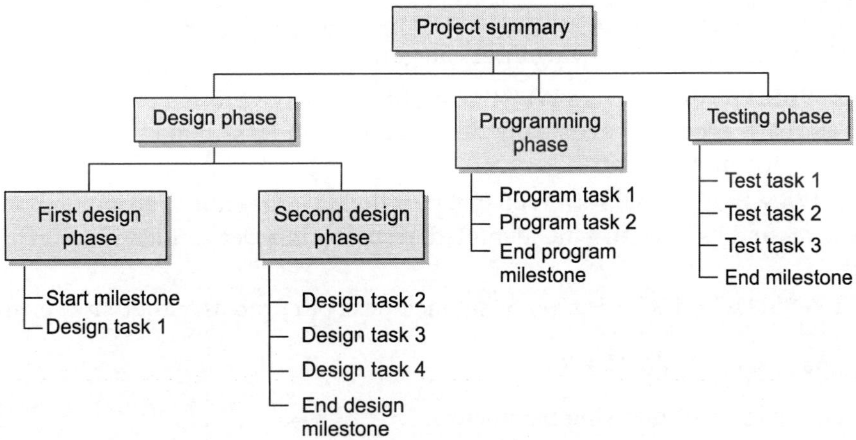

Fig. 4.2 Exmple of WBS

4.1.4 When to Use WBS

A work breakdown structure is an essential element in project planning and project management. In the quality planning process, WBS begins with a generalized goal and then identifies progressively finer levels of actions needed to accomplish the goal. In the quality improvement process, the tool is especially useful for creating an implementation plan to remedy identified process problems. For WBS to accurately reflect the project, however, it is essential that the team using it have detailed understanding of the tasks required.

4.1.5 How to Use WBS

The basic steps to use Work Breakdown Structure are discussed as follows:

1. **Identify the primary requirement or objective:** This should be a clear item, based on customer requirements, to which the entire team agrees. Write this requirement at the top of the chart.

2. **Subdivide the requirement statement into major secondary categories:** These branches should represent requirements, products, or activities that directly lead to the primary objective or that are directly required to fulfill the overall requirement. The team should continually ask, "What is required to meet this condition?", "What happens next?", and "What needs to be addressed?" Write the secondary categories below the primary requirement statement. Using sticky notes at this stage makes later changes easier to accomplish.
3. **Break each major heading into greater detail:** As you move from top to bottom in the WBS, products and activities should become more and more specific. Stop the breakdown when each task is tiny enough to be easily completed and evaluated for accuracy.

   If the team does not have enough knowledge to continue at some point, identify the individuals who can supply the information and continue the breakdown later with those individuals present.
4. **Review the WBS for logic and completeness:** Make sure that each subheading and path has a direct cause-and-effect relationship with the one before. Examine the paths to ensure that no obvious products or actions have been left out. Also ensure that the development of listed products or completion of listed actions will indeed lead to the anticipated results.

4.1.6 Types of WBS

WBS can be classified into the following three categories:

1. **Process WBS:** Process WBS is a WBS that partitions a large process into smaller and smaller processes. Each process is eventually decomposed into tasks that can be assigned to individuals for accomplishment.
2. **Product WBS:** Product WBS is a WBS that partitions a large entity into its components. Each components and its interfaces are identified, resulting in a clearer identification of the larger system.
3. **Hybrid WBS:** Hybrid WBS is a WBS that includes both process and product elements.

4.1.7 Parameters to Build WBS

WBS can be built using the following parameters:

1. **System structure:** If the system is broken into modules then they become the anchor to build WBS. This can be further linked to the delivery and implementation plan
2. **Functions:** If the system is largely function driven, then WBS can be built around it's application, which is designed to deliver functions.
3. **Organizational units:** If the system can be visualized after modeling by structure and or functions into organizational units, than WBS can be anchored onto organizational units
4. **Life cycle phases:** Disregarding the earlier three parameters, one can follow the life cycle phase and build WBS for each phase starting from inception till delivery to the customer.

   The choice of WBS parameters largely depends upon the nature, complexity and the development and implementation strategy.

4.1.8 Role of WBS

The role of the WBS is to:

- Partition the major project deliverables into smaller components to improve the accuracy of cost estimates.

- Provide a mechanism for collecting and organizing actual costs.
- Provide a mechanism for performance measurement and control.

4.1.9 WBS Characteristics

1. Each WBS is a well-defined statement, having specific goals to be achieved.
2. The activities in WBS are standard life cycle activities, which when completed achieve the goal.
3. WBS should be detailed enough to monitor and track the progress of development.
4. Each WBS has a milestone, suggesting a goal that can be traced back to SRS and RDD.
5. Goals and milestones should be quantifiable, measurable and controllable.
6. The breakdown of WBS into sub-activities should be such that it's scheduling is easier, resource allocation is clearly possible, and responsibility to complete the activity can be fixed with an individual.
7. The activities are such that their performance can be measured to control planned efforts, resources, costs and time allocation.
8. Several outputs together achieve a milestone; a number of milestones together achieve goals; and multiple goals convergence achieves the major customer deliverable.

4.1.10 Use of WBS

The Work Breakdown Structure (WBS) is used for defining work packages and developing and tracking the cost and schedule for the project. The work is broken down into tasks, each of which has a manager, a responsible institution, costs and schedule, technical scope, and, to the extent possible, a specific geographic piece of the machine.

4.1.11 Applications of the Different Types WBS

1. **Process WBS:** The process WBS is used by project managers to manage their software engineering projects. The WBS presents a "picture "of the activities that have to be accomplished to ensure a successful software project.

   The *top level* of the WBS identifies the project by name. The *second level* of the WBS identifies the major work elements to be done, such as planning, organizing, requirements analysis, design, coding, testing and so forth. The *third level* describes the more detailed activities that must be completed in order to accomplish the second level activities.

   The *lowest level* process elements in a WBS represent tasks. A task is the smallest unit of management accountability for work assigned. These small units of management's accountability are specified in "work packages". A work packages is a task specification that is suitable for assignment to one or two person for a duration of one or two weeks.
2. **Product WBS:** The product WBS is a primary tool of systems engineers and software engineers. A product WBS illustrates the components and interfaces of the product to be developed or produced and relates the elements of the product to each other and to the end product. The product WBS specifies the hardware, software and data that together completely define a project deliverable. The top level of the product WBS identifies the product by name. Other elements of a product WBS are discrete, identifiable items of hardware, software and data.

3. **Hybrid WBS:** Many practitioners combine the product and process elements of a project into one WBS. Some design the WBS by beginning with process elements and interleaving product with process elements; others begin with product elements and interleave the processes; other intermix product and processes on the same levels A process—product WBS begins with a process, alternates process and product elements, and terminates with the products elements. The rationale behind this approach is that processes produce products. Sub products is turn, require development processes. The terminal elements of this hybrid WBS are product components.
This approach is used by managers who first want to determine, and second, want to control project cost and schedule for each product elements. Activities that can not be attached to a particular product element, such as quality assurance and project management, are identified as stand—alone processes.
4. **WBS dictionary:** Each elements of a WBS is defined in a WBS dictionary. The elements are usually identified by their names and decimal numbers. Dictionary entries for process elements are work packages or pointers to work packages; entries for product elements are the requirements allocated to those elements or pointers to the requirements.

4.2 PROJECT LIFE CYCLE

Project Life Cycle is a collection of generally sequential project phases whose name and number are determined by the control needs of the organization or organizations involved in the project. A life cycle can be documented with a methodology.

The project life cycle is a part of the product life cycle covering the period from project initiation (also know as project authorization) to project closure (or termination).

A project life cycle is a collection of project phases. A project phases vary by project industry, but some general phases include concept, development, implementation, and closeout. The first two phases (concept and development) focus on planning and are often referred to as project feasibility the last two phases (implementation and close out) focus on delivering the actual work and often referred to as project acquisition.

Figure 4.3 provides a summary framework for the general phases of the project life cycle.

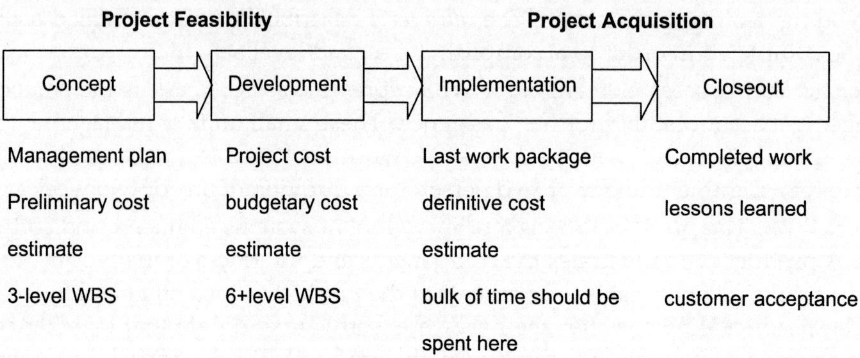

Fig. 4.3 Framework of project life cycle

1. **Concept phase:** In the concept phase the committee would be able to deliver a report and presentation on its findings. The report and presentation would be an example of a deliverable—a product produced as part of a project.

2. **Development phase:** After the concept phase is completed, the next project phase is of development phase. In the development phase the project team creates a more detailed project plan, a more accurate cost estimate, and a more thorough WBS. In the example under discussion, suppose the concept phase report suggested that requiring students to have laptops was one means of increasing the use of technology on campus. The project team could then further expand this idea in the development phase. They would have to decide if students would purchase or lease the laptops, what type of hardware and software the laptops would require, how much to charge students, how to handle training and maintenance, how to integrate the use of the new technology with current courses and so on. If, however the concept phase report showed that the laptop idea was not a good idea for the college, then increasing the use of technology by requiring laptops would no longer be considered in the development phase. This phased approach minimizes the time and money spent developing inappropriate project. A project idea must pass the concept phase before evolving during the development phase.
3. **Implementation phase:** The third phase of the project life cycle is called implementation. In this phase, the project team delivers the required work and creates a definitive or very accurate cost estimate. Suppose tom Walter's college took the idea of requiring students to have laptops through the development phase. during the implementation phase, the project team would need to obtain the required hardware and software, install the necessary network equipment, deliver the laptops to the students, create a process for collecting fees, provide training to students, faculty, and staff, and so on. Other people on campus would also be involved in the implementation phase. Faculty would need to consider how best to take advantage of the new technology. The recruiting staff would have to update their materials to reflect this new feature of the college. Security would need to address new problems that might result from having students carry around expensive equipment. The bulk of a project team's efforts and the most money are usually spent during the implementation phase of projects.
4. **Closeout phase:** The last phase of the project life cycle is called closeout. In the closeout phase, all of the work is completed, and there should be some sort of customer acceptance of the entire project. The project team should document their experiences on the project in a lessons—learned report. If the laptop idea made it all the way through the implementation phase and all students received laptops, the project team would then complete the project by closing out any related to gather opinions on how the project fared. They would ensure that any contracts with vendors were completed and appropriate payments had been made. They would transition future work related to the laptop project to other parts of the organization. The project team could also share their lessons learned with other college campuses who are considering doing the same thing.

4.3 THE PRODUCT LIFE CYCLE

The product life cycle is the period from the concept to the end of a product. The product life cycle models vary considerably with the nature of product *e.g.*, the product life cycle for building a bridge is significantly different than that for developing a software product. Product development life cycle is a part of the product life cycle.

Just like the product life cycles, the projects also follow a project life cycle.

Product life cycle model applies to all projects (regardless of the product), *e.g.*, initiation, planning, execution, monitoring and control, closure.

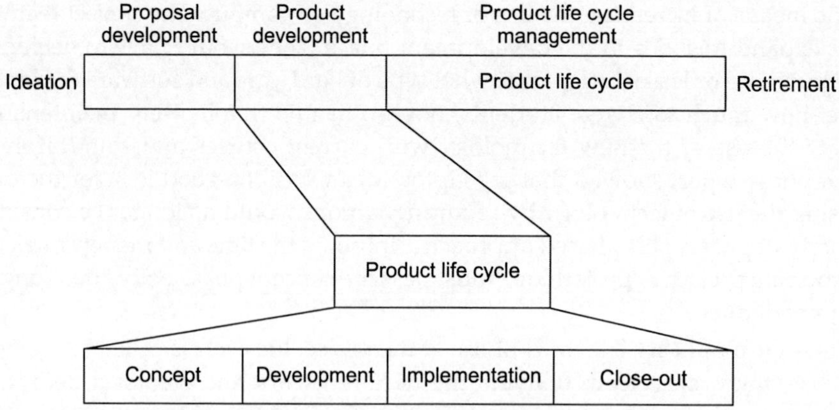

Fig. 4.4 The product life cycle and the project life cycle

Figure 4.4 shows the product life cycle and where one project life cycle could fit in. Understanding each of these life cycles and their relationships can help us to better define the start and finish of a project. In addition, we will gain a better understanding of how people measure product and project performance.

The product life cycle starts with an idea and ends with retirement of the product. Let us look at a software product as an example. Suppose that a sales representative for a Software Company calls on the human resources department of employees' contributions to their pensions. This finding gives the idea to develop an application for that client and sell it to them. The product is launched, and it proves to provide value, it may (or may not) enjoy a long period of demand. It is possible that underfurnished product technology become old, and the company decides to no longer support the product; this marks the end of that product's life and the end of its life cycle.

5

PROJECT SCHEDULING AND ITS TECHNIQUES

5.1 PROJECT SCHEDULING

Scheduling for software engineering project's can be viewed by two different perspectives. In the ***first,*** an end date for release of a computer-based system has already been established. The software organization is constrained to distribute effort within the prescribed time frame.

The ***second*** view of software schedule is that rough chronological bounds have been discussed but that the end date is set by the software engineering organization. Effort is distributed to make best use of resources, and an end date is defined after careful analysis of the software.

Unfortunately, the first situation is encountered far more frequently than the second.

The project schedule is the core of the project plan. It is used by the project manager to commit people to the project and show the organization how the work will be performed. It enables the project manager to identify risk points, understand the proper linkage of events assists in the resource planning and allows the Project Manager to establish goals for the team and the project. Before a project schedule can be related, the project manager must have a Work Breakdown Structure (WBS), an effort estimate for each task, and a source list with availability for each resource.

Thus a *project schedule*:

- It is a calendar that links the tasks to be done with the resources that will do them.
- It is the means by which the project manager brings the team and the project under control.

5.1.1 Definitions

Project Scheduling is the process of converting a general or outline plan for a project into a time-based graphic presentation given information on available resources and time constraints.

OR

Project Scheduling is the process of identifying and organizing the tasks of a project into a sequence of events ensuring a harmonious completion of the venture. These events are dependent on the results of their preceding activities, thus interlinking all the activities of the project. This interdependency provides for a major need of effective project scheduling.

OR

Software project schedule is an action that distributes estimated effort across the planned project duration by allocating the effort to specific software engineering tasks.

5.1.2 Basic Principles of Project Schedule

A number of basic principles guide software project schedule:

1. **Compartmentalization:** The project must be compartmentalized into a number of manageable activities and tasks. To accomplish compartmentalization, both the product and the process are refined.
2. **Interdependency:** The interdependency of each compartmentalized activity or task must be determined. Some tasks must occur in sequence, while others can occur in parallel. Some activities cannot commence until the work product produced by another is available. Other activity can occur independently.
3. **Time allocation:** Each task to be scheduled must be allocated some number of work units (*e.g.*, person-days of effort). In addition, each task must be assigned a star date and a completion date that is a function of the interdependencies and whether work will be conducted on a full time basis.
4. **Effort validation:** Every project has a defined number of people on the software team. As time allocation occurs, you must ensure that no more than the allocated number of people has been scheduled at any given time.
5. **Defined responsibilities:** Every task that is scheduled should be assigned to a specific team member.
6. **Defined outcomes:** Every task that is scheduled should have a defined outcome for software projects; the outcome is normally a work product or a part of a work product. Work products are often combined in deliverables.
7. **Defined milestones:** Every tasks or a group of tasks should be associated with a project milestones. A milestone is accomplished when one or more work products has been reviewed for quality and has been approved.

5.1.3 Scheduling Objectives

The goal of defining the schedule is for the project team to have a complete understanding of all the work that needs they must accomplish, by defining the schedule the project also develops an understanding of the constraints, dependencies and sequence of the activities.

5.1.4 Scheduling Terminology and Techniques

5.1.4.1 Scheduling Terminology

Some basic terminology related to scheduling is given below:

1. **Scheduling:** A scheduling is the mapping of task onto time. Each task has a start and an end time. We can thus plan the deadlines for individual deliverables.
2. **Task:** A task is a well defined work assignment for a role.

3. **Activities:** Group of related tasks is called as activities. A project manager assigns a task to role.
4. **Work product:** It is a tangible item that results from a task. For example, an objective models a class diagram, a piece of source code, a document etc.
5. **Work package:** The specification of work to be accomplished in completing a task or activity is described in a work package.
6. **Event:** Something that cause a system or objective to change state. For example, a message the condition becoming time of completion of an activity.
7. **Synchronization points:** The points in a project schedule that require the team to synchronize the contents of products, complete tasks and reduce defects.
8. **Thrashing:** The performing of unproductive work associated with a software project is known as thrashing.
9. **Task status:** The status of a specific task relative to the task goals and completion.
10. **Network:** A network is a graphical representation of a project plan, showing the interrelationships of various activities.

5.1.4.2 Scheduling Techniques

Scheduling techniques can be broadly divided into two main categories:

1. **Network diagram:** PERT and CPM.
2. **Bar chart:** Milestone chart and Gantt charts.

These scheduling techniques are discussed in the following sections.

5.2 NETWORK DIAGRAMS

Network diagrams play a very important role in the project scheduling. This is one of the most important scheduling techniques applied in various fields of project development.

Network analysis/diagrams entails a group of techniques for presenting information relating time and resources so as to assist in the planning, scheduling and controlling of projects.

The information usually represented by a network includes the sequences, interdependencies, interrelationships and criticality of various activities of the project.

5.2.1 Objectives of Network Analysis

The various objectives of network analysis are:

1. Powerful tools for planning, scheduling and control.
2. Minimization of total cost.
3. Minimization of total time.
4. Minimization of cost for a given total time.
5. Minimization of time for a given cost.
6. Minimization of idle resources.
7. To minimize production delays, interruptions and conflicts.

5.2.2 Applications of Network Analysis

Network analysis nowadays can be used in scheduling the projects of almost every field. Some of its applications are mentioned as follows:

1. Construction of a dam or canal system in a region.
2. Construction of a building or a highway.
3. Maintenance of aeroplanes or oil refinery.
4. Space flight.
5. Missile development.
6. Assembly line scheduling.
7. Cost control of a project using PERT/CPM.
8. Designing a prototype of a machine.
9. Development of supersonic planes.
10. Research and development.
11. Budget and auditing procedures.
12. Planning of political campaigns.
13. Strategic and tactical military planning.
14. Market penetration programmes.
15. Find the best traffic flow pattern in a large city.
16. Preparing inventory plans.
17. Organization of big conferences, public works etc.
18. Shifting of manufacturing plant from one side to another.

5.2.3 Rules for Drawing Network Diagrams

There are a number of rules in connection with the handling of events and activities of a project network that should be followed while constructing network diagram. These include:-

1. Each activity is represented by one and only one arrow in the network

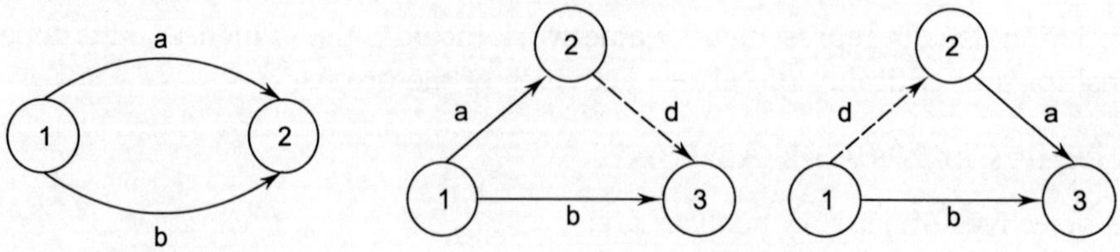

(*a*) Wrong (*b*) Right

Fig. 5.1 Representation of an activity

2. No two events can be identified by the same end events.
3. The flow of the diagram should be from left to right.
4. Activities are represented by arrows (→) and events are represented by circles (O).
5. Arrows should not cross each other.
6. Arrows should be kept straight and should not be curved or bent.
7. Dangling must be avoided in a network diagram.
8. The dummy activity should be introduced only if it extremely necessary.

9. All events should be numbered in ascending order.
10. No event numbers can be repeated.
11. No event can occur until every activity preceding it has been completed.
12. An activity succeeding an event cannot be started until that event has occurred.
13. The network has only one starting point (event) and one ending point which is known as ending/terminal event.

5.2.4 Fulkerson's Rule for Labeling Network Diagrams

The various rules for labeling network diagrams are:

1. Initial or start event is numbered as 1.
2. Delete all arrows emerging from all numbered events. This will create at least one new start event and this must be numbered in ascending order.
3. Continue numbering of all the events till we reach the last event out of which no activity will emerge.

5.2.5 Errors in Network Diagrams

Three types of errors are most commonly observed in drawing network diagrams:

1. **Dangling:** To disconnect an activity before the completion of all the activities in a network diagrams is known as dangling. As shown in Fig. 5.2, activities (5–10) and (6–7) are not the last activities in the network and hence these are dangling activities.

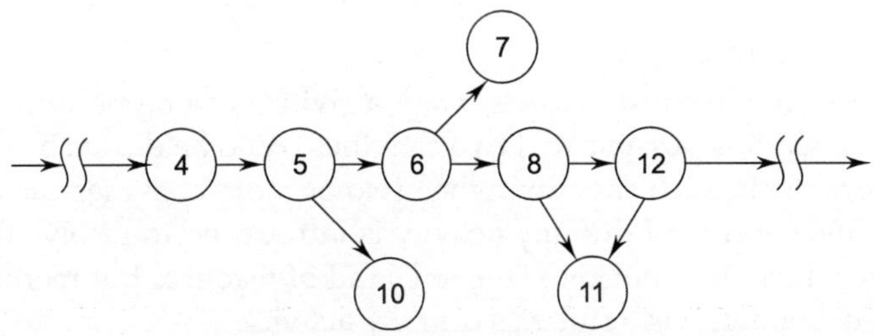

Fig. 5.2 Dangling error diagram

2. **Looping/cycling:** Drawing an endless loop in a network is known as error of looping or cycling error. This is shown in Fig. 5.3 as follows:

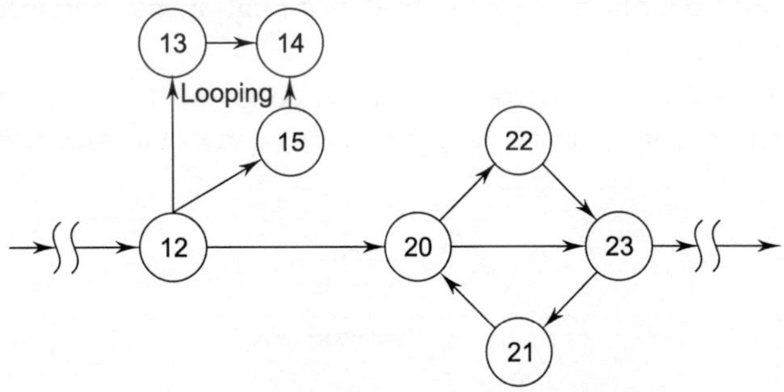

Fig. 5.3 Looping or cycling error diagram

3. **Redundancy:** Unnecessary inserting the dummy activity in network logic is known as the error of redundancy as shown in the Fig. 5.4 as follows:

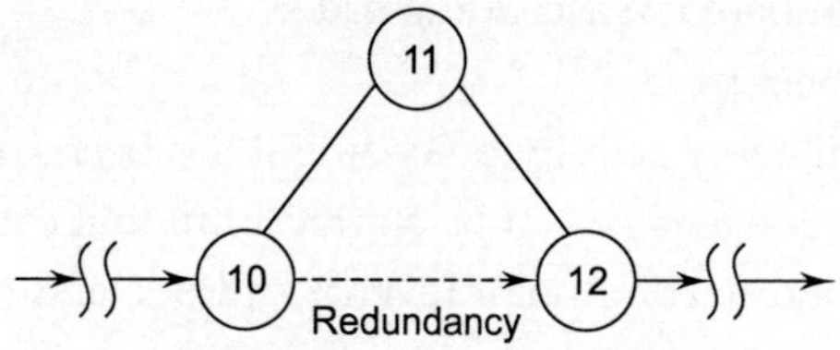

Fig. 5.4 Redundancy error

5.2.6 Terminologies in Project Management

1. **Activity:** An individual operation which has an end and a beginning and which utilizes resources is called activity. An arrow is used to represent an activity with it's head indicating the direction of progress in project.

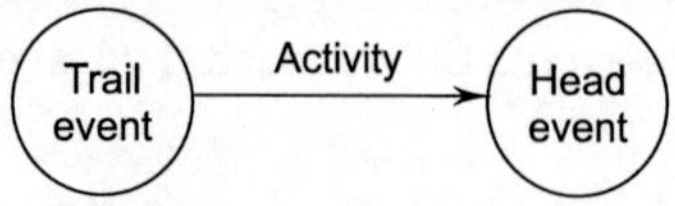

The activities are divided into four categories

(*a*) **Predecessor activity:** Activities that must be completed immediately prior to the start of another activity are called as Predecessor Activity.

(*b*) **Successor activity:** Activities that cannot be started until one or more of other activities are completed, but immediately succeed them are called Successor Activity.

(*c*) **Concurrent activity:** Activities which can be accomplished concurrently are known as concurrent activities.

(*d*) **Dummy activity:** In most projects many activities can be performed concurrently or simultaneously. It is possible that two activities could be drawn by the same beginning and end events. In such situation when two or more activities can be performed concurrently, the concept of dummy activity is introduced to resolve this problem. Thus, an activity which does not consume any kind of resource but merely depicts the technological dependence is termed as dummy activity.

Dummy Activities is inserted in the network to clarify the activity pattern in the following two situations:

- To make activities with common starting and finishing points distinguishable.
- To identify and maintain proper precedence relationship between activities those are not connected by events.

Example: Consider a situation where A and B are concurrent activities C is dependent on A and D is dependent on both A and B. Such a situation can be handled using a dummy activity as follows:

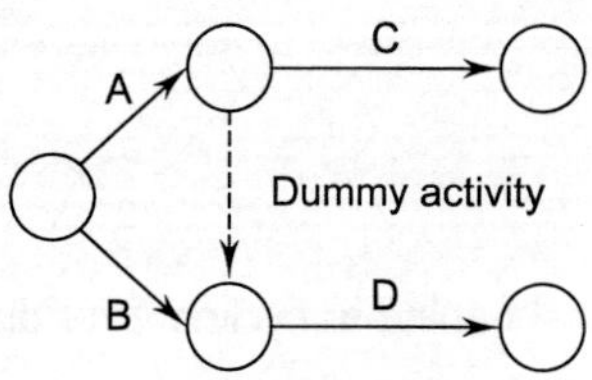

Fig.5.5 Example of dummy activity

2. **Event:** An Event is an instant of time at which an activity starts and finishes. An event is represented by circle (O) in a network which is known as node or connector. The event can be classified into 3 categories:
   (*a*) **Merge event:** When more than one activity comes and joins an event such an event is known as merge event.
   (*b*) **Burst event:** When more than one activity leaves an event, such event is known as burst event.
   (*c*) **Merge and burst event:** An activity may be a merge and burst event at the same time with respect to some activities it may be a burst event.

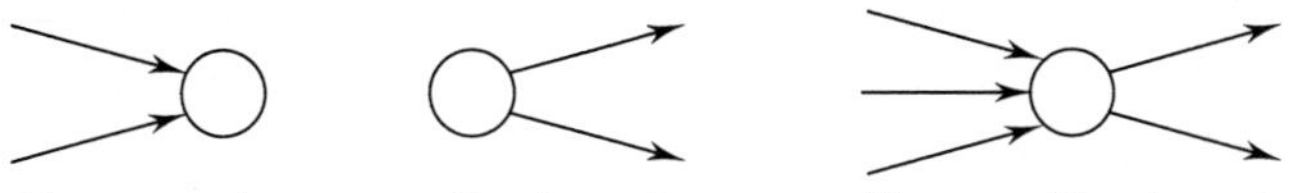

Fig. 5.6 Types of event

3. **Float:** Float can be described as the free time associated with an event. Hence, float or slack is that time by which an activity can be delayed without delaying the entire project. Activities which do not have any float or slack time are the activities which cannot be delayed without delaying the project. These activities are called the critical activities. Hence along the critical path the float or slack is zero.

Types of Float

(*a*) **Total float:** The amount of time by which the completion of an activity could be delayed beyond the earliest expected completion time without affecting the overall project duration time. Mathematically, total float of an activity (*i-j*) is the difference between the latest start time and earliest start time of that activity. Hence the total float $(T_f)_{ij}$ can be calculated by the formula:

$$(T_f)_{ij} = \text{(Latest start-Earliest start) for activity } (i\text{-}j) \text{ or}$$
$$(T_f)_{ij} = (L_s)_{ij} - (ES)_{ij}$$

This float is concerned with overall project duration

(*b*) **Free float:** The amount of time by which the completion of an activity could be delayed beyond the earliest expected completion time without affecting the earliest start of a succeeding activity. Mathematically, free float of an activity (*i-j*) is the difference between the earliest time for event *j* and the earliest time for event *i*. Hence, free float can be calculated by the formula:

$$(F_f)_{ij} = \text{Earliest time for event } j - \text{Earliest time for event } i.$$

This float is concerned with the commencement of the succeeding activity.

(*c*) **Independent float:** The amount of time by which the start of an activity can be delayed without affecting the earliest start time of any immediately following activities, assuming that the preceding activity has finished at its latest finish time. Mathematically, independent float of an activity (*i-j*) denoted by $(I_f)_{ij}$ can be calculated by formula:

$$(I_f)_{ij} = (E_j - L_i) - D_{ij}$$

The negative I_f is always taken zero. This float is concerned with prior and subsequent activities.

(*d*) **Critical path:** Critical path can be defined as "the sequence of critical activities in a network".

OR

The critical path is the longest path in the network from starting event to ending event and defines the minimum time required to complete the project.

By the term path we mean a sequence of activities such that it begins at the starting event and end at the final event. The length of a path is the sum of the individual times of the activities lying on a path.

If the activities on a critical path are delayed by a day, the project would also be delayed by a day unless the times of the future activities are reduced by a day by different means. The critical path is denoted by double or darker lines to make distinctions from other non-critical paths. The critical path identifies all critical activities of the project.

Features of Critical Path

1. If the project has to be shortened, then some of the activities on that path must also be shortened.
2. The variation in the actual performance from the expected activity duration time will be completely reflected in one to one fashion in the anticipated completion of the whole project.

Methods/ Steps to Determine Critical Path

1. Determination of Earliest Time
2. Determination of Latest Time
3. Computation of Float
4. To identify critical path *i.e.*, paths which have zero float.

5.3 TYPES OF NETWORK DIAGRAMS

Network diagrams play a very vital role in project management. Project management is necessary to ensure that a project is completed within the estimated budget, within the allocated time and perform to satisfaction. PERT and CPM are two techniques used in project management.

5.3.1 Critical Path Method (CPM)

Critical Path Method (CPM) was developed by M.R. Walker in the 1950s by the DuPont Corporation as a project management method designed to address the challenge of shutting down chemical plants for maintenance and then restarting the plants once the maintenance had been completed. Given the complexity of the process, they developed the Critical Path Method (CPM) for managing such projects. These methods were widely used by DuPont for many engineering functions.

The Critical Path Method (CPM) or critical path analysis is a mathematically based algorithm for scheduling a set of project activities. It emphasizes the relationship between applying more men or other resources to shorten the duration of given jobs in a project and the increased cost of these additional resources. Today, it is commonly used with all forms of projects, including construction, software development, research projects, and product development, engineering, and plant maintenance, among others. Any project with interdependent activities can apply this method of scheduling.

CPM models the activities and events of a project as a network. Activities are depicted as nodes on the network and events that signify the beginning or ending of activities are depicted as arcs or lines between the nodes. The following Fig. 5.7 depicts an example of a CPM network diagram:

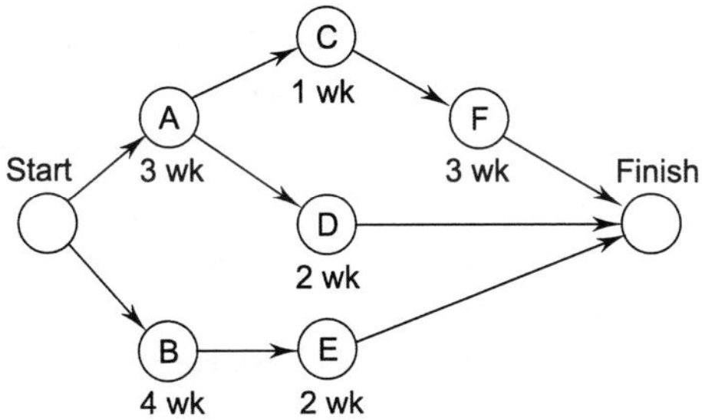

Fig. 5.7 Example of CPM diagram

5.3.1.1 Procedure to Determine the Critical Path

1. List all the jobs and draw the network diagrams.
2. Indicate the duration for each activity in the network.
3. Calculate the earliest start time and earliest finish time for each event.
4. Tabulate the various times such as normal time, start time and latest time on the arrow diagram.
5. Determine the total float for each activity by taking the difference between the earliest start and latest start time.
6. Identify the critical activities and connect them with the beginning event and ending event in the network diagram by darker or double lines arrows which give the critical path.
7. Calculate the total project duration.

5.3.1.2 Steps in CPM Project Planning

The following are the basic steps used in the CPM Project Planning:

1. **Specify the individual activities:** From the work breakdown structure, a listing can be made of all the activities in the project. This listing can be used as the basis for adding sequence and duration information in later steps.
2. **Determine the sequence of the activities:** Some activities are dependent on the completion of others. A listing of the immediate predecessors of each activity is useful for constructing the CPM network diagram.
3. **Draw the network diagram:** Once the activities and their sequencing have been defined, the CPM diagram can be drawn. CPM originally was developed as an *Activity On Node* (AON) network, but some project planners prefer to specify the activities on the arcs.
4. **Estimate activity completion time:** The time required to complete each activity can be estimated using past experience or the estimates of knowledgeable persons. CPM is a deterministic model that does not take into account variation in the completion time, so only one number is used for an activity's time estimate.
5. **Identify the critical path:** The critical path is the longest-duration path through the network. The significance of the critical path is that the activities that lie on it cannot be delayed

without delaying the project. Because of its impact on the entire project, critical path analysis is an important aspect of project planning.

The critical path can be identified by determining the following four parameters for each activity:

- ***ES - earliest start time:*** The earliest time at which the activity can start given that its precedent activities must be completed first.
- ***EF - earliest finish time***: Equal to the earliest start time for the activity plus the time required to complete the activity.
- ***LF - latest finish time:*** The latest time at which the activity can be completed without delaying the project.
- ***LS - latest start time:*** Equal to the latest finish time minus the time required to complete the activity.

The *slack time* for an activity is the time between its earliest and latest start time, or between its earliest and latest finish time. Slack is the amount of time that an activity can be delayed past its earliest start or earliest finish without delaying the project.

The critical path is the path through the project network in which none of the activities have slack, that is, the path for which ES=LS and EF=LF for all activities in the path. A delay in the critical path delays the project. Similarly, to accelerate the project it is necessary to reduce the total time required for the activities in the critical path.

6. **Update CPM diagram:** As the project progresses, the actual task completion times will be known and the network diagram can be updated to include this information. A new critical path may emerge, and structural changes may be made in the network if project requirements change.

5.3.1.3 Advantages of CPM

CPM provides the following advantages:

1. Helps the top management to concentrate their attention to the critical activities and there completion in time.
2. Provides a best way of planning and scheduling a construction project.
3. Provides a graphical view of the project.
4. Gives the complete information about the importance, duration, size and performance of an activity.
5. Predicts the time required to complete the project.
6. Shows which activities are critical to maintaining the schedule and which are not.

5.3.1.4 Disadvantages of CPM

CPM provides the following disadvantages:

1. Based on assumption of known time for each of the activity in the project which may not be true in real life situations.
2. Do not use statistical techniques in determining time estimates.
3. Entire evaluation of the project is to be repeated and a new critical path is to be found out when certain changes are done in the network.
4. Suitable for a situation which has a definite start and definite finish.

5.3.2 PERT

Complex projects require a series of activities, some of which must be performed sequentially and others that can be performed in parallel with other activities. This collection of series and parallel tasks can be modeled as a network.

In 1957 the Critical Path Method (CPM) was developed as a network model for project management. CPM is a deterministic method that uses a fixed time estimate for each activity. While CPM is easy to understand and use, it does not consider the time variations that can have a great impact on the completion time of a complex project.

The *Program Evaluation and Review Technique* (PERT) is a network model that allows for randomness in activity completion times. PERT was developed in 1958 by U.S. Navy for managing its Polaris Missile Project having thousands of contractors. It has the potential to reduce both the time and cost required to complete a project. It is a very useful device for planning time and resources of a project.

PERT is an event-oriented approach as it mainly concerned with various events in a project. PERT deals with the probability of completion of a project in particular time as the time of various activities involved cannot be known accurately. It is the only time an activity is expected to take for completion which can best be calculated.

The *main objective* is the analysis through PERT is to find out the completion for a particular event within specified date.

The following Fig. 5.8 depicts an example of a PERT chart:

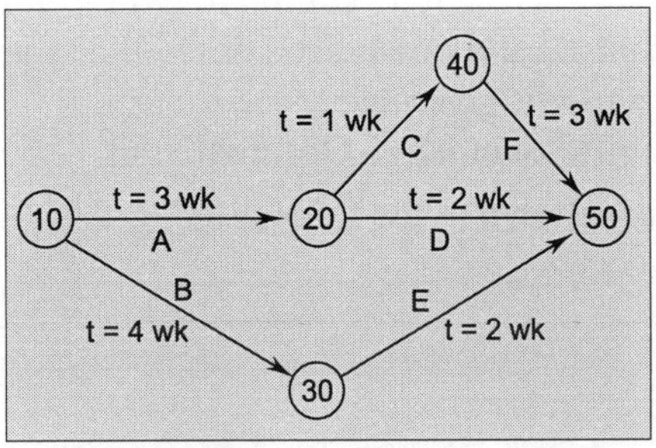

Fig. 5.8 Example of PERT chart

5.3.2.1 Steps in the Pert Planning Process

PERT planning process involves the following steps:

1. **Identify activities and milestones:** The activities are the tasks required to complete the project. The milestones are the events marking the beginning and end of one or more activities. It is helpful to list the tasks in a table that in later steps can be expanded to include information on sequence and duration.
2. **Determine activity sequence:** This step may be combined with the activity identification step since the activity sequence is evident for some tasks. Other tasks may require more analysis to determine the exact order in which they must be performed.
3. **Construct the network diagram:** Using the activity sequence information, a network diagram can be drawn showing the sequence of the serial and parallel activities. For the original activity-on-arc model, the activities are depicted by arrowed lines and milestones are depicted by circles or "bubbles".

If done manually, several drafts may be required to correctly portray the relationships among activities. Software packages simplify this step by automatically converting tabular activity information into a network diagram.

4. **Estimate activity times:** Weeks are a commonly used unit of time for activity completion, but any consistent unit of time can be used. A distinguishing feature of PERT is its ability to deal with uncertainty in activity completion times. For each activity, the model usually includes three time estimates: the optimistic value, the pessimistic value and the most likely value.
   (*a*) **Optimistic time (*a* or t_o):** It is generally the shortest possible time in which the activity can be completed. It is common practice to specify optimistic times to be three standard deviations from the mean so that there is approximately a 1% chance that the activity will be completed within the optimistic time. It assumes that everything goes very well.
   (*b*) **Most likely time (*m* or t_m):** It is the estimate of the normal time the activity would take. It assumes normal delays. Note that this time is different from the *expected time.*
   (*c*) **Pessimistic time (*b* or t_p):** It represents the longest time that an activity could take if everything goes wrong. Three standard deviations from the mean is commonly used for the pessimistic time.

   PERT assumes a beta probability distribution for the time estimates. For a beta distribution, the expected time for each activity can be approximated using the following weighted average:

   Expected time (t_e) = (Optimistic + 4 × Most likely + Pessimistic)/6

   This expected time may be displayed on the network diagram.

   To calculate the ***variance*** for each activity completion time, if three standard deviation times were selected for the optimistic and pessimistic times, then there are six standard deviations between them, so the variance is given by:

   Variance = [(Pessimistic – Optimistic)/6]^2

   These three time values are shown in the following Fig. 5.9

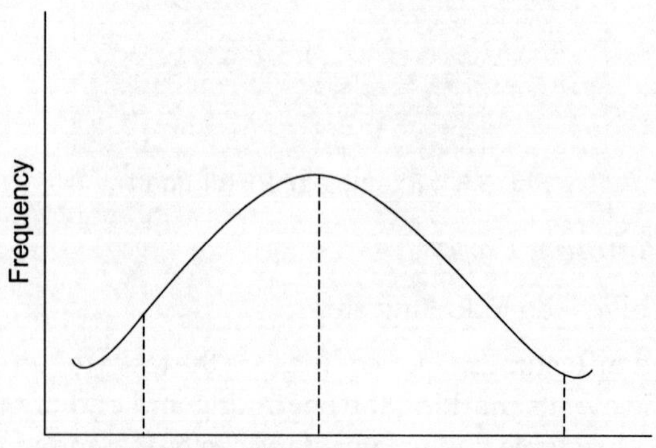

Fig. 5.9 Time distribution curve

5. **Determine the critical path:** The critical path is determined by adding the times for the activities in each sequence and determining the longest path in the project. The critical path determines the total calendar time required for the project. If activities outside the critical path speed up or slow down (within limits), the total project time does not change. The amount of time that a non-critical path activity can be delayed without delaying the project is referred to as *slack time.*

If the critical path is not immediately obvious, it may be helpful to determine the following four quantities for each activity:

- ES - Earliest Start time
- EF - Earliest Finish time
- LS - Latest Start time
- LF - Latest Finish time.

These times are calculated using the expected time for the relevant activities. The earliest start and finish times of each activity are determined by working forward through the network and determining the earliest time at which an activity can start and finish considering its predecessor activities. The latest start and finish times are the latest times that an activity can start and finish without delaying the project. LS and LF are found by working backward through the network. The difference in the latest and earliest finish of each activity is that activity's slack. The critical path then is the path through the network in which none of the activities have slack.

The variance in the project completion time can be calculated by summing the variances in the completion times of the activities in the critical path. Given this variance, one can calculate the probability that the project will be completed by a certain date assuming a normal probability distribution for the critical path. The normal distribution assumption holds if the number of activities in the path is large enough for the central limit theorem to be applied.

Since the critical path determines the completion date of the project, the project can be accelerated by adding the resources required to decrease the time for the activities in the critical path. Such a shortening of the project sometimes is referred to as *project crashing*.

6. **Update as project progresses:** Make adjustments in the PERT chart as the project progresses. As the project unfolds, the estimated times can be replaced with actual times. In cases where there are delays, additional resources may be needed to stay on schedule and the PERT chart may be modified to reflect the new situation.

5.3.2.2 *Advantages of PERT*

PERT provides the following advantages:

1. Forces management to plan carefully and study how the various parts fit into whole project.
2. Provides a forward looking type of control.
3. Make possible the pressure for action at the right time.
4. Focuses attention on critical elements of the project.
5. Suggest areas for increasing efficiency, reduction of costs and profit improvements.
6. Minimize production delays, interruptions and conflicts by scheduling and budgeting resources.

5.3.2.3 *Disadvantages of PERT*

PERT provides the following disadvantages:

1. Difficulty arises while securing the realistic time estimates.
2. It is also sometimes troublesome to develop a clear logical network.

3. Planning and implementation of network require personnel trained in network methodology.
4. The activity time estimates are somewhat subjective and depend on judgement. In cases where there is little experience in performing an activity, the numbers may be only a guess. In other cases, if the person or group performing the activity estimates the time there may be bias in the estimate.
5. Even if the activity times are well-estimated, PERT assumes a beta distribution for these time estimates, but the actual distribution may be different.
6. Even if the beta distribution assumption holds, PERT assumes that the probability distribution of the project completion time is the same as that of the critical path. Because other paths can become the critical path if their associated activities are delayed, PERT consistently underestimates the expected project completion time.

The underestimation of the project completion time due to alternate paths becoming critical is perhaps the most serious of these issues. To overcome this limitation, Monte Carlo simulations can be performed on the network to eliminate this optimistic bias in the expected project completion time.

5.3.3 Difference Between Pert and CPM

S. No.	PERT	CPM
1	PERT was developed for managing the Polaris Missile Project by the US Navy	CPM was developed to plan and control the maintenance of chemical plants by DuPont Company
2	PERT technique was applied to Research and Development projects	CPM technique was used towards construction projects
3	PERT is particularly useful for non-repetitive and complex projects in which time estimates are uncertain	CPM is best utilized for repetitive and non-complex projects in which time estimates can be made with some measure of certainty
4	PERT restricts its attention to the time variables	CPM includes time-cost trade-offs
5	PERT is probabilistic in nature and as such is used more in Research and Development projects	CPM is deterministic and finds application mostly in construction projects.

5.3.4 Basic Steps in PERT/CPM Techniques

Project Scheduling by PERT/CPM consist of four main steps:

1. **Planning:** The planning phase is started by splitting the total project into small projects. These smaller projects, in turn, are divided into activities and are analyzed by the department or a section. The relationship of each activity with respect to other activities are defined and established, and the corresponding responsibilities and the authority are also stated. Thus, the possibility of overlooking any task necessary for the completion of the project is reduced substantially.
2. **Scheduling:** The ultimate objective of the scheduling phase is to prepare a time chart showing the start and finish times for each activity as well as its relationship to other activities of the project. Moreover, the schedule must pinpoint the critical path (in view of time) activities which require special attention if the project is to be completed in time. For non-critical activities, the schedule must show the amount of slack or float times which can be used

advantageously when such activities are delayed or when limited resources are to be utilized effectively. In this phase, it is possible to resource requirements such as time, manpower, money, machines etc.

3. **Allocation of resources:** Allocation of resources is performed to achieve the desired objective. A resource is a physical variable such as labour, finance, equipment and space which will impose a limitation on time for the project. When resources are limited and conflicting, demands are made for the same type of resources a systematic method for allocation of resources become essential. Resource allocation usually incurs a compromise, and the choice of this compromise depends on the judgement of managers.
4. **Controlling:** The final phase in project management is controlling. Critical path methods facilitate the application of the principle of management by expectation to identifying areas that are critical to the completion of the project. By having progress reports from time to time and updating the network continuously, a better financial as well as technical control over the project is executed. Arrow diagrams and time charts are used for making periodic progress reports. If necessary, new course of action is determined for the remaining portion of project.

5.3.5 Use of PERT/CPM for Management

1. The PERT/CPM techniques help the management in properly planning the complicated projects, controlling working plan and also keeping the plan up to-date. These are also helpful in searching the potential spots and in taking corrective measures.
2. The network techniques provide a number of checks and safeguards against going astray in developing the plan for the project. Thus there are little chances of over-sight of certain activities and events.
3. These techniques help the management in reaching the goal with minimum time and least cost and also in forecasting the probable project duration and the associated cost.
4. The networks clearly designate the responsibility of different supervisors of an activity himself knows the time schedule precisely and also the supervisors of the other activities with whom he has to cooperate.
5. The flexibility of the network permits the management to make the necessary alterations and improvements as and when they are needed. These allocations can be made during the deployment of resources or reviewing.
6. Applications of network techniques has resulted in better managerial control, better utilization of resources, improved communication and progress reporting, and better decision-making.
7. Applications of PERT/CPM techniques have resulted in saving of time which directly results in saving of cost. Also, saving in time or early completion of the project results in earlier return of revenue and introduction of the product or process ahead of the competitors, resulting in increased profits.

5.3.6 Applications of PERT/CPM Techniques

Though the list containing the PERT/CPM application areas is very large, but these techniques are very widely used in the following typical areas:

1. **Building construction:** It is one of the largest areas in which the network techniques of project management have found its applications.

2. **Administration:** Networks are used by the administration for streamlining paperwork system, for making major administrative changes in the system, for long range planning and for developing staffing plans, etc.
3. **Manufacturing:** The design development and testing of new machines, installing machines and plant layouts are a few examples of its applications to the manufacturing function of a firm.
4. **Maintenance planning:** Maintenance and shutdown of power plants, chemical plants, steel furnaces and overhauling of large machines can be carried out by using PERT techniques.
5. **Research and development:** The research and development is the most extensive area where PERT techniques are used for development of new products, processes and systems.
6. **Inventory planning:** Installation of production and inventory control, acquisition of spare parts, etc, have been greatly helped by network techniques.
7. **Marketing:** Networks are also used for advertising programmes for development and launching of new products and for planning their distribution.

5.4 BAR CHARTS

Planning is one of the main secrets to successful project implementation, as anyone who has been involved in relocation or major project knows.

The key to good planning is simply to get the team talking and thinking about what needs to be done, and then use charts to communicate that to others.

Two simple planning techniques are useful to Project Teams; *Milestone Plans* and *Bar or Gantt charts* shown below.

- *Milestone Plans* focus mainly on the end-dates by which something needs to be complete or by which certain objectives need to be achieved.
- *Bar or Gantt Charts* focus more on the activities to be carried out to complete the project.

Both are invaluable in forcing a Project Team to think through the detail of what needs to be done, what the priorities and linkages are, and then as a means of communicating intentions to others in a diagram or picture. The different types of Bar charts which are used in project scheduling are discussed in the following sections:

5.4.1 Milestone Chart

The milestone chart is the simplest scheduling method. The method is best applied to small projects being performed by only a few people because it does not exhibit the interrelationships among the activities. This approach has been used to summarize complex schedule containing many tasks.

Milestone chart is a chart that shows the high-level picture of a project's scheduled and actual milestone start and completion dates.

A milestone plan indicates which intermediate:

A *Milestone Chart* is a Project Control Chart that graphically depicts key events along a timescale, usually with triangles representing each event. It can depict a single event or a culmination of events. It can mark specific points in the project where checks can be made to see if the project is on time and where it should be. The best place to locate milestones is at the completion of a major activity.

5.4.1.1 *When to Use it*

Milestone charts are used

- During the planning phase to provide a broad-brush picture of the implementation's expected progress.
- During implementation to track milestone activity.

5.4.1.2 *How to Use it*

Fill in the chart by recording key events that are identified as milestones or that need approvals before the change can proceed. Include key task events as well as events that have to be tracked for other than project progress, for example, those events that senior management have identified for special review.

A sample format for a milestone chart follows:

Milestone	Scheduled Start	Actual Start	Scheduled Completion	Actual Completion

5.4.1.3 *Advantage and Disadvantage of Milestone Chart*

The ***advantages*** of the milestone chart are the ease and minimal cost of preparation. The ***disadvantage*** is that a milestone chart shows only completion dates. This may result in uncertainty over activity start dates and interrelationships for all but very simple projects. Comparing the actual completion dates with the targets completion dates provides only a general indication of overall schedule status. This approach does not provide sufficient status. This approach does not provide sufficient feedback to the project manager for control of even moderately complex project.

5.4.2 Gantt Charts

A Gantt chart is an excellent tool in the hands of project managers who wish to visualize, schedule, and track scheduled and actual progress of projects. Its graphical nature allows executives and non-managers to readily understand project flow, without a requiring a complete tutorial in project management.

Gantt charts may be simple versions created on graph paper or more complex automated versions created using project management applications such as Microsoft Project or Excel. Thus,

- Gantt chart is one of the simplest and oldest techniques for tracking project progress
- A Gantt chart is a graphical representation of the duration of tasks against the progression of time.
- A Gantt chart is a useful tool for planning and scheduling projects.
- A Gantt chart is helpful when monitoring a project's progress.
- Gantt-charts are advantageous in that they are simple to understand and easy to change.
- Gantt charts are most commonly used for exhibiting program progress or defining specific work required to accomplish an objective. They often include such items as listing of activities, activity duration, schedule dates, and progress-to-date.

- Gantt charts are a project planning tool that can be used to represent the timing of tasks required to complete a project.
- A **Gantt chart** is a type of bar chart that illustrates a project schedule.

The Gantt is frequently used for smallest projects (less than 25 activities) and overcomes some disadvantages of milestone charts. This type of schedule is perhaps the most widely used scheduling technique.

Although is not possible to show the interdependence among activities on the chart. It is easier to show possible overlapping of activities than with either a CPM or PERT network. In many cases CPM and PERT network are translated directly onto a Gantt calendar chart. The Gantt chart can then be used to estimate resource and budget requirement versus time. This is done by identifying the amount of resources or budget needed per unit of time for each activity and calculating the total for all activities occurring doing a specified time period.

5.4.2.1 History

Henry Gantt (1861–1919), a mechanical engineer, management consultant, and industrial advisor developed Gantt charts in the 1910's. Henry Laurence Gantt came up with the prototype of the Gantt chart around World War I. Not as commonplace as they are today, Gantt charts were innovative and new during the 1920's, where Gantt charts were used on large construction projects like the Hoover Dam started in 1931 and the Eisenhower National Defense Interstate Highway System started in 1956.

Now, a staple project management tool and buzzword in the repertoire of modern project management tools today, Gantt charts are routinely deployed by the project managers, planners, and system developers. Working on projects without them is unthinkable, except in the rare case when the inherently nature of the work does not require them.

Henry L. Gantt's global contribution to the modern project management is honored today through the "The Henry Laurence Gantt Medal". This medal, established in 1929, is awarded for distinguished achievement in management and service to the community. This chart is used also in Information Technology to represent data that has been collected.

5.4.2.2 Definitions

Gantt chart is a type of floating bar chart usually used in project management to show resources or tasks over time.

OR

In production planning and control, Gantt chart is a type of bar chart depicting the work planned and done in relation to time; each division of space represents both a time interval and the amount of work to be done during that interval.

OR

Gantt chart is a chart which provides a graphical illustration of a schedule that helps to plan, coordinate, and track specific tasks in a project.

OR

Gantt chart is a graphic device that depicts tasks, machines, personnel, or whatever resources are required to accomplish a job on a calendar-oriented grid.

OR

A Gantt chart is basically a bar chart used in project management to show tasks, milestones, and even dependencies between tasks.

OR

Gantt chart is a graphical representation of a project that shows each task as a horizontal bar whose length is proportional to its time for completion.

5.4.2.3 Gantt Chart Role in Project Planning

For larger projects, a work breakdown structure would be developed to identify the tasks before constructing a Gantt chart. For smaller projects, the Gantt chart itself may used to identify the tasks.

The strength of the Gantt chart is its ability to display the status of each activity at a glance. While often generated using project management software, it is easy to construct using a spreadsheet, and often appears in simple ASCII formatting in e-mails among managers.

For sequencing and critical path analysis, network models such as CPM or PERT are more powerful for dealing with dependencies and project completion time. Even when network models are used, the Gantt chart often is used as a reporting tool.

5.4.2.4 Purpose

A **Gantt chart** helps organize a plan to implement a new project or process. It documents what is to be accomplished, who will be involved, and when each step will take place. It also acts as documentation for an implementation plan. It will show at a quick glance the order of implementation, and areas that overlap. Additionally it provides guidance for projecting and allocating resources.

5.4.2.5 Representation of Gantt Charts

Gantt's scheduling tool takes the form of a horizontal bar graph and is known as a **Gantt chart**, a basic sample of which is shown below in Fig. 5.10.

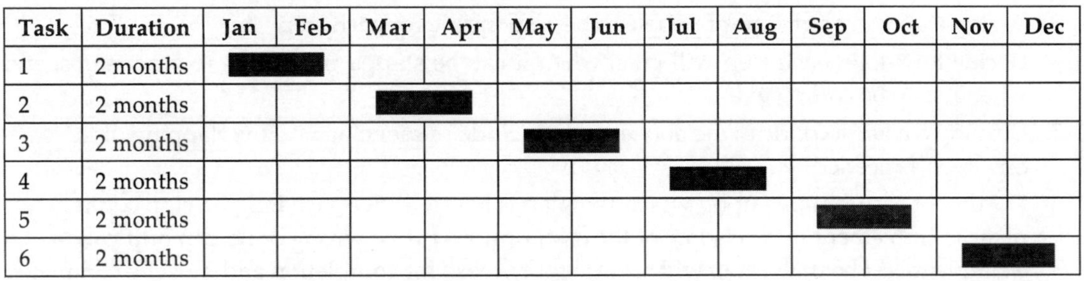

Fig. 5.10 Gantt chart format

The horizontal axis of the Gantt chart is a time scale, expressed either in absolute time or in relative time referenced to the beginning of the project. The time resolution depends on the project —the time unit typically is in weeks or months. Rows of bars in the chart show the beginning and ending dates of the individual tasks in the project.

In the above example, each task is shown to begin when the task above it completes. However, the bars may overlap in cases where a task can begin before the completion of another, and there may be several tasks performed in parallel. For such cases, the Gantt chart is quite useful for communicating the timing of the various tasks. Fig. 5.11 depicts the overlapping of the activities with respect to elapsed time as in this other activity can start before the preceding activity is completed.

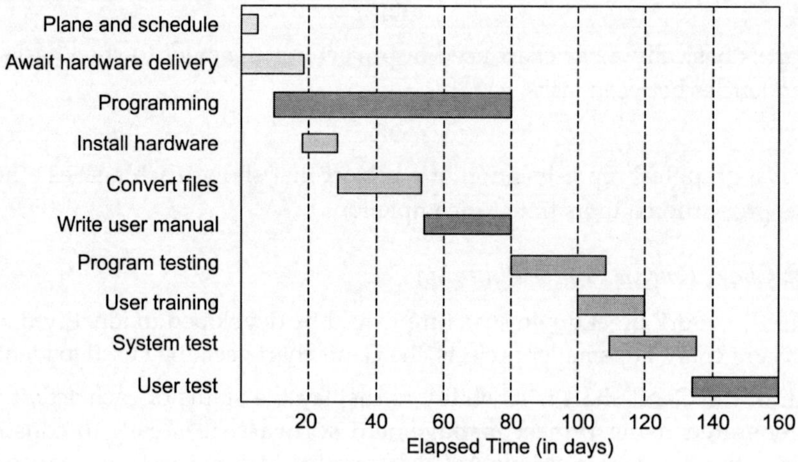

Fig. 5.11 Gantt chart format

For larger projects, the tasks can be broken into subtasks having their own Gantt charts to maintain readability.

5.4.2.6 *Basic Steps/Process in Drawing Gantt Charts*

In constructing a Gantt chart, keep the tasks to a manageable number (no more than 15 or 25) so that the chart fits on a single page. More complex projects may require subordinate charts which detail the timing of all the subtasks which make up one of the main tasks. For team projects, it often helps to have an additional column containing numbers or initials which identify that who is on the team, is responsible for the task.

The following are the basic steps which are generally used in drawing Gantt charts:

1. Develop a list of all tasks to be carried out as part of implementation.
2. Organize listed tasks in sequential order.
3. Assign a person or groups of people to be responsible for each step.
4. Decide how long each step will take, when it can be started in relation to other steps, and when it is to be completed.
5. Develop a chart to portray the above steps. Include sequencing and overlapping of the various steps as needed.
6. Document assumptions upon which the plan is based. Where needed, develop contingency plans to implement in case some of the assumptions prove wrong or need modification. An example might be that a step will require four weeks for completion and must be completed prior to beginning the next step. If that step actually takes six weeks what would be the contingency plan to ensure that the next step was not delayed.

5.4.2.7 *Practical Application of Gantt Charts*

These charts are generally introduced during the planning and scheduling stage of projects. A visual tool, the charts allow us to obtain a bird's eye view of the project in its totality. From beginning to the end, the charts force us to:

1. Make a realistic assessment of the end-time of the project.
2. Sequence our tasks (or phases, or activities) — one after the other, as well as in parallel.

3. Think in terms of task dependencies - which task is dependent on what.
4. Concentrate on the necessary resources, both when and where, throughout the run of the project.

Once the Gantt charts are drawn up, and project execution begins, we start comparing our actual, ground-level performance against what was planned. This comparison is possible by checking the field reports against the Gantt charts. Thus, *we get to benefit from them in two immediate ways*:

1. **To monitor work in progress:** At the minimum, a percentage of completion can be worked out, by taking a snapshot of the progress "right-now", and comparing it with the chart, for the "right-now" point of time. If there are any slip-ups in terms of time or cost, we are forced to question our optimism (or hope?) that the tasks would get completed earlier than they actually did, at the planning stage. This introspection helps in more realistic planning for a now more matured manager in their future projects.
2. **To also consider ways to speed up future tasks:** While there is still time, to ensure completion by the total project's estimated deadline. Perhaps resources (better manpower, more funds, or additional material) need to be allocated much in advance for a task that is going to be initiated later down the line? Perhaps some tasks may be rescheduled in a more efficient manner, in order to meet some unforeseen contingencies that have occurred after the project started?

5.4.2.8 Benefits of Gantt Chart

While they might have become popular as a visual representation of timed tasks, Gantt charts offer ten specific benefits for project managers and their teams.

1. **Clarity:** One of the biggest benefits of a Gantt chart is the tool's ability to boil down multiple tasks and timelines into a single document. Stakeholders throughout an organization can easily understand where teams are in a process while grasping the ways in which independent elements come together toward project completion.
2. **Communication:** Teams can use Gantt charts to replace meetings and enhance other status updates. Simply clarifying chart positions offers an easy, visual method to help team members understand task progress. To see other ways to compile status information, check out these series of articles.
3. **Motivation:** Some teams or team members become more effective when faced with a form of external motivation. Gantt charts offer teams the ability to focus work at the front of a task timeline, or at the tail end of a chart segment. Both types of team members can find Gantt charts meaningful as they plug their own work habits into the overall project schedule.
4. **Coordination:** For project managers and resource schedulers, the benefits of a Gantt chart include the ability to sequence events and reduce the potential for overburdening team members. Some project managers even use combinations of charts to break down projects into more manageable sets of tasks.
5. **Creativity:** Sometimes, a lack of time or resources forces project managers and teams to find creative solutions. Seeing how individual tasks intertwine on Gantt charts often encourages new partnerships and collaborations that might not have evolved under traditional task assignment systems.
6. **Time management:** Most managers regard scheduling as one of the major benefits of Gantt charts in a creative environment. Helping teams understand the overall impact of project delays can foster stronger collaboration while encouraging better task organization.
7. **Flexibility:** Whether you use Excel to generate Gantt charts or you load tasks into a more precise chart generator, the ability to issue new charts as your project evolves lets you react

to unexpected changes in project scope or timeline. While revising your project schedule too frequently can eliminate some of the other benefits of Gantt charts, offering a realistic view of a project can help team members recover from setbacks or adjust to other changes.

8. **Manageability:** For project managers handling complex assignments, like software publishing or event planning, the benefits of Gantt charts include externalizing assignments. By visualizing all of the pieces of a project puzzle, managers can make more focused, effective decisions about resources and timetables.
9. **Efficiency:** Another of the benefits of Gantt charts is the ability for teams members to leverage each other's deadlines for maximum efficiency. For instance, while one team member waits on the outcome of three other tasks before starting a crucial piece of the assignment, he or she can perform other project tasks. Visualizing resource usage during projects allows managers to make better use of people, places, and things.
10. **Accountability:** When project teams face major organizational change, documenting effort and outcomes becomes crucial to career success. Using Gantt charts during critical projects allows both project managers and participants to track team progress, highlighting both big wins and major failures. During professional review periods, team members who frequently exceed expectations can leverage this documentation into larger raises or bonuses.

5.4.2.9 Limitations

Some of the limitations of Gantt charts are:

1. They do not show the interdependencies of the activities and therefore do not represent a "network" of activities.
2. Planning and scheduling are considered simultaneously.
3. These are essentially a manual graphical procedure so it is not suitable for large projects.
4. They have a tendency to quickly become outdated and to lose their usefulness.
5. Gantt charts does not show how tasks must be ordered (precedence) but simplify show when a task should begin and should end.
6. Gantt chart is often more useful to for depicting relatively simple projects or sub projects of a large project, the activities of a single worker, or for monitoring the progress of activities compared to scheduled completion dates.

5.4.3 Ball Chart

After collecting data about the project progress, a manager needs some way of presenting that data in most effective way. Ball chart is one such mechanism. In these charts, the circles indicate stat and completion points for activities. Initially, these circles contain the original scheduled dates. When revisions are done, these are added as second dates in an appropriate circle until an activity is actually started or completed. Thus, circles will contain only two dates—the original and the most recent target dates or the original and actual dates.

A some what more striking way of showing whether or not targets have been is to use a ball chart as in Fig. 5.12. In this version of the ball chart, the indicates start and completion points for activities. The circles initially contain the original scheduled dates. Whenever revisions are produced these are added second dates in the appropriate circle until an activity is actually started. When the relevant date replace the revised estimates (in bold and most recent dates, or the original and actual dates.

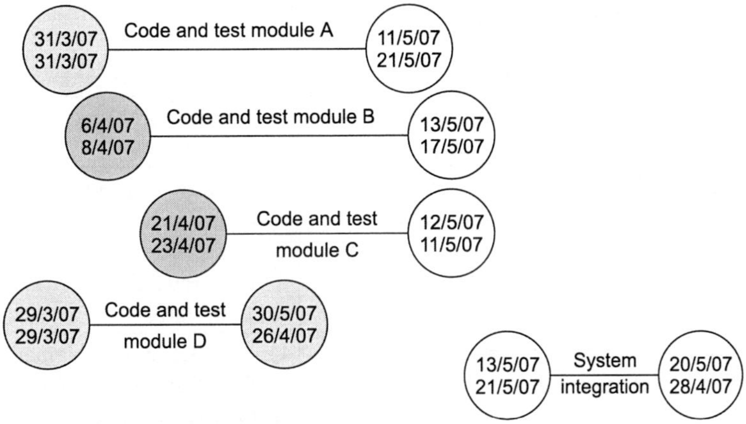

Fig. 5.12 The ball wall chart provides an incentive for meeting targets

Where the actual start or finish date for an activity is later than the target date, the circle is coloured red (dark grey in Fig. 5.12)—where an actual date is on time or earlier than the target then the circle is coloured green (light grey in Fig. 5.12)

Such charts are frequently placed in a prominent position and the colour—coded balls provide a constant reminder to the project team. Where more than one team is working in close proximity, such a highly visible record of achievement can encourage competitiveness between teams.

Another advantage of ball charts over Gantt and slip chart is that they are relatively easy to keep up to date only the dates and possibly colours need to be changed, whereas the others need to be redrawn each time target dates are revised.

5.5 COMPARISON OF SCHEDULING TECHNIQUES

5.5.1 Milestone Technique

Criteria	Strengths	Weaknesses
Applicability	Only small errors in measurement are likely to occur if activity durations are short.	No explicit technique for depicting interrelationships.
Reliability	Simplicity of system affords some reliability.	Frequently unreliable because judgment of estimator may change over time numerous estimates in a large project, each with some unreliability may lead to errors in judging status.
Implementation	Easiest of all systems because it is well understood.	Difficult to implement for the control of operation where time standards do not ordinarily exist and must be developed.
Simulation Capabilities	-------	No significant capability.
Updating Status	Easy to update periodically Not necessary to use computer.	-------
Flexibility	-------	Poor accommodation of frequent logic changes.
Cost	Data gathering , processing and display relatively inexpensive.	The chart tends to be inflexible Program changes require new charts.

5.5.2 Gantt Chart Technique

Criteria	Strengths	Weaknesses
Applicability	Only small errors in measurement are likely to occur if activity durations are short.	No explicit technique for depicting interrelationships.
Reliability	Single duration estimate for each activity avoids errors due to over complexity.	Frequently unreliable because judgment of estimator may changes over time. Numerous estimates in a large project, each with some unreliability, may lead to errors in judging status.
Implementation	Easiest of all system in some respects because it is well understood.	Quite difficult to implements for the control of operations where time standards do not ordinarily exist and must be developed.
Simulation Capabilities	------------	No significant capability.
Updating Status	Easy to update graphs periodically if no major program changes Not necessary to use computer.	May have to redo graph because of inability to update current charts.
Flexibility	Can also be used for estimating resource requirements.	If significant logic changes occur frequently numerous charts must be completely reconstructed.
Cost	Data gathering and processing relatively inexpensive. Display can be inexpensive if existing graphs can be updated and if inexpensive materials are used.	The graph tends to be inflexible. Program changes require new graphs which are time consuming and costly. Expensive display devices are frequently used.

5.5.3 CPM Technique

Criteria	Strengths	Weaknesses
Applicability	Accurately depicts work sequence and interrelationships among activities.	No formula is provided to estimate probable time to completion; consequently, the technique is as valid as the estimator. The margin of error is generally less on project with little uncertainty.
Reliability	Single duration estimate for each activity avoids errors due to over complexity.	Numerous estimates in a large projects, each with some unreliability, may lead to significant errors in judging overall project status.
Implementation	Graphic display of work sequence and activity interrelationships is desired by manager's of complex projects.	Relatively difficult to explain to those unused to approach. Complexity of schedule may intimidate clients.
Simulation capabilities	Excellent for simulating alternative plans if computerized, especially when coupled with time-cost-resources aspects.	Requires computer for all but very small projects.
Updating status	Good capability, Activities are clearly identified and time estimates can be obtained as needed.	Schedules for even moderately complex projects require use of computer.

Flexibility	Portions of the network can be easily changed to reflect scope changes if computerized. Can be used to estimate resource requirement if plotted on time scale.	Schedule for even moderately complex projects require use of computer.
Cost	Can reduce overall project costs significantly through better planning and control.	Considerable data are required to use CPM as both a planning and status reporting tool and a computer is almost invariable required. Therefore, the cost outlay can be fairly extensive.

5.5.4 PERT Technique

Criteria	Strengths	Weaknesses
Applicability	Pert, like CPM, is capable of depicting work sequence. The use of three time estimates should make it more accurate than any other technique.	Overly complex for small projects.
Reliability	Probabilistic duration estimates may be more accurate than single estimate.	Securing three duration estimates for each activity requires more information which could introduce additional error.
Implementation	Graphic display of sequence and event interrelationships is desired by managers of complex projects.	The complete PERT system is quite complex, and therefore, difficult to implement. May intimidate first time users and client.
Simulation capabilities	Excellent for simulating alternative plans if computerized, especially when coupled with time – cost – resources aspects.	Requires computer for all but very small projects.
Updating status	Events are clearly identified and elapsed times can be obtained as needed.	Estimation of activity durations is quite time consuming and calculation of expected times requires use of a computer.
Flexibility	As the project changes over time, the network and new time estimates can be readily adjusted to reflect changes. Can be used to estimate resource requirements if plotted on time scale.	Schedules for even moderately complex projects require use of computer.
Cost	Can reduce overall project costs significantly through better planning and control.	More data and more computation are required than in any other system; hence the system is very costly.

6

Project Monitoring and Control

Project monitoring and control is a key phase in the project management cycle. Properly executing this process will contribute significantly to successful project completion. It consists of all those processes which are performed to observe project execution so that potential problems can be identified in a timely manner and corrective actions can be taken, when necessary to control the execution of the project.

In multi-phase projects, the monitoring and controlling process also provides feedback between project phases, in order to implement corrective or preventive actions to bring the project into compliance with the project management plan.

6.1 PROJECT MONITORING

Monitoring a project means exercising a complete control over the project to ensure that targets are met, finding out what is happening and comparing it with current targets. If there is a mismatch between the planned outcomes and actual ones then:

1. Either re-planning is done to bring the project back on target.
2. The target is revised.

This project cycle is shown in Fig. 6.1.

So it is clear that firstly initial project plan is created. The project information is gathered. Then, we compare the monitoring progress against the plan (targets). If it is satisfactory then the project is completed else we need to revise the plan and compare again. So it is a continuous process.

6.1.1 Why do we Monitor?

- Simply because we know that things don't always go according to plan (no matter how much we prepare).
- To detect and react appropriately to deviations and changes to plans.

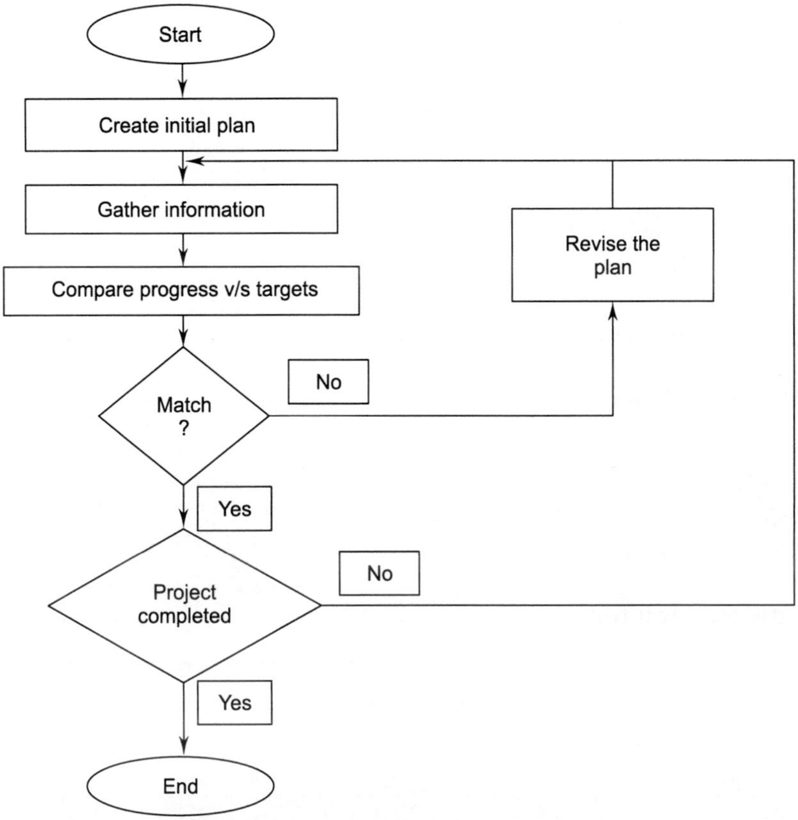

Fig. 6.1 Project control and monitoring cycle

6.1.2 What do we Monitor?

- Men (human resources)
- Machines
- Materials
- Money Space
- Time
- Tasks
- Quality/Technical Performance.

6.1.2.1 Inputs and Outputs

The various inputs and outputs which we monitor during a project are:

Inputs

- Time
- Money
- Resources
- Material Usage
- Tasks
- Quality/Technical Performance.

Outputs

- Progress
- Costs
- Job starts
- Job completion
- Engineering/design changes
- Variation Order (VO).

6.1.3 When do we Monitor?

- End of the project
- Continuously
- Regularly
- Logically
- While there is still time to react
- As soon as possible
- At task completion
- At pre-planned decision points (milestones)

6.1.4 Where do we Monitor?

- At head office?
- At the site office?
- On the spot?
- Depends on situation and the 'whats'

6.1.5 How do we Monitor?

- Through meetings with clients, parties involved in project (Contractor, supplier,etc.)
- For schedule - Update CPA, PERT Charts, Update Gantt Charts
- Using Earned Value Analysis
- Calculate Critical Ratios
- Milestones
- Reports
- Tests and inspections
- Delivery or staggered delivery
- PMIS (Project Management InfoSys) Updating

6.1.6 Monitoring Project Work

1. Project work (initiation, planning, execution and closing) needs to be monitored.
   (*i*) Also, corrective (or preventive) actions need to be taken wherever necessary.
2. Monitoring involves:
   (*i*) Collecting, measuring, and disseminating performance data
   (*ii*) Comparing actual project performance with the plan
   (*iii*) Tracking risks
   (*iv*) Monitoring of approved changes
   (*v*) Monitoring accurate project database
   (*vi*) Timely reporting of information
   (*vii*) Assessing trends to help in process improvements
   (*viii*) Identifying preventive and corrective actions.
3. Continuous monitoring:
   (*i*) Gives an insight into project's health.
   (*ii*) Also brings out areas requiring special attention.

6.2 PROJECT CONTROLLING

Project Controlling is the process that keeps the project moving towards its objectives, and ensuring that it stays as close to the plan as possible.

Project management, functional management and upper management must all provide an active support to the control system. Importance of control system should be driven to all project workers, *i.e.*, show them how they benefit from it. Control system must be objective, impersonal and uniformly applied.

Figure 6.2 illustrates a model of the project control cycle and shows how, once the initial project plan has been published. Project control is a continual process of monitoring progress against the plan and, where necessary revising the plan to take account of deviations. It also illustrates the important steps that must be taken after completion of the project so that the experience gained in any one project can feed into the planning stages of future projects, thus allowing us to learn from past mistakes.

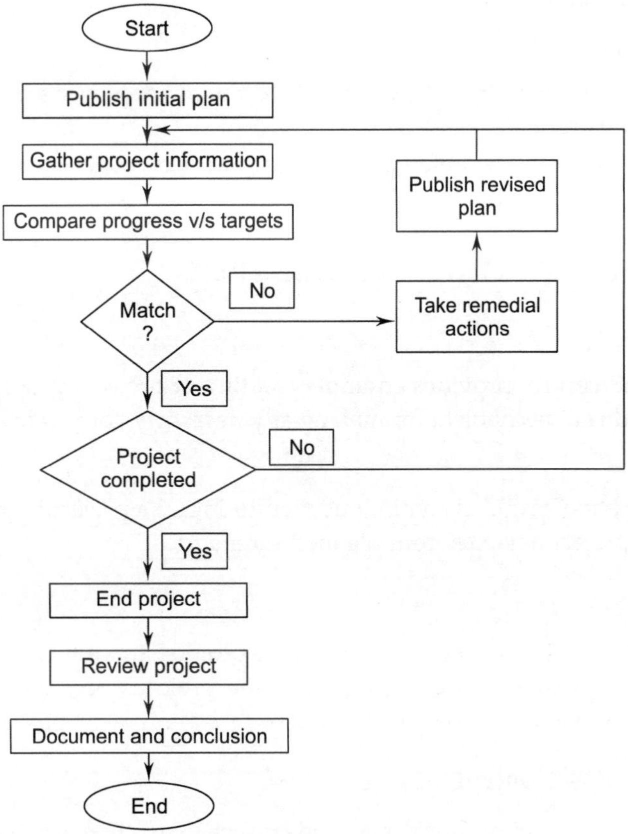

Fig. 6.2 Project control cycle

6.2.1 Project Control Process

Project Control process is concerned about:

1. Reviewing or verifying validity of technical objectives
2. Confirming the continued need for project

3. Timing the project with the operational requirements
4. Over-seeing resources expenditure
5. Comparing the "actual" with the "plan".

In general, the project control process consists of three phases:

1. Setting performance standards
    - **Expressed as:** Technical specifications, budgets, schedules etc.
    - **Based on:** User requirements, project plan, SOW etc.
2. Comparing actual performance with standards
    - Compare actuals with budgets, schedule, specifications, resources
    - Make projections (forecasts) for remaining work
3. Taking necessary corrective actions (as appropriate)
    - Shift project goals, alter project plans, re-deploy resources

6.2.2 Types of Project Control

There are two types of project control:

1. **External project control:** This refers to the "additional" deployer's (say clients) system for monitoring and control
2. **Internal project control:** This refers to the performers (say contractors) system for monitoring and control

6.3 PROJECT MONITORING AND CONTROL

6.3.1 Definition

Project monitoring and control provides an understanding of project's progress, identifies deviation from the plan and is a mechanism for making any necessary corrective actions.

OR

Project Monitoring and Control is continuous monitoring of a project in order to determine if, and when any given project deviates from planned estimates.

6.3.2 Purpose

The purpose of project monitoring and controlling is to provide an understanding of and communicate the project's progress, thus identifying when the project's performance deviates significantly from the plan so that appropriate corrective and preventive actions are taken.

6.3.3 Monitoring V/S Control

The difference between the project monitoring and project controlling are discussed as follows:

Monitoring:

- **Collecting, recording and reporting** information concerning any and all aspects of project performance that the project manager or others in the organization wish to know.
- Project Monitoring is that aspect of project management which is performed throughout the project.

Controlling:

- Controlling uses data supplied by the monitoring process to bring actual performance into approximate alignment with planned performance.
- Project Controlling is that aspect wherein corrective and preventive actions are taken.

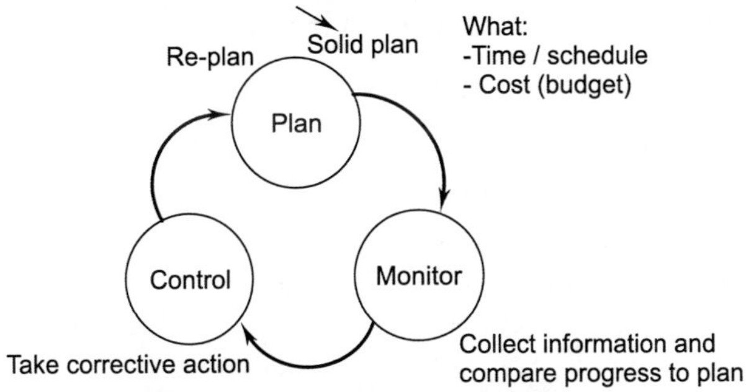

Fig. 6.3 Plan → Monitor → Control cycle

6.3.4 Monitoring and Control: Inputs, T/T, Outputs

Inputs

1. Project management plan
2. Work performance information
3. Rejected change requests.

Tools and Techniques

1. Project management methodology
2. Project management information system
3. Earned value management
4. Expert judgement.

Outputs

1. Recommended corrective actions
2. Recommended preventive actions
3. Forecasts
4. Recommended defect repair
5. Requested changes.

6.3.5 Role of Monitoring in Project Control

1. Monitoring function consists of two activities:
    - Data collection
    - Information reporting
2. Data collection and information reporting system is established simultaneously while setting the performance standards.
3. Data for project monitoring must be directly related to plans, budget, schedules, deliverables and standards.
4. Typical sources for project monitoring data include invoices, time cards, change notices, test reports, expert opinions etc.

- **Caution:** While collecting data, an economic balance needs to be struck between too much data and too little data.

5. Timing for data collection and information distribution is also important. Providing adequate information (not too much or too little) at the right frequency is the key.

6.3.6 Monitoring and Controlling Process Group

Monitoring and Controlling Group Processes:

- Observe the project execution
- Analyze situation and identify problems
- When necessary take corrective actions.

Note: The project performance is measured regularly

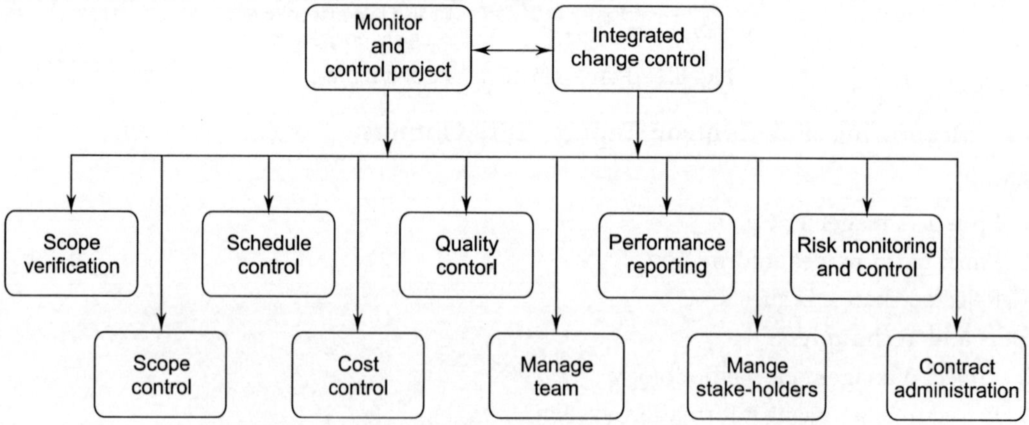

Fig. 6.4 Project monitoring and controlling process group

6.3.7 Dimensions of Project Monitoring and Control

Monitoring function consists of two activities:

(*i*) Data collection

(*ii*) Information reporting.

Both are established simultaneously. Data for project monitoring must be directly related to plans, budget, schedule, deliverables and standards. Typical sources for project monitoring data include invoices, time cards, change notices, test reports, expert opinions etc.

How can we do Project Monitoring and Control?

The various dimensions by which we can monitor and control the project are:

1. **Measuring the technical progress:** Measuring the technical progress requires size metrices for each time. For example:

   (*i*) Number of LOC under baseline (Development Team)

   (*ii*) Number of defects found (Test Team)

   (*iii*) Number of critical use cases that have been demonstrated (Architecture Team).

   Size metrices and quality metrice must be viewed together while measuring technical progress.

2. **Measuring stability:** Measuring stability means measuring the rate of new change requests corresponding to the defects in the system. Once an initial version of the system is baselined, change requests are issued to control and track changes to the baseline. If the work completion indicates that the project is almost finished but the rate of change requests is still high then the project may not be achieving its target quality goals.
3. **Measuring modularity:** Measuring modularity can be another dimension of project monitoring and control. We talk in terms of the breakage. It is the measure of the impact of a change on the baseline. (It is measured in terms of LOC, Number of files, Function Points etc).
4. **Measuring maturity:** Measuring maturity is another dimension of project monitoring and control. As we know that Mean Time Between Failures (MTBF) measures the time between discovered defects during testing. The maturity of a project increases as the project moves towards completion.
5. **Measuring financial status:** Another dimension can be measuring of the financial status. The project manager can compare the planned costs against the actual costs to assess the financial health of the project.

7 EARNED VALUE ANALYSIS

Earned Value Management (EVM) technique is used to track the Progress and Status of a Project and Forecasts the likely future performance of the Project. It integrates the scope, schedule and cost of a project. This technique can be used to show past performance of the project, current performance of the project and predict the future performance of the project by use of statistical techniques.

The EVA technique is used in several countries to get better cost and schedule control. A variety of terminology is used as a descriptot for this approach. These include Earned Value Analysis (EVA), Earned Value Management (EVM), Earned Value Management System (EVMS) and Earned Value Technique (EVT). The most comprehensive trend analysis technique is the Earned Value method.

It is generally true that past performance is a good indicator of future performance and as such Earned Value is a very useful tool for predicting the outcome of projects in terms of time to completion, cost to completion and expected final costs. The ***project baseline*** is an essential component of EVM and serves as a reference point for all EVM related activities.

- Earned value indicates how much of the budget and time should have been spent, with regards to the amount of work done to date.
- Earned Value provides the project manager with an objective way of measuring performance and predicting future outcomes.
- Earned Value enable the project manager to report progress with greater confidence and highlight any overrun earlier. This in turn enables the management team to make cost and time allocation decisions earlier than would otherwise be the case.
- EVM provides quantitative data for project decision-making.

In a nutshell Earned Value is an approach where you monitor the project plan, actual work and work-completed value to see if a project is on track.

7.1 HISTORY OF EVA

EVM emerged as a financial analysis specialty in United States Government programs in the 1960s. In 1967 the Department of Defense (DoD) established the Cost/Schedule Control Systems Criteria

(C/SCSC) to standardize contractor requirements for reporting cost and schedule performance on major contracts. A basic tenet of C/SCSC is the concept of Earned Value Management.

It has since become a significant branch of project management. In the late 1980s and early 1990s, EVM emerged as a project management methodology to be understood and used by managers and executives, not just EVM specialists. Today EVM has become an essential part of every project tracking.

7.1.1 EVM Rewards and Recognition

According to the NASA Headquarters Library, the first version of Earned Value Management (EVM) was developed by the Defence Department (DoD) to track its programmes during the sixties. Since 2005, EVM has been a part of general federal project risk management. Today EVM is a mandatory requirement of the US government. The Office of Management and Budget (OMB) promotes use of EVM as a preferred performance-based management system to manage software projects. EVM is also used in the private sector by companies in a variety of industries, consulting firms and educational establishments.

Some of the most well known organisations practicing EVM are:

- NASA
- Project Management Institute (PMI)
- Society of Cost Estimating and Analysis
- Defence Acquisition University
- Federal Acquisition Institute
- Acquisition Management (UK).

Based on reports of the General Accounting Office (GAO) in August 1996 a memorandum of understanding concerning common cost and schedule management for acquisitions was signed by Australia, Canada, and the United States. This gives international recognition to EVM worldwide.

7.2 DEFINITIONS

EVA is a valuable technique to determine real gains and losses on projects and provides a means to balance gains/losses and maximize the gains.

OR

Earned Value Management is a methodology for determining cost and schedule performance of a project by comparing "planned" work with "accomplished" work in terms of the dollar value assigned to the work.

OR

Earned Value Analysis is based on assigning a 'value' to each task or work package based on the original expenditure forecasts.

OR

Earned Value Analysis is ***"a measure of progress of a project".***

OR

Earned Value Analysis is a technique for performing quantitative analysis of progress does exist.

OR

Earned Value Analysis is a systematic project management process used to find variances in projects based on the comparison of worked performed and work planned.

OR

Earned Value Analysis (EVA) is a project performance measurement technique that integrates scope, time, and cost data based on the baseline of cost performance versus achievement; the project manager can find the earned value. A baseline is the original project plan and its cost measured by units in WBS. The actual performance will be compared with the plan and its cost to find the earned values.

OR

According to **Humphrey.**

The EVS provides a common value scale for every [software project] task, regardless of the type of work being performed. The total hours to do the whole project are estimated, and every task is given an earned value based on its estimated percentage of the total.

OR

According to **The User's Guide for Microsoft Project 98**, EVA can be defined as,.

"A measure of the cost of work performed up to the status date or today's date. Earned value uses your original cost estimates and your actual work to date to show whether the actual costs incurred are on budget."

OR

Englert and Associates, Inc defines it as, "A method for measuring project performance. It compares the amount of work that was planned with what was actually accomplished to determine if cost and schedule performance is as planned."

OR

Project Magazine defines it as, "A methodology used to measure and communicate the real physical progress of a project taking into account the work complete, the time taken and the costs incurred to complete that work."

OR

Field Operative defines it as, "The physical work accomplished plus the authorized budget for this work. The sum of the approved cost estimates, (which may include overhead allocation), for activities, (or portions of activities), completed during a given period, usually project-to-date".

7.3 EARNED VALUE ANALYSIS

The financial status of a project can be assessed using earned value. It enables us to assess both the cost and schedule of a project using one chart. Consider the following graph which is shown in Fig. 7.1.

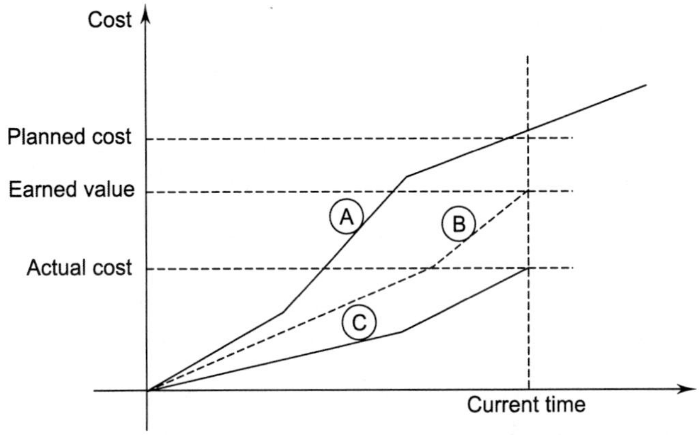

Fig. 7.1 Cost v/s time curve

We have shown three curves-A, B and C in the graph. Thin line (Curve A) shows the planned costs of the project over time. A project that is on budget and on schedule would follow the same line very closely.

Thick line (Curve-C) shows the actual costs of the project overtime. However, these two curves are not sufficient to understand the financial state of the project. So, we plot the third curve *i.e.*, dotted line (Curve-B) that shows the earned value. It represents the value of work we completed so far. The earned value is measured by adding the planned costs of the task that have been completed. In the curve of Fig. 7.1, we observe that the earned value is between the actual cost and the planned cost. It shows that the project is under budget and late. Also, if the earned value had been above the planned costs, then the project would have been under budget and early.

Note:

1. An earned value above actual costs indicates that more work was accomplished for the same amount of money *i.e.*, the project is under budget.
2. An earned value below actual costs indicates that not as much work was completed as planned *i.e.*, the project is late.

EVA has gained popularity in recent year. EVA is based on assigning a "value" to each task or work package, based on the original expenditure forecasts. EVA is also known as the budgeted cost of work performed.

Successful implementation of Earned Value Management principles can result in:

- Better visibility in to program performance.
- Reduce cycle time to deliver of product.
- Increased accountability.
- Reduced risk.

7.4 NEED OF EVA

The need of EVA is as follows:

1. There is a need of a different measure of progress for different task.
2. There is a need for a uniform unit of measure.
3. Progress of many tasks is to be rolled-up into an overall project status.

7.5 ROLE OF EVA IN RISK MANAGEMENT

Content of this section has been referred from the paper titled "**Use of Earned Value Management to Mitigate Software Development Risk**" by **Paul E. Young.**

The American Heritage Dictionary defines risk as "the possibility of suffering harm or loss".

Donald Reifer adds that risk "refers to those factors, both technical and managerial, that are threats to success and/or a major source of problems on software-intensive projects." He further defines Risk Management as "the process of identifying these threats, analyzing them, quantifying their effects, and implementing plans that counteract their negative effects."

Risk Management: Barry Boehm defines the practice of Risk Management in terms of two primary activities, each with three subsidiary steps. The first activity, risk assessment, consists of risk identification, risk analysis, and risk prioritization. The second activity, risk control, includes risk-management planning, risk resolution and risk monitoring. It is in primarily in two of these activities, risk identification and risk monitoring, that Earned Value Management can play an important role.

Risk Identification: Under his methodology, Boehm views risk identification as a means of producing a list of possible items which might jeopardize a project's success. The list is produced early in a project's development using techniques such as checklists, decision-driver analysis, assumptions analysis and decomposition. The list is updated periodically during the life of the project utilizing similar techniques.

Using Earned Value Management for risk identification, on the other hand, involves comparing actual task cost and schedule performance against estimated values. This is accomplished using cost and schedule variance to assess work package performance against the plan. The earned value practitioner is alerted to a potential risk area whenever that task or task area cost or schedule variance exceeds a predetermined value. Although not absolute confirmation that the work package is in trouble- the cost or schedule variance could be due to a delay in reporting or some other cause- an assessment of earned value does provide an early indicator of cost and/or schedule problems that can indicate an area of program risk.

Although different from Boehm's up-front risk assessment approach, earned value can be combined with his "crystal ball" technique of risk identification to maximize risk management efforts. First, Boehm's methodology is used to identify a list of potential risk elements. This list is then used to increase the level of tracking of those elements judged to be at a high risk. By increasing the granularity and frequency of tracking potential high risk tasks, Earned Value Management can help confirm problem areas sooner and thus speed risk mitigation efforts.

Risk Monitoring: According to Boehm, "Risk monitoring involves tracking the project's progress toward resolving its risk items and taking corrective action where appropriate." Earned Value Management can play an important role in this area also. The project manager can monitor the impact risk-management planning and risk resolution activities have on task performance utilizing the same methods he utilized to alert him to the risk items initially. In addition, if the risk resolution involves rework or additional program tasks, these tasks should be subjected to Earned Value Management as well in order to determine their performance against the modified plan.

7.6 NORMALIZED EARNED VALUE

Transformation from one tangible state (the desire) to another tangible state (the software) with intermediate states being somewhat intangible, we choose unity (1 or 100% complete) to represent the position of transformation at completion. The initial position of the transformation is assumed to be zero (0% complete). We define any value that represents a specific position on the continuum of intermediate position values as *normalized earned value*. For example, if a project's position in the direction of the progress is 0.5 (50% complete), then that project's normalized earned value is said to be 0.5 or 50%. If a project has been assigned (estimated to be) some budgeted *monetary* value (measured in units of currency such as *rupees*) or some budgeted *effort* value (measured in units of *labour*), then the project's earned value may be expressed as the project of its normalized earned value and its total budgeted monetary value or total budgeted effort value respectively.

We can define displacement mathematically by the following formula:

$$\Delta r(t_1, t_2) = r(t_2) - r(t_1)$$

Where

t_1 = some *initial* point in time;

t_2 = some *final* point in time where $t_2 \geq t_1$;

$r(t_1)$ = the initial position vector; the position vector at time t_1;

$r(t_2)$ = the final position vector; the position vector at time t_2;

$\Delta r(t_1, t_2)$ = the displacement vector from the initial position to the final position.

Within the progress dimension S, the magnitude of the displacement vector $|\Delta r(t_1, t_2)|$, quantifies a change in normalized earned value from the position at some time t_1 to the position at some later time t_2.

7.7 EARNED VALUE INDICATORS

EVA provides the means for integrated management of schedule, progress and cost based on 3 variables: Planned Value (PV), Earned Value (EV) and Actual Costs (AC), as well as the related indexes Schedule Performance Index (SPI) and Cost Performance Index (CPI). EVA inspires the participants to pay more attention to costs and progress, motivates the participants to discuss the cost elements with more intensity and optimize the costs resulting in a project that was finished on time and on budget.

The **main EVA variables (indicators) / Basic Parameters** are:

- BCWS (Budgeted Cost of Work Scheduled)/PV (Planned Value)
- BCWP (Budgeted Cost of Work Performed)/EV (Earned Value)
- ACWP (Actual Cost of Work Performed)/AC (Actual Cost).

Earned value can be compared to actual cost and budgeted cost to determine variance and predict future performance.

Variances

- Schedule Variance (SV)
- Cost Variance (CV)

- Budget Variance (BV)
- Time Variance (TV).

Performance Indices

- SPI (Schedule Performed Index)
- CPI (Cost Performance Index)
- BPI (Budget Performance Index)
- TPI (Time Performance Index)
- XPI (Composite Performance Index).

7.7.1 Basic Parameters of EVA

EVA concentrates on three basic parameters:

- How much work SHOULD have been done so far (BCWS);
- How much money has ACTUALLY been spent to progress the project so far (ACWP) and
- What is the VALUE of work that has been accomplished so far (BCWP)?

By comparing these values, assessments can be made about how efficient a project is and where problems may lie. It is used for an objective assessment of cost AND schedule performance can be gained. Instead of simply concentrating on how much time has been taken to achieve progress, earned value looks at how much value has been achieved so far.

The basic Earned Value Analysis variables (indicators) are discussed as follows:

7.7.1.1 BCWS (Budgeted Cost of Work Scheduled)/PV (Planned Value)

BCWS is defined as the original budgeted cost for the item. It is the cost of each task or work package as per the budget.

OR

BCWS, also called the budget, is that portion of the approved total cost estimate planned to be spent on an activity during a given period.

OR

BCWS is the amount expressed in Pounds (or hours) of work to be performed as per the schedule plan.

OR

Planned Value (PV) or BCWS is the total cost of the work scheduled /Planned as of a reporting date.

OR

BCWS shows ***"How much work (person-hours) you planned to have accomplished at a given point in time"*** (this is from the WBS in your plan). In other words, the Budgeted Cost of Work Scheduled (BCWS) is the sum of all the budgeted estimates for the work scheduled to be completed by today (or by any specific date or given time period).

For the purpose of WBS control, BCWS is plotted against time scale in a graphical form. This is done by plotting cumulative cost of work scheduled for the entire project on y-axis and time scale on x-axis. It covers the estimated time of completion of project. At any time on x-axis, the corresponding point on y-axis shows the budgeted cost of all work packages to be carried out upto that time (completely or partially). This curve is known as BCWS curve and is shown in Fig. 7.2.

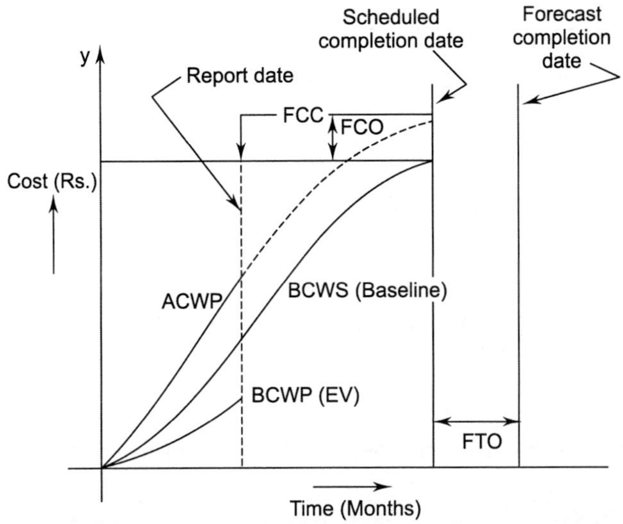

Fig. 7.2 BCWS, BCWP, ACWP and cost and time overrun prediction

In this graph, FCO shows the forecast overcost. FTO shows the forecast time overrun. ACWP, BCWS, and BCWP have their usual meanings as discussed in this chapter.

For units of currency (rupees):

$$\text{BCWS}_{rp}(t) = \sum_{j=1}^{n} \text{Activity}_j \text{ planned cost}$$

Where,

Activity_j = Must in order to count, be planned for completion by time t.

n = Total no. of activities in the project

For units of labour:

$$\text{BCWS}_{\text{L}}(t) = \sum_{j=1}^{n} \text{Activity}_j \text{ planned Effort}$$

Where,

Activity_j = Must in order to count, be planned for completion by time t.

n = Total no. of activities in the project

For a normalized (% of BAC) measurement:

$$\text{BCWS}_{\%}(t) = \frac{\text{BCWS}_{rp}(t)}{\text{BAC}_{rp}} \equiv \frac{\text{BCWS}_{\text{L}}(t)}{\text{BAC}_{\text{L}}}$$

OR

PV = BAC * % of planned work

% Completed planned

The percentage of work which was planned to be completed by the Reporting Date. This is calculated using the following formula

% Completed planned = PV / BAC

7.7.1.2 BCWP (Budgeted Cost of Work Performed)/EV (Earned Value)

BCWP is the sum of the budgets for completed work packages and completed work portions of open work packages.

OR

BCWP, also called the Earned Value (EV), is the percentage of work actually completed multiplied by the planned cost.

OR

BCWP is the sum of the BCWS values for all work tasks that have actually been completed by a point in time on the project schedule.

OR

Earned Value (EV) or BCWP is the total cost of the work completed/performed as of a reporting date.

OR

Budgeted Cost for Work Performed (BCWP)/Earned Value (EV) is the amount expressed in Pounds (or hours) on the actual worked performed.

OR

BCWP is the value of the work earned (accomplished). It is also known as the Earned Value (EV)

OR

BCWP is *"the value (person-hours) in terms of your base budget of what you have accomplished at a given point in time (or, % complete X Planned Value)"*. The BCWP is calculated by adding up the budgeted cost of every activity that has been completed. In other words, BCWP is the sum of the budgets for completed work packages and completed portions of open work packages.

For units of currency (rupees):

$$\text{BCWP}_{rp}(t) = \sum_{l=1}^{n} \text{Completed Activity}_l \text{ planned cost}$$

Where,

Activity$_l$ = Must in order to count, be completed by time t.

m = Total no. of completed activities in the project

For units of labour:

$$\text{BCWP}_{\text{L}}(t) = \sum_{l=1}^{n} \text{Completed Activity}_l \text{ planned Effort}$$

Where,

Activity$_l$ = Must in order to count, be completed by time t.

m = Total no. of completed activities in the project

For a normalized (% of BAC) measurement:

$$\text{BCWP}_{\%}(t) \equiv \frac{\text{BCWP}_{rp}(t)}{\text{BAC}_{rp}} \equiv \frac{\text{BCWP}_{\text{L}}(t)}{\text{BAC}_{\text{L}}}$$

OR

BCWP or EV = BAC * % of Actual work

Earned Value is also known as Performance Measurement, Management by Objectives, Budgeted Cost of Work Performed and Cost Schedule Control Systems.

Difference between BCWS and BCWP: The difference between the BCWS and BCWP is that the former represents the budget of the activities that were planned to be completed and the later represents the budget of the activities that actually were completed.

7.7.1.3 ACWP (Actual Cost of Work Performed)/AC (Actual Cost)

ACWP is the actual costs incurred in accomplishing the work performed within a given time period. For equitable comparison, ACWP is only recorded for the work performed to date against tasks for which a BCWP is also reported.

OR

ACWP also called as Actual Cost, are the total direct or indirect cost incurred in accomplishing work on an activity during a given period.

OR

ACWP is the sum of the effort actually expended on work tasks that have been completed by a point in time on the project schedule.

OR

Actual Cost (AC) or ACWP is the total cost taken to complete the work as of a reporting date.

OR

Actual Cost of Work Performed (ACWP)/Actual Cost (AC) is the sum of all costs (in Pounds) actually accrued for a task to date.

OR

ACWP shows ***"How much work (person-hours) you have actually spent at a given point in time"***. To calculate the Actual Cost of Work Performed (ACWP), add up the actual cost for all the work that has been completed so far on the project. ACWP is plotted against time scale for effective WBS control as depicted in Fig. 7.2. The ACWP can be equal, more or less than BCWP. This depends on following conditions:

- ACWP=BCWP (When project continues as per plan)
- ACWP > BCWP (When there is cost over-run)
- ACWP < BCWP (When there is cost under-run)

For units of currency (rupees):

$$\text{ACWP}_{rp}(t) = \sum_{k=1}^{n} \text{Activity}_k \text{ Actual Accumulated cost}$$

Where,

n = Total no. of activities in the project

For units of labour:

$$\text{ACWP}_{\text{L}}(t) = \sum_{k=1}^{n} \text{Activity}_k \text{ Actual Accumulated Effort}$$

Where,

$$n = \text{Total no. of activities in the project}$$

For a normalized (% of BAC) measurement:

$$ACWP_{\%}(t) \equiv \frac{ACWP_{rp}(t)}{BAC_{rp}} \equiv \frac{ACWP_{L}(t)}{BAC_{L}}$$

% Completed Actual

The percentage of work which was actually completed by the Reporting Date. This is calculated using the following formula.

% Completed Actual = AC / EAC

All these three elements can be derived from Work Breakdown Structure by associating the costs to each of the tasks. For a big project it will be a tedious task to calculate these elements manually. Scheduling software's like Microsoft Project is used to calculate these three elements.

7.7.2 Variance

Variance shows any schedule or cost deviation from a specific plan. It is used within an organization to verify the budget and schedule for a project. Also used frequently as a key component of plan reviews and performance measurement. Must compare scheduling and budget variance at the same time.

Schedule variance: deviations from work planned—not a measure of changes in cost.

Cost variance: deviations from the budget- not a measure of work scheduled v/s work completed.

7.7.2.1 Schedule Variance (SV)

Schedule Variance (SV) is very important factor to measure project performance. Schedule Variance indicates how much ahead or behind schedule the project is.

Schedule Variance (SV) is the Budgeted Cost of Work Performed (BCWP) minus the budgeted cost of work scheduled. In other words, schedule variance shows the difference between the scheduled completion of an activity and the actual completion of that activity.

Schedule Variance (SV) can be defined as ***"the difference between the work scheduled (BCWS) and the work actually performed (BCWP)"***. The schedule variance is calculated in terms of the difference in dollar value between the amount of work that should have been completed in a given time period and the work actually completed.

For a given time (t), the Schedule variance is given by the formula:

$$SV = EV - PV$$

or

$$SV = BCWP - BCWS$$

For units of currency (rupees):

$$SV_{rp}(t) \equiv BCWP_{rp}(t) - BCWS_{rp}(t)$$

For units of labour:

$$SV_{L}(t) \equiv BCWP_{L}(t) - BCWS_{L}(t)$$

For a normalized (% of BAC) measurement:

$$SV_{\%}(t) \equiv BCWP_{\%}(t) - BCWS_{\%}(t)$$

It indicates the degree to which the value of completed work differs from that planned. It is shown in Fig. 7.3.

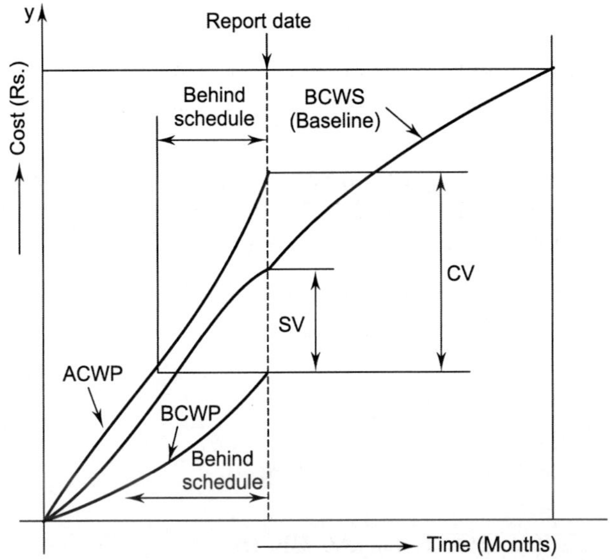

Fig. 7.3 Project cost/schedule progress report

In the above figure CV shows the cost variance to date. SV is the schedule variance. We have used the word "baseline" with BCWS. It is actually a baseline budget. It is based on the project plan and shows the forecast growth in EV through time.

Interpretation: The formula mentioned above gives the variance in terms of cost which will indicate how much cost of the work is yet to be completed as per schedule or how much cost of work has been completed over and above the scheduled cost.

- If SV < 0, means the project is behind of schedule
- If SV > 0, means the project is ahead of schedule
- If SV = 0, means the project is on scheduled time.

Schedule variance %: Schedule Variance % indicates how much ahead or behind schedule the project is in terms of percentage. Schedule Variance % can be calculated as using the following formula:

SV % = Schedule Variance (SV)/Planned Value (PV)

OR

SV % = SV/BCWS

Interpretation: The formula mentioned above gives the variance in terms of percentage which will indicate how much percentage of work is yet to be completed as per schedule or how much percentage of work has been completed over and above the scheduled cost.

- If SV% < 0, means the project is % behind of schedule
- If SV% > 0, means the project is % ahead of schedule
- If SV% = 0, means the project is on scheduled time.

7.7.2.2 Cost Variance (CV)

Cost Variance (CV) is very important factor to measure project performance. Cost Variance (CV) indicates how much over or under budget the project is.

Cost Variance (CV) is the Budgeted Cost of Work Performed (BCWP) minus the actual cost of work performed. In other words, cost variance shows the difference between the estimated cost of an activity and the actual cost of that activity.

Cost Variance (CV) can be defined as ***"the difference between the planned cost of work performed (BCWP) and actual cost incurred for the work (ACWP)"***. This is the actual dollar value by which a project is either over-running or under-running its estimated cost.

For a given time (t), the Cost variance is given by the formula:

$$CV = EV - AC$$

or

$$CV = BCWP - ACWP$$

For units of currency (rupees):

$$CV_{rp}(t) = BCWP_{rp}(t) - ACWP_{rp}(t)$$

For units of labour:

$$CV_L(t) = BCWP_L(t) - ACWP_L(t)$$

For a normalized (% of BAC) measurement:

$$CV_{\%}(t) = BCWP_{\%}(t) - ACWP_{\%}(t)$$

It indicates the accuracy of the original cost estimates. It is shown in the graph of Fig. 7.3.

Interpretation: The formula mentioned above gives the variance in terms of cost which will indicate how less or more cost has been to complete the work as of date.

- If $CV < 0$, means the project is over cost/budget
- If $CV > 0$, means the project is under cost/budget
- If $CV = 0$, means the project is costs as estimated.

Cost Variance %: Cost Variance % indicates how much over or under budget the project is in terms of percentage.

Cost Variance % can be calculated as using the following formula:

$$CV\,\% = \text{Cost Variance (CV)}/\text{Earned Value (EV)}$$

OR

$$CV\,\% = CV/BCWP$$

Interpretation: The formula mentioned above gives the variance in terms of percentage which will indicate how much less or more money has been used to complete the work as planned in terms of percentage.

- If $CV\% < 0$, means the project is % over cost/budget
- If $CV\,\% > 0$, means the project is % under cost/budget.

7.7.2.3 Budget Variance

It is the difference between planned and actual. In it positive values are favourable and negative values are unfavourable.

For units of currency (rupees):

$$BV_{rp}(t) = BCWS_{rp}(t) - ACWP_{rp}(t)$$

For units of labour:

$$BV_L(t) = BCWS_L(t) - ACWP_L(t)$$

For a normalized (% of BAC) measurement:

$$BV_{\%}(t) = BCWS_{\%}(t) - ACWP_{\%}(t)$$

7.7.2.4 *Time Variance*

It is the difference in elapsed calendar time between time now and time where plan function equals earned function evaluated at time now. In it positive values are favourable and negative values are unfavourable.

For units of elapsed calendar time:

$$TV_t(t) = t_{BCWS_{rp}(t)=BCWP_{rp}(t)} - t = t_{BCWS_L(t)=BCWP_L(t)} - t$$

$$= t_{BCWS_{\%}(t)=BCWP_{\%}(t)} - t$$

For a normalized (% of BAC) measurement:

$$TV_{\%}(t) = \frac{t_{BCWS_{rp}(t)=BCWP_{rp}(t)} - t}{t_{BCWS_{rp}(t)=BCWP_{rp}(t)}} = \frac{t_{BCWS_L(t)=BCWP_L(t)} - t}{t_{BCWS_L(t)=BCWP_L(t)}}$$

$$= \frac{t_{BCWS_{\%}(t)=BCWP_{\%}(t)} - t}{t_{BCWS_{\%}(t)=BCWP_{\%}(t)}}$$

7.7.3 Performance Indices

7.7.3.1 *SPI (Schedule Performed Index)*

Schedule Performance Indicator is an index showing the efficiency of the time utilized on the project.

OR

Schedule Performance Index is the ratio of work performed to work scheduled and can be used to estimate the projected time to complete the project.

OR

SPI is defined as ***"the ratio of the earned value (or BCWP) to that planned value (or BCWS)". It can be used to estimate the projected time to complete the project. Mathematically,***

$$SPI = EV/PV \text{ or } BCWP/BCWS$$

For units of currency (rupees):

$$SPI(t) = \frac{BCWP_{rp}(t)}{BCWS_{rp}(t)}$$

For units of labour:

$$SPI(t) = \frac{BCWP_L(t)}{BCWS_L(t)}$$

For a normalized (% of BAC) measurement:

$$SPI(t) = \frac{BCWP_{\%}(t)}{BCWS_{\%}(t)}$$

Interpretation: The formula mentioned above gives the efficiency of the project team in utilizing the time allocated for the project.

- SPI = 1, BCWP = BCWS (project on time)
- SPI <1, BCWP < BCWS (performing less than planned / time overrun / project team is less efficient in utilizing the time allocated to the project)
- SPI > 1, BCWP > BCWS (performing more than planned / time underrun / project team is very efficient in utilizing the time allocated to the project).

7.7.3.2 CPI (Cost Performance Index)

Cost Performance Indicator is an index showing the efficiency of the utilization of the resources on the project.

OR

Cost Performance Index is the ratio of work performed to actual costs and can be used to estimate the projected cost of completing the project.

OR

CPI is defined as ***"the ratio of the earned value (or BCWP) to actual cost (or ACWP)". It can be used to estimate the projected cost of completing the project. Mathematically,***

$$CPI = EV/AC \text{ or } BCWP/ACWP$$

For units of currency (rupees):

$$CPI(t) = \frac{BCWP_{rp}(t)}{ACWP_{rp}(t)}$$

For units of labour:

$$CPI(t) = \frac{BCWP_{L}(t)}{ACWP_{L}(t)}$$

For a normalized (% of BAC) measurement:

$$CPI(t) = \frac{BCWP_{\%}(t)}{ACWP_{\%}(t)}$$

Interpretation: The formula mentioned above gives the efficiency of the utilization of the resources allocated to the project.

- CPI = 1 (Performance is as planned and on budget)
- CPI < 1 (Poor Performance but spending more than planned (over budget)/efficiency in utilizing the resources allocated to the project is not good)
- CPI > 1 (Better performance but spending less than planned (under budget)/efficiency in utilizing the resources allocated to the project is good).

CPI can be used to produce revised cost estimate for the project. It is also called Estimate at Completion (EAC). **Estimate at Completion (EAC)** is the ***"actual costs incurred by the project to date, plus an estimate of the costs for work remaining"***. At the start of the project BAC and EAC will be equal. Only as actual costs (ACWP) vary from planned costs (BCWP) will EAC vary from BAC.

EAC is calculated as follows:

$$EAC = \text{Budget at Completion (BAC)}/CPI$$

Where, BAC is the current projected budget for the project.

NOTE: Budget at Completion (BAC) is the sum of all of the budgets allocated to a program.

7.7.3.3 BPI (Budget Performance Index)

It is the ratio of amount planned to amount spent. Budget efficiency achieved from project start to time *t*. In it values greater than unity are favourable, values less than unity are unfavourable.

For units of currency (rupees):

$$\text{BPI (t)} = \frac{\text{BCWS}_{rp}\ (t)}{\text{ACWP}_{rp}\ (t)}$$

For units of labour:

$$\text{BPI (t)} = \frac{\text{BCWS}_{\text{L}}\ (t)}{\text{ACWP}_{\text{L}}\ (t)}$$

For a normalized (% of BAC) measurement:

$$\text{BPI (t)} = \frac{\text{BCWS}_{\%}\ (t)}{\text{ACWP}_{\%}\ (t)}$$

7.7.3.4 TPI (Time Performance Index)

Time efficiency achieved from project start to time *t*. In it values greater than unity are favourable, values less than unity are unfavourable.

For units of currency (rupees):

$$\text{TPI}\ (t) = \frac{t_{\text{BCWS}_{rp}\ (t) = \text{BCWP}_{rp}\ (t)}}{t}$$

For units of labour:

$$\text{TPI}\ (t) = \frac{t_{\text{BCWS}_{\text{L}}\ (t) = \text{BCWP}_{\text{L}}\ (t)}}{t}$$

For a normalized (% of BAC) measurement:

$$\text{TPI}\ (t) = \frac{t_{\text{BCWS}_{\%}\ (t) = \text{BCWP}_{\%}\ (t)}}{t}$$

7.7.3.5 XPI (Composite Performance Index)

Combined cost and schedule efficiency achieved from project start to time *t*. In it values greater than unity are favourable, values less than unity are unfavourable.

$$\text{XPI (t)} = \sqrt{\text{CPI}\ (t)\ \text{SPI}\ (t)}$$

7.8 OTHER INDICATORS OF EVA

7.8.1 Budget at Completion

The starting point for project's performance measurement is the Budget at Completion. This measure is a primary output of the estimation process and represents what is expected to be spent by the project. The plan that is associated with this value is generally known as the baseline plan or simply the baseline. In normalized unit system BAC is always assume to be unity (1 or 100%). The currency (rupees) and labour variance of this value may change during the coarse of a project as a result of re-planning or re-baselining.

For units of currency (rupees):

$$BAC_{rp} = \sum_{j=1}^{n} Activity_j \text{ planned cost}$$

Where,

$$n = \text{Total no. of activities in the project}$$

For units of labour:

$$BAC_L = \sum_{j=1}^{n} Activity_j \text{ planned Effort}$$

Where,

$$n = \text{Total no. of activities in the project}$$

For a normalized (% of BAC) measurement:

$$BAC_{\%} = \Delta r \left| \left(t_{start}, t_{finish} \right) \right| = 1 = 100\%$$

Budget at Completion (BAC) is the sum of all of the budgets allocated to a program. In addition to the PMB, there generally is an amount of management reserve, which is a portion of the total program budget not allocated to specific work packages and withheld for management control purposes. The BAC consists of the PMB plus all management reserves.

Performance Measurement Baseline (PMB) is the sum of all work packages Budgeted Cost of Work Scheduled (BCWS) for each time period, calculated for the total program duration. The PMB forms the time-phased budget plan against which project performance is measured.

7.8.2 Variance at Completion (VAC)

Variance of TOTAL cost of the work and expected cost.

$$VAC = BAC - EAC.$$

7.8.3 Estimate at Completion (EAC)

EAC is the expected TOTAL cost required to finish complete work.

$$\begin{aligned} EAC &= BAC/CPI \\ &= AC + ETC \\ &= AC + ((BAC - EV)/CPI) \text{ (typical case)} \\ &= AC + (BAC - EV) \text{ (atypical case).} \end{aligned}$$

Here atypical means it is assumed that similar variances will not occur in the future.

7.8.4 Estimate to Complete (ETC)

ETC is the expected cost required to finish all the REMAINING work.

$$ETC = EAC - AC$$

$$= (BAC/CPI) - (EV/CPI)$$
$$= (BAC - EV)/CPI.$$

7.9 BENEFITS OF EVA

EVM contributes to:

- Preventing scope creep
- Improving communication and visibility with stakeholders
- Reducing risk
- Profitability analysis
- Project forecasting
- Better accountability
- Performance tracking.

7.10 EXAMPLE OF EARNED VALUE AND VARIANCE

7.10.1 Example 1

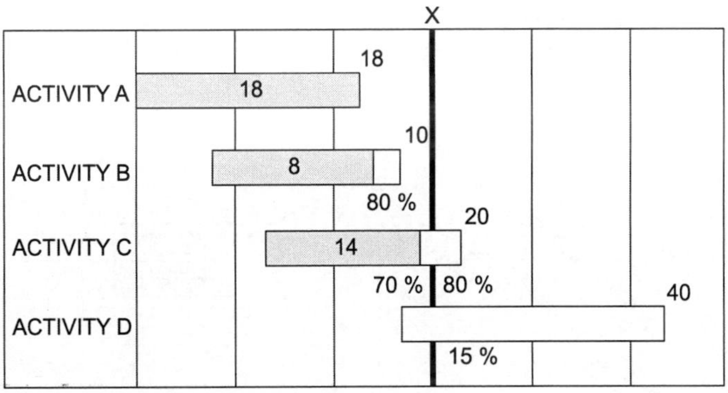

Solution:

On Day X:

- PLANNED VALUE (BCWS) = 18 + 10 + 16 + 6 = 50
- EARNED VALUE (BCWP) = 18 + 8 + 14 + 0 = 40
- ACTUAL COST (ACWP) = 45 (from your project tracking)

Therefore:

- Schedule Variance = BCWP – BCWS = 40 – 50 = – 10 (behind schedule)
- Schedule Performance Index = 40/50 = 0.8, or 80% of plan (a B-, at best)
- Cost Variance = BCWP – ACWP = 40 – 45 = – 5
- Cost Performance Index = 40/45 = 0.89, or your getting an 89$ return on every $ (person-hour) spent on this project.

The calculated values of EVA indicators can be represented graphically which is shown as follows:

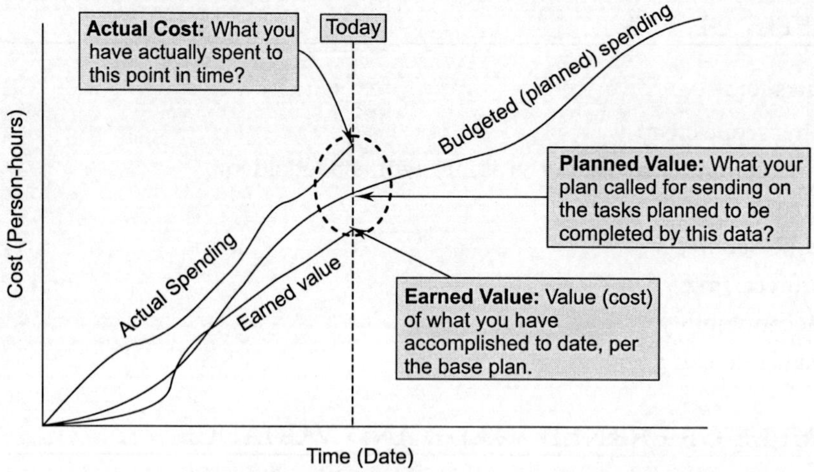

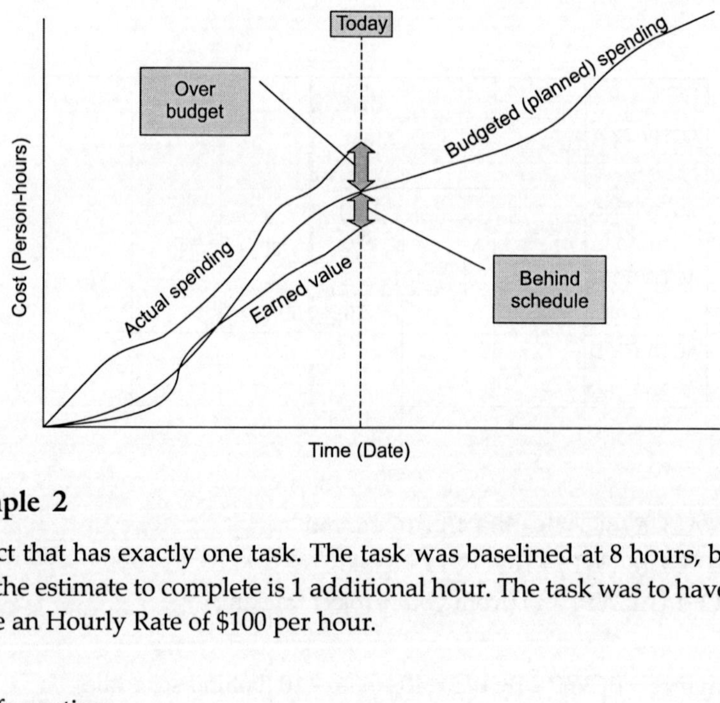

7.10.2 Example 2

Assume a project that has exactly one task. The task was baselined at 8 hours, but 11 hours have been spent and the estimate to complete is 1 additional hour. The task was to have been completed already. Assume an Hourly Rate of $100 per hour.

Solution:

Using this information:

Hourly Rate = $100

1. **PV or BCWS** = Hourly Rate * Total Hours Planned or Scheduled
   PV = $800 ($100 * 8 hours)
2. **AC or ACWP** = Hourly Rate * Total Hours Spent
   AC = $1100 ($100 * 11 hours)
3. **EV or BCWP** = Baselined Cost * % Complete Actual
   EV = $734 (baseline of $800 * 91.7% complete)

(NOTE % Complete Actual (below) to get the 91.7%)

4. **BAC** = Baselined Effort-hours * Hourly Rate
   BAC = $800 (8 hours * $100)
5. **EAC** = AC + ETC
   EAC = $1200 (1100 + 100)
6. **VAC** = BAC – EAC
   VAC = – $400 ($800 – $1200)
7. **% Completed Planned** = PV / BAC
   % Complete Planned = 100% ($800 PV / $800 BAC)
8. **% Completed Actual** = AC / EAC
   % Complete Actual = 91.7% ($1100 AC / $1200 EAC)
9. **SV** = Earned Value (EV) – Planned Value (PV)
   SV = –$100 ($700 EV – $800 PV)
10. **SPI** = Earned Value (EV)/Planned Value (PV)
    SPI = 0.88 ($700 EV / $800 PV)
11. **CV** = Earned Value (EV) – Actual Cost (AC)
    CV = –$400 ($700 EV – $1100 AC) indicating a cost overrun
12. **CPI** = Earned Value (EV)/Actual Cost (AC)
    CPI = 0.64 ($700 EV / $1100 AC) indicating over budget

7.10.3 Example 3

A project has a budget of £10M and schedule for 10 months. It is assumed that the total budget will be spent equally each month until the 10th month is reached. After 2 months the project manager finds that only 5% of the work is finished and a total of £1M spent.

Solution:

1. PV = £2M
   EV = £10M * 0.05 = £0.5M
   AV = £1M
2. CV = EV – AC = 0.5 – 1 = –0.5M
   CV% = 100 * (CV/EV) = 100*(–0.5/0.5) = –100% overrun
3. SV = EV – PV = 0.5 – 2 = –1.5 months
   SV% = 100 * (SV/PV) = 100*(–1.5/2) = –75% behind
4. CPI = EV/AC = 0.5/1 = 0.5
   SPI = EV/PV = 0.5/2 = 0.25
5. EAC = BAC/CPI = 10/0.5 = £20M
   ETC = (BAC – EV) / CPI = (10 – 0.5)/0.5 = £19M
6. Time to compete = (10 – 0.5)/0.25 = 38 Months

This project will take TOTAL £20M (19 + 1) and 40 (38 + 2) Months to complete.

Let's work a calculation of Earned value to see how this metric works:

7.10.4 Example 4

A work task on a very large software project schedule is "Develop, Review & Publish Test Plan". Four software engineers are assigned to this task, & it is estimated to take them, three weeks to complete with the work evenly distributed across weeks. The budget for this task is Rs. 120k, allocated evenly by week. The first week, only two of the engineers were available. The second and third weeks, all four engineers were available.

Week 1: Test Plan			
Cost	*Amount*	*Progress*	*Amount*
Planned	40k	Planned	30%
Actual	20k	Actual	20%

The following chart contains Earned Value information about this task for the first week.

Planned value : 40k

Actual cost : 20k

Earned Value : PV * rate of performance = 40k * 20/30 = 26.6k

Cost Variance = 26.6k – 20k = 6.6k

Schedule Variance = 26.6k – 40k = –13.4k

Cost Performance Index = 26.6/20 = 1.33 = 133%

Schedule Performance Index = 26.6/40 = 0.665 = 66.5%

Note that in this example, the Cost Performance Index is greater than 100% and therefore costs are running below budget. It makes sense, because not all labour costs are being spent.

The Schedule Performance Index is less than 100%. However since the task is running behind schedule.

During this week, the Test Plan activity is off track.

While Earned Value has value at the task level, it is particularly powerful when taken at time intervals (say, monthly), and at project kill points.

To complete an Earned Value calculation at the project level, calculations would be made for all tasks already completed or in play, and then summed for a cumulative value. That way, while we might be running behind on some tasks, if we are running ahead on others our project might be OK overall.

Consequences found: From the calculation done, we came to know the following points:

- First of all, the calculation only works if good planning information is in place and strong metrics are being used to track actuals. Of course, good project management practices should be producing this data.
- Second, percentage completion values can be meaningless or unavailable. What does it mean to say a task is 75% complete? Many organizations get around this by simplifying things in the following way:
  - If a task has not been started, it is 0% complete
  - If a task has been started but not finished, it is 50%
  - If a task has been finished, it is 100% complete.

This simplification can be pretty powerful. By one estimate, for a one-year project with weekly reporting and an average work packet size of one week, simplified completion estimates produce a 1% error rate.

7.11 INTERPRETATION OF EARNED VALUE INDICATORS

EVA with three main indicators (BCWS, BCWP and ACWP) has yet not gained any universal acceptance as far as software projects are concerned. This is because a half constructed house has a value but a half developed software project has virtually no value at all.

Accordingly to **Martin**, "The usefulness of EV measurements in project management is controversial". The most enthusiastic managers regard it the best way to prevent surprises and as a most workable tool. Others consider the information helpful in managing the project but not worth the cost of obtaining it. Still others say the information becomes available too late or there are better ways to obtain it. The most critical managers view it as a complete waste of time.

Earned value indicators that are variances or ratios can help us determine if there is enough money left in the budget and if the project will finish on time.

Variance: The difference between baseline and scheduled task or resource information they usually occur when we set a baseline plan and begin entering actual information into our schedule. Variance can occur in work, costs and schedule. Such as a Cost Variance (CV) can be either positive or negative:

- A positive variance indicates that the project is ahead of schedule or under budget. Positive variance might enable us to reallocate money and resources from tasks or projects with positive variances to tasks or projects with negative variances.
- A negative variance indicates that project is behind schedule or over budget and we need to take action. If a task or project has a negative CV, we might have to increase our budget or accept reduced profit margins.

Ratio: Ratios such as the Cost Performance Index (CPI) and the Schedule Performance Index (SPI) can be greater than 1 or less than 1:

- A value that's greater than 1 indicates that the project is ahead of schedule or under budget.
- A value that's less than 1 indicates that we're behind schedule or over budget. For example, an SPI of 1.5 means that we've taken only 67 percent of the planned time to complete a portion of a task in a given time period and a CPI of 0.8 means that we've spent 25 percent more time on a task than was planned.

7.12 ERROR TRACKING

"Error tracking allows you to compare current work with past efforts and provides a quantitative indication of the quality of the work being conducted".

Throughout the software process, a project team creates work products (*e.g.*, requirements specifications or prototype, design documents, source code). But the team also creates (and hopefully corrects) errors associated with each work product. If error-related measures and resultant metrics are collected over many software projects, a project manager can use these data as a baseline for comparison against error data collected in real time. Error tracking can be used as one means for assessing the status of a current project.

To review briefly, the software team performs formal technical reviews (and, later, testing) to find and correct errors, E, in work products produced during software engineering tasks. Any errors that are not uncovered (but found in later tasks) are considered to be defects, D. Defect removal efficiency has been defined as

$$DRE = E/(E+D)$$

DRE is a process metric that provides a strong indication of the effectiveness of quality assurance activities, but DRE and the error and defect counts associated with it can also be used to assist a project manager in determining the progress that is being made as a software project moves through its scheduled work tasks.

Let us assume that a software organization has collected error and defect data over the past 24 months and has developed averages for the following metrics:

- Errors per requirements specification page, E_{req}
- Errors per component-design level, E_{design}
- Errors per component-code level, E_{code}
- DRE-requirements analysis
- DRE-architectural design
- DRE-component level design
- DRE-coding.

As the project progresses through each software engineering step, the software team records and reports the number of errors found during requirements, design, and code reviews. The project manager calculates current values for E_{req}, E_{design}, and E_{code}. These are then compared to averages for past projects. If current results vary by more than 20% from the average, there may be cause for concern and there is certainly cause for investigation.

For example, if *E*req = 2.1 for project X, yet the organizational average is 3.6, one of two scenarios is possible:

1. The software team has done an outstanding job of developing the requirements specification.
   or
2. The team has been lax in its review approach.

If the second scenario appears likely, the project manager should take immediate steps to build additional design time12 into the schedule to accommodate the requirements defects that have likely been propagated into the design activity.

These error tracking metrices can also be used to better target review and/or testing resources. For example, if a system is composed of 120 components, but 32 of these component exhibit E_{design} values that have substantial variance from the average, the project manager might elect to dedicate code review resources to the 32 components and allow others to pass into testing with no code review. Although all components should undergo code review in an ideal setting, a selective approach (reviewing only those modules that have suspect quality based on the E_{design} value) might be an effective means for recouping lost time and/or saving costs for a project that has gone over budget.

The more quantitative your approach to project tracking and control, the more likely you'll be able to foresee potential problems and respond to them proactively. Use earned value and tracking metrics.

8

SOFTWARE REVIEWS

8.1 INTRODUCTION

Software reviews are a "filter" for the software engineering process. That is, reviews are applied at various points during software development and serve to uncover errors and defects that can then be removed. Software reviews "purify" the software engineering activities that we have called *analysis, design,* and *coding*. "Software reviews means viewing your software again".

8.2 WHY WE NEED SOFTWARE REVIEWS?

Freedman and Weinberg discuss the need for reviews this way: Technical work needs reviewing for the same reason that pencils need erasers: *To err is human.* The second reason we need technical reviews is that although people are good at catching some of their own errors, large classes of errors escape the originator more easily than they escape anyone else.

8.3 DEFINITIONS

A review can be defined as:

"A meeting at which the software element is presented to project personnel, managers, users, customers or other interested parties for comment or approval".

OR

"A software review process can be defined as a critical evaluation of an object".

OR

A review is a process or meeting during which a work product, or a set of work products, is presented to project personnel, managers, users, customers, or other interested parties for comment or approval.

OR

A software review is

"A process or meeting during which a software product is [examined by] project personnel, managers, users, customers, user representatives, or other interested parties for comment or approval".

In this context, the term "software product" means "any technical document or partial document, produced as a deliverable of a software development activity", and may include documents such as contracts, project plans and budgets, requirements documents, specifications, designs, source code, user documentation, support and maintenance documentation, test plans, test specifications, standards, and any other type of specialist work product.

8.4 PURPOSE OF SOFTWARE REVIEW

The purpose of any review is:

- To discover errors in analysis, design, and coding, testing and implementation phase of software development cycle.
- To see whether procedures are applied uniformly and in a manageable manner.

The reviews predominantly are at three stages: ***first,*** Requirement Review, ***then*** Design Review and ***finally*** Technical Review. Every organization has review guidelines and there is a set procedure for each review. The review is performed by an authorized person, review meetings are held, an issues list is made, and decisions and actions are taken to resolve them. The issues and the solutions are rechecked in the next meeting. Table 8.1 shows the main reviews and the focus in each of them.

Table 8.1 Main reviews, its participants and their focus

Review	*Participants*	*Focus*
Requirement	Customer, Project Manager, Users	Meeting the Requirement and software specification.
Design	Project manager, system designer, solution architect, and customer	Architecture, Performance, Deliverables
Technical	Project manager, designer, solution Architect.	Quality, Standards and Deliverables

8.5 OBJECTIVES FOR SOFTWARE REVIEWS

Reviews objectives are:

- To ensure that the software element conforms to its specifications.
- To ensure that the development of the software element is being done as per plans, standards and guidelines applicable for the project.
- To ensure that the changes to the software element are properly implemented and affect only those system areas identified by the change specification.

8.6 VARIETIES OF SOFTWARE REVIEWS

Software reviews may be divided into three categories:

- ***Software peer reviews*** are conducted by the author of the work product, or by one or more colleagues of the author, to evaluate the technical content and/or quality of the work.
- ***Software management reviews*** are conducted by management representatives to evaluate the status of work done and to make decisions regarding downstream activities.
- ***Software audit reviews*** are conducted by personnel external to the software project, to evaluate compliance with specifications, standards, contractual agreements, or other criteria.

8.7 IEEE 1028 GENERIC PROCESS FOR FORMAL REVIEWS

IEEE Std 1028 defines a common set of activities for "formal" reviews (with some variations, especially for software audit). The sequence of activities is largely based on the software inspection process originally developed at IBM by **Michael Fagan**. Differing types of review may apply this structure with varying degrees of rigour, but all activities are mandatory for inspection:

1. **Entry Evaluation:** The Review Leader uses a standard checklist of entry criteria to ensure that optimum conditions exist for a successful review.
2. **Management Preparation:** Responsible management ensure that the review will be appropriately resourced with staff, time, materials, and tools, and will be conducted according to policies, standards, or other relevant criteria.
3. **Planning the Review:** The Review Leader identifies or confirms the objectives of the review, organises a team of Reviewers, and ensures that the team is equipped with all necessary resources for conducting the review.
4. **Overview of Review Procedures:** The Review Leader, or some other qualified person, ensures (at a meeting if necessary) that all Reviewers understand the review goals, the review procedures, the materials available to them, and the procedures for conducting the review.
5. **Individual Preparation:** The Reviewers individually prepare for group examination of the work under review, by examining it carefully for *anomalies* (potential defects), the nature of which will vary with the type of review and its goals.
6. **Group Examination:** The Reviewers meet at a planned time to pool the results of their preparation activity and arrive at a consensus regarding the status of the document (or activity) being reviewed.
7. **Rework/follow-up:** The Author of the work product (or other assigned person) undertakes whatever actions are necessary to repair defects or otherwise satisfy the requirements agreed to at the Examination meeting. The Review Leader verifies that all action items are closed.
8. **Exit Evaluation:** The Review Leader verifies that all activities necessary for successful review have been accomplished, and that all outputs appropriate to the type of review have been finalized.

8.8 TYPES OF REVIEWS

- ***Inspection*** is a very formal type of peer review where the reviewers are following a well-defined process to find defects.
- A ***Desk-check*** is a simple review in which the author of a work product distributes it to one or more reviewers.

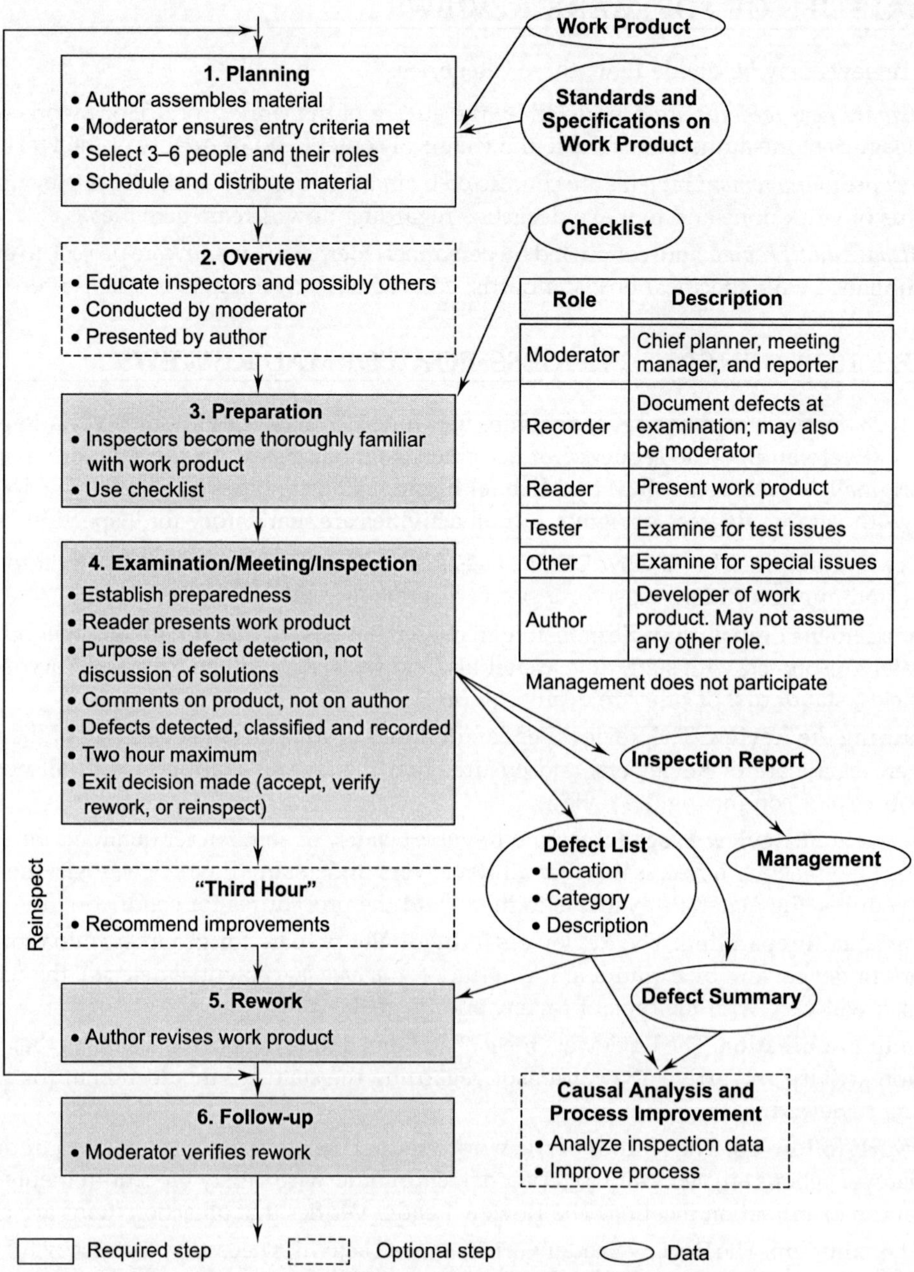

Fig. 8.1 The software inspection process (IEEE Std 1028)

- *Walkthrough* is a form of peer review where the author leads members of the development team and other interested parties through a software product and the participants ask questions and make comments about defects.
- *Code review* is systematic examination (often as peer review) of computer source code.
- *Pair programming* is a type of code review where two persons develop code together at the same workstation.

- *Technical review* is a form of peer review in which a team of qualified personnel examines the suitability of the software product for its intended use and identifies discrepancies from specifications and standards.

8.8.1 Code Inspection

A code inspection, originally introduced by Fagan (1976) at IBM, is similar to a walkthrough but is more formal. Fagan's experiment, three separate inspections were performed: one following design, but prior to implementation: one following implementation, but prior to unit testing; and one following unit testing. The inspection following unit testing was not considered to be cost effective in discovering errors; therefore, it is not recommended.

"Software inspection is an industry-proven process for improving software product quality and reducing development time and cost."

An inspection is one of the most common sorts of review found in software projects. The organization aspects of code inspection are similar to those of code walk-through (*i.e.*, the number of participants, duration of the meeting, psychological attitudes of the participants, etc., should be about the same), but there is a difference in goals.

In code inspection, the analysis is aimed explicitly at the discovery of commonly made errors. In such a case, it is useful to state beforehand the type of error for which we are searching. For instance, consider the classical error of writing a procedure that modifies a formal parameter and calling the procedure with a constant value as the actual parameter.

The following is a list of some classical programming errors, which can be checked during code inspection:

1. Use of un-initialized variables.
2. Jumps into loops
3. Non-terminating loops
4. Incompatible assignments
5. Array indices out of bounds
6. Improper storage allocation and de-allocation
7. Mismatches between actual and formal parameters in procedure calls
8. Use of incorrect logical operators or incorrect precedence among operators
9. Improper modification of loop variables
10. Comparison of equality of floating-point values, etc.

8.8.1.1 Participants in Software Inspection

An inspection team consists of four persons who play the roles of Moderator, Reader, Recorder and Author.

1. *Moderator*: The moderator must be technically very competent. He / She is the person who leads the inspection process, places the meeting; coaches other team members, deals with scheduling a meeting place and disseminating materials before the meeting, and follows up on rework.
2. *Reader*: The reader takes the team through the code by paraphrasing its operation.
3. *Recorder*: A recorder notes each error on a standard format. This frees the other team members to focus on thinking deeply about the code.

4. *Authors*: The author's role is to understand the errors found and to illuminate unclear areas. As code inspections are never confrontational, the Author should never be in a position of defending the code.

8.8.1.2 Checklist for Code Inspection

Inspections or reviews are more formal and conducted with the help of some kind of checklist. The steps in the inspections or reviews are:

1. Are the numbers of actual parameters and formal parameters in agreement?
2. Do the type attributes of actual and formal parameters match?
3. Do the dimensional units of actual and formal parameters match?
4. Are the numbers attributes, and ordering of arguments to built-in functions correct?
5. Are constants passed as modifiable arguments?
6. Are global variable definitions and usage consistent among modules?
7. Application of a checklist specially prepared for development plan, SRS, design and architecture
8. Nothing observation: ok, not ok, with comments on mistake or inadequacy.
9. Repair-rework.
10. Checklists prepared to countercheck whether the subject entity is correct, consistent and complete in meeting the objectives.

8.8.1.3 Advantages of Code Inspection

1. Lists all potential design flows that can make s/w code less maintainable and costly to develop.
2. Indicates all defects otherwise difficult to testing and usage
3. A detailed error feedback is provided to individual programmers. So that it makes easier for them to make changes in the code.

8.8.1.4 Objectives of Software Inspection

The objectives of a software inspection is:

- To detect defects in documents or code.
- For all of the inspectors to reach consensus on a work product and approve it for use in the project.
- To repair all of the defects so that everyone on the inspection team can approve the work product.

Commonly inspected work products include software requirements specifications and test plans. In an inspection, a work product is selected for review and a team is gathered for an inspection meeting to review the work meeting by reading the work product and nothing each defect. In an inspection, a defect is any part of the work product that will keep an inspector from approving it. For example, if the team is inspecting a software requirements specification, each defect will be text in the document which an inspector disagrees with.

8.8.1.5 Issues of Code Inspection

One issue in inspection implementation is whether or not there should be a reader who paraphrases the product. And other define inspection processes that do not include paraphrasing. The main advantage of paraphrasing is that it provides an opportunity for synergistically finding new defects that were not found by individuals. The advantage of not paraphrasing is that the meeting can take much less time, which is significant because meetings can consume a great deal of valuable time. Published experiments comparing the relative advantages of paraphrasing versus not paraphrasing are needed.

Another issue in inspection implementation is whether or not the meeting should be eliminated entirely or replaced with depositions (a series of meetings of the moderator, author and one other inspector). Some experiments have suggested that meetings do not significantly add to the defect detection ability of the inspection process.

8.8.2 Deskchecks/Buddy-Checks

A deskcheck is a simple review in which the author of a work product distributes it to one or more reviewers. In a deskcheck, the author sends a copy of the work product to selected project team members. The team members read it, and then write up defects and comments to send back to the author. Unlike an inspection, a deskcheck does not produce written logs which can be archived with the document for later reference. There is no follow-up meeting or approval process. It is simply a way for one team member to check another's work. Deskchecks are not formal reviews (where "formal" simply means that it generates a written work product which meets a certain standard and is archived with the rest of the project documentation); there is no standard for the results of the deskcheck. The reviewers simply review the work product and return the results. There is no moderator, and there is not necessarily any consensus generated.

8.8.2.1 Where Deskchecks are Useful

Deskchecks can be used as ***predecessors to inspections***. In many cases, having an author of a work product pass his work to a peer for an informal review will significantly reduce the amount of effort involved in the inspection. Many defects can be caught by a single person reviewing a document. Approval and consensus is built later on during the inspection meeting; this is simply a way of saving effort. After a deskcheck, many authors will feel much more comfortable sending their document into an inspection—it will often help the author to be more objective and to take the inspection comments less personally.

There are times when a full inspection is neither necessary nor useful. Some work products do not benefit enough to warrant the attention of an entire inspection team because they do not need consensus or approval. In these cases, the author simply needs input from others to prevent defects, but does not require that they approve the document. In these cases, the deskcheck is a useful review practice.

8.8.2.2 Advantages of Desk Chechking

1. The main advantage of this method is that since it is done by the programmer who has complete knowledge of both the programming language as well as the code that he has written.
2. It is done by one individual only. So, there are no scheduling overheads.
3. The defects are detected and corrected with minimum time today.

8.8.2.3 Disadvantages of Desk Chechking

1. A developer will never pin-point any defects in his own code.
2. Developers generally prefer to write new code rather than do any form of testing.
3. This method is inconsistent and depends on a single person.
4. It is an informal method.

8.8.2.4 *Example of Deskchecks*

The illustration below (Fig. 8.2) contains an example of comments from a deskcheck which was used by a tester to find defects in an automation script. In this case, the entire review was performed via e-mail: the author mailed the script to the reviewer, and the reviewer read it and e-mailed the comments back to the author. These comments are much simpler than the inspection log. In an inspection, each log entry must either resolve a defect or indicate that it is an open issue which must be resolved. Deskcheck comments can simply point out issues or raise questions without having to supply solutions or promise a resolution. There was no follow-up or approval, and the reviewer had no more contact with this script.

Reviewer's Name:	Sophie (senior QA engineer)
Author's Name:	Dean (junior QA engineer)
Title:	Contract Certification – automated test script #TP-491-A
Review Date:	8/12/03
No. of Review Hours:	2

Location	*Comments*
Global	Script does not adequately copy databases in when the data changes
Case 14	The test plan logs in as "Administrator", this script logs in as "Admin"
Case 52, 53	What exactly is printed? It's not clear, you should be looking for specific data.
Case 61	The test plan tests all of the preferences, but the script only tests the first five.
Global	Script does not adequately copy databases in when the data changes

Fig. 8.2 Sample deskcheck comments

8.8.3 Code Walk Through

A code walk-through is an informal analysis of code as a cooperative, organized activity by several participants. The analysis is based mainly on the game of "playing the computer." That is, participants select some test cases (the selection could have been done previously by a single participant) and simulate execution of the code by hand. This is the reason for the name walk-***through***: participants "walk through the code" or through any design notation. These are a popular form of peer review process, and are generally viewed as not being as "powerful" as inspections.

In software engineering, a **walkthrough** or **walk-through** is a form of software peer review "in which a designer or programmer leads members of the development team and other interested parties through a software product, and the participants ask questions and make comments about possible errors, violation of development standards, and other problems"

In general, the following prescriptions are recommended:

- Everyone's work should be reviewed on a scheduled basis.
- The number of people involved in the review should be small (three to five).
- The participants should receive written documentation from the designer a few days before the meeting.
- The meeting should last a predefined amount of time (a few hours).
- Discussion should be focused on the discovery of errors, not on fixing them, nor on proposing alternative design decisions.

- Key people in the meeting should be the designer, who presents and explains the rationale of the work, a moderator for the discussion, and a secretary, who is responsible for writing a report to be given to the designer at the end of the meeting.

In order to foster cooperation and avoid the feeling that the designers are being evaluated, managers should not participate in the meeting.

8.8.3.1 *Definitions*

"Walkthrough is reviews of a software product (design specifications, code, test procedures, and so on) conducted by the peers of the group being reviewed."

OR

"Walkthroughs are a critique of a software product by the producer's press for the sole purpose of finding errors".

OR

"Code walk through is an informal code analysis technique. In this technique, after a module has been coded, successfully compiled and all syntax errors eliminated".

OR

A walkthrough is performed as a step by step simulation of the code with a sample set of input.

OR

Yourdon defines a walkthrough as

"a group peer review of products." the reviews are to find defects, but suggestions that do not involve defects are permitted.

OR

Daniel Freedman and Gerald Weinberg define

"a walkthrough as a review that is characterized by the producer of the reviewed material being present and guiding the progression of the review."

OR

Walkthroughs are similar to inspections in that they are also peer reviews that are used to detect defects. Usually, however, the person leading the review meeting and presenting the product is the producer of that product.

8.8.3.2 *Objectives of Walkbrough*

In general, a walkthrough has one or two broad objectives: to gain feedback about the technical quality or content of the document; and/or to familiarize the audience with the content.

Other objectives of walkthrough are:

- To evaluate a software element mainly "to find defects, omissions, and contradictions to improve the software element and to consider alternative implementations". Other important implementation include "exchange of techniques and style variations, and education of the participants.
- A walkthrough may point out efficiency and readability problems in the code, modularity in the design or unstable design specifications.
- To discover the algorithmic and logical errors in the code.

8.8.3.3 *When to use a Walkthrough?*

Walkthroughs should be used for early evaluation of documents, models, designs and code in the Software Requirements (SR), Architectural Design (AD), and Detailed Design and production (DD) phases. Wakthroughs are used when the author of a work product needs to take into account the perspective of someone who does not have the technical expertise to review the document.

8.8.3.4 *Participants in a Walkthrough*

A walkthrough is normally organized and directed by the author of the technical document. Any combination of interested or technically qualified personnel (from within or outside the project) may be included as seems appropriate.

IEEE 1028 recommends three specialist roles in a walkthrough:

- The ***Author***, who presents the software product in step-by-step manner at the walk-through meeting, and is probably responsible for completing most action items;
- The ***Walkthrough Leader***, who conducts the walkthrough, handles administrative tasks, and ensures orderly conduct (and who is often the Author); and
- The ***Recorder***, who notes all anomalies (potential defects), decisions, and action items identified during the walkthrough meeting.

8.8.3.5 *Elements of a Walkthrough*

- Small group, including responsible project leader.
- Well-defined, controlled agenda.
- Typically the project leader "walks through" the work product.
- Reviewers raise issues and identify potential problems.
- A written record is maintained.
- At conclusion, the group decides on the status of the product: accept, reject, accept provisionally.

8.8.3.6 *Guidelines of walkthrough*

These guidelines can help an author lead a successful walkthrough meeting:

- Verify that everyone is present who needs to review the work product. This could include users, stakeholders, engineering leads, managers and other interested people.
- Verify that everyone present understands the purpose of the walkthrough meeting, and how the material is going to be presented.
- Describe each section of the material to be covered by the walkthrough.
- Present the material in each section, ensuring that everyone present understands the material being presented.
- Lead discussion to identify missing any sections or material.
- Document all issues that are raised by walkthrough attendees.

After the meeting, the author should follow up with individual attendees who may have had additional information or insights. The document should then be corrected to reflect any issues that were raised.

8.8.3.7 *Advantage of Walkthrough*

The various advantages of walkthrough are:

1. A large amount of material can be examined in a short period of time, little time is demanded of the participants, and the review is often educational.
2. It improves project team communication and project morale by involving team members in the walkthrough process.
3. The earlier bugs are found in the life cycle of a product, the cheaper and easier they are to fix.

8.8.3.8 *Disadvantage of Walkthrough*

The various disadvantages of walkthrough are:

1. Unfortunately it can be difficult to conduct walkthroughs in a way that explores substantial issues.
2. It takes time, not only for person actively working on the project, but also for other people who usually under deadline pressure themselves.

8.8.4 Code Review

Code review is a systematic examination (often as peer review) of computer source code intended to find and fix mistakes overlooked in the initial development phase, improving both the overall quality of software and the developers' skills. Code review for a model is carried out after the module is successfully compiled and the all the syntax errors have been eliminated. Code reviews are extremely cost-effective strategies for reduction in coding errors and to produce high quality code.

A code review is a special kind of inspection in which the team examines a sample of code and fixes any defects in it. In a code review, a defect is a block of code which does not properly implement its requirements, which does not function as the programmer intended, or which is not incorrect but could be improved (for example, it could be made more readable or its performance could be improved). In addition to helping teams find and fix bugs, code reviews are useful for both cross-training programmers on the code being reviewed and for helping junior developers learn new programming techniques.

Select the code sample: The first task in a code review is to select the sample of code to be inspected. It's impossible to review every line of code, so the programmers need to be selective about which portion of the code gets reviewed. Many teams have found that it takes about two hours to review 400 lines of code (in a high-level language such as Java), although this estimate differs dramatically from team to team and depends on the complexity of the code being reviewed. At that rate, there is no way a team could review all of the code for a software project. Nor would the team want to—in any program, there is a good deal of uninteresting code that looks very similar to the code already developed in previous applications, which has a lower risk of containing as many defects.

Hold the review session: The team selection and preparation in a code review are similar to any other kind of inspection. An inspection team of three to ten people must be selected. Each of these people must be technically capable of reading and understanding the code being reviewed. Before the meeting the moderator distributes the code sample to each inspector, who does individual preparation exactly as in the inspection.

8.8.4.1 *Types of Code Review*

Code review practices fall into two main categories: formal code review and lightweight code review.

1. **Formal code review:** Formal code review, such as a Fagan inspection, involves a careful and detailed process with multiple participants and multiple phases. Formal code reviews are the traditional method of review, in which software developers attend a series of meetings and review code line by line, usually using printed copies of the material. Formal inspections are extremely thorough and have been proven effective at finding defects in the code under review.
2. **Lightweight code review:** Lightweight code review typically requires less overhead than formal code inspections, though it can be equally effective when done properly. Lightweight reviews are often conducted as part of the normal development process:
    - ***Over-the-shoulder*:** One developer looks over the author's shoulder as the latter walks through the code.
    - ***E-mail pass-around*:** Source code management system e-mails code to reviewers automatically after checkin is made.
    - ***Pair programming*:** Two authors develop code together at the same workstation; such is common in Extreme Programming.
    - ***Tool-assisted code review*:** Authors and reviewers use specialized tools designed for peer code review.

8.8.4.2 Code Review Checklist

The following attributes should be verified during a code review:

1. **Clarity**
    - Is the code clear and easy to understand?
    - Did the programmer unnecessarily obfuscate any part of it?
    - Can the code be refactored to make it clearer?
2. **Maintainability**
    - Will other programmers be able to maintain this code?
    - Is it well-commented and documented properly?
3. **Accuracy**
    - Does the code accomplish what it is meant to do?
    - If an algorithm is being implemented, is it implemented correctly?
4. **Reliability and Robustness**
    - Is the code fault-tolerant? Is it error-tolerant?
    - Will it handle abnormal conditions or malformed input?
    - Does it fail gracefully if it encounters an unexpected condition?
5. **Security**
    - Is the code vulnerable to unauthorized access or malicious use or modification?
6. **Scalability**
    - Could the code be a bottleneck that prevents the system from growing to accommodate increased load, data, users or input?
7. **Reusability**
    - Could this code be reused in other applications?
    - Can it be made more general?

8. **Efficiency**
    - Does the code make efficient use of memory, CPU cycles, bandwidth or other system resources?
    - Can it be optimized?

8.8.4.3 Difference between Code Review and Inspection

The main difference between a code review and any other kind of inspection is in the review session. While code review session is similar to the inspection meeting (see "Page-by-page review" above), there are a few important differences:

1. One important difference is that in addition to the moderator, there is a code reader who reads the code aloud during the meeting. The purpose of the reader is simply to keep the team's place during the inspection; the team should have already read the code and identified defects during their preparation.
2. Another important difference between code reviews and document inspections is that the code review is much more focused on detecting defects, and less on fixing them.
3. In the code review, the moderator needs to be especially careful not to let the meeting turn into a problem-solving session. Programmers love to solve problems. It's easy for them to get caught up in a small detail and turn the meeting into an analysis of a minute problem that covers just a few lines of code.

8.8.5 Pair Programming

Pair programming is an agile software development technique in which two programmers work together at one workstation. One types in code while the other reviews each line of code as it is typed in. The person typing is called the ***driver***. The person reviewing the code is called the ***observer (or navigator)***. The two programmers switch roles frequently (possibly every 30 minutes or less). Pair Programming, in part, is a way to do effective, real-time, responsive inspection, which supports higher quality, which supports reduced schedule pressure.

Pair programming can be used for both coding and testing. Pair testing is an extension of pair programming concept and pair programming is the part of extreme programming (XP). An Extreme Programming Practice in which two engineers participate in one development effort at one workstation. Each member performs the action the other is not currently doing: While one types in unit tests the other thinks about the class that will satisfy the test.

A single, unsubstantiated, unscientific, undergraduate's survey has shown that, after training for the "PeopleSkills" involved, two programmers are more than twice as productive as one for a given task.

"Laurie Williams" of the University of Utah in Salt Lake City has shown that paired programmers are only 15% slower than two independent individual programmers, but produce 15% fewer bugs. Since testing and debugging are often many times more costly than initial programming, this is an impressive result."

8.8.5.1 Benefits of Pair Programming

Benefits of pair programming are discussed as follows:

1. *Design quality*: Shorter programs, better designs, fewer bugs. Program code must be readable to both partners, not just the driver, in order to be checked in. Pairs typically consider more

design alternatives than programmers working solo, and arrive at simpler, more-maintainable designs, as well as catch design defects very early.

2. *Reduced cost of development*: With bugs being a particularly expensive part of software development, especially if they're caught late in the development process, the large reduc-tion in defect rate due to pair programming can significantly reduce software development costs.
3. *Learning and training*: Knowledge passes easily between pair programmers: they share knowledge of the specifics of the system, and they pick up programming techniques from each other as they work. New hires quickly pick up the practices of the team through pairing.
4. *Overcoming difficult problems*: Pairs often find that seemingly "impossible" problems become easy or even quick, or at least possible, to solve when they work together.
5. *Improved morale*: Programmers report greater joy in their work and greater confidence that their work is correct.
6. *Decreased management risk*: Since knowledge of the system is shared among programmers, there is less risk to management if one programmer leaves the team.
7. *Increased discipline and better time management*: Programmers are less likely to skip writing unit tests, spend time web-surfing or on personal e-mail, or other violations of discipline, when they are working with a pair partner. The pair partner "keeps them honest".
8. *Resilient flow*: Pairing leads to a different kind of flow than programming alone, but it does lead to flow. Pairing flow happens more quickly: one programmer asks the other, *"What were we working on?"* Pairing flow is also more resilient to interruptions: one programmer deals with the interruption while the other keeps working.
9. *Fewer interruptions*: People are more reluctant to interrupt a pair than they are to interrupt someone working alone.
10. *Decreased risk of RSI*: The risk of repetitive stress injury is significantly reduced, since each programmer is using a keyboard and mouse approximately half the time they were before.
11. *Mentoring*: Everyone, even junior programmers, has knowledge that others don't. Pair programming is a painless way of spreading that knowledge.
12. *Team cohesion*: People get to know each other more quickly when pair programming. Pair programming may encourage team jelling.

8.8.5.2 Drawbacks of Pair Programming

1. *Work preference*: Some developers prefer to work alone.
2. *Intimidation*: A less experienced or less confident developer may feel intimidated when pairing with a more experienced developer and participate less as a result.
3. *Tutoring cost*: Experienced developers may find it tedious to tutor a less experienced developer. Experienced developers working alone may be capable of producing code that is clean and accurate at the outset, and the benefits of pairing might not be worth the cost of an additional developer in some situations. This may apply more especially when producing more trivial parts of the system.
4. *Egos and potential conflict*: Personality conflicts can result in one or both developers feeling awkward or uncomfortable. Differences in coding style may result in conflict.
5. *Cost*: There are varying opinions as to whether two developers can be as productive when working together as when working separately.

8.8.5.3 Types of Pair Programming

Pair programming can be divided into two broad categories:

1. *Remote pair programming*: It is also known as virtual pair programming or distributed pair programming, is the practice of pair programming where the two programmers comprising the pair are in different locations, working via a collaborative real-time editor, shared desktop, or a remote pair programming IDE plugin.

   Remote pair programming might be useful to do pair programming with offshore teams or in open source projects with distributed contributors.
2. *Ping pong pair programming*: Some agile teams use a different style of pair programming called "ping pong pair programming". In this pattern, the observer writes a failing unit test, the driver modifies the code to pass the unit test(s), the observer writes a new unit test, and so on. This loop continues as long as the observer is able to write failing unit tests. The technique can result in the driver role switching as often as a few minutes or less.

8.8.6 What is Formal Technical Review?

Formal technical review is a software quality assurance activity performed by software engineering practitioners to improve software product quality. The product is scrutinized for completeness, correctness, consistency, technical feasibility, efficiency, and adherence to established standards and guidelines by the client organization.

The FTR serves as a training ground, enabling junior engineers to observe different approaches to software analysis, design and implementation. Each FTR is conducted as a meeting and will be successful only if it is properly planned, controlled and attended.

8.8.6.1 Objectives of Formal Technical Review

The various objectives of formal technical review are as follows:

- To uncover errors in logic or implementation.
- To ensure that the software has been represented accruing to predefined standards.
- To ensure that software under review meets the requirements.
- To make the project more manageable.

For the success of formal technical review, the following are expected:

- The schedule of the meeting and its agenda reach the members well in advance.
- Members review the material and its distribution
- The reviewer must review the material in advance.

8.8.6.2 The Review Meeting

The meeting should consist of two to five people and should be restricted to not more than 2 hours (preferably). The aim of the review is to review the product / work and the performance of people. When the product is ready, the producer (developer) informs the project leader about the completion of the product and requests for review. The project leader contacts the review leader for the review. The review leader asks the reviewer to perform an independent review of the product / work before the scheduled FTR.

8.8.6.3 Result of FTR

- Meeting decision
  1. Whether to accept the product/ work without any modification
  2. Accept the product/work with certain changes
  3. Reject the product/ work due to error.
- Review summary report
  1. What was reviewed?
  2. Who reviewed it?
  3. Findings of the review
  4. Conclusion.

8.8.7 Difference between Walkthrough and Inspection/Review

1. The basic difference between the two is that a walkthrough is less formal and has only a few steps, whereas inspections and reviews are more formal and logically sequential with many steps.
2. Both processes are undertaken before actual development, and hence they are conducted on documents such as development plan, SOW, RDD and SRS, design document and broad WBS to examine their authenticity, completeness, correctness and accuracy.
3. Both are costly but the cost incurred is comparatively much lower than the cost of repair at a much later stage in the development cycle.
4. Another difference between a walkthrough and an inspection is that the former is less formal and quick; whereas inspection is more formal, takes more time, and is far more systematic.
5. A walkthrough differs from software technical reviews in its openness of structure and its objective of familiarization. It differs from software inspection in its ability to suggest direct alterations to the product reviewed, its lack of a direct focus on training and process improvement, and its omission of process and product measurement.
6. Walkthrough also permits suggestions for general improvement to be made during the main meeting as well as other goals. While inspection concentrate (during the main meeting) on finding defects.
7. Inspections are typically more structured than walkthroughs.

9

SOFTWARE TESTING

9.1 INTRODUCTION TO TESTING

Testing is a set of activities that can be planned in advance and conducted systematically. For this reason a template for software testing-a set of steps into which we can place specific test case design techniques and testing methods-should be defined for the software process.

A number of software testing strategies have been proposed in the literature. All provide the software developer with a template for testing and all have the following generic characteristics:

- To perform effective testing, a software team should conduct effective formal technical reviews. By doing this, many errors will be eliminated before testing commences.
- Testing begins at the component level and works "outward" toward the integration of the entire computer-based system.
- Different testing techniques are appropriate at different points in time.
- Testing is conducted by the developers of the software and (for large projects) an independent test group.
- Testing and debugging are different activities, but debugging must be accommodated in any testing strategy.

A strategy for software testing must accommodate low-level tests that are necessary to verify that a small source code segment has been correctly implemented as well as high-level tests that validate major system functions against customer requirements. A strategy must provide guidance for the practitioner and a set of milestones for the manager. Because the steps of the test strategy occur at a time when deadline pressure begins to rise, progress must be measurable and problems must surface as early as possible.

9.2 DEFINITIONS

Testing is the process of analyzing a software item to detect the differences between existing and required condition (*i.e.*, bugs) and to evaluate the features of the software items. (IEEE 1993).

OR

Testing is the process of analyzing a program with the intent of finding errors. (Myers 1979)

OR

"Testing is the process of executing a program with the intent of finding errors".

9.3 TESTING OBJECTIVES

The testing objective is to test the code, whereby there is a high probability of discovering all errors.

This objective also demonstrates that the software functions are working according to Software Requirement Specifications (SRS) with regard to functionality, features, facilities and performance. It should be noted, however, that testing will detect errors in the written code, but it will not show an error if the code does not address a specific requirement stipulated in SRS but not coded in the program.

Testing objectives are:

1. Testing is a process of executing a program with the intent of finding an error.
2. A good test case is one that has a high probability of finding an as-yet-undiscovered error.
3. A successful test is one that uncovers an as-yet-undiscovered error.

9.4 TESTING PRINCIPLES

There are many principles that guide software testing. Before applying methods to design effective test cases, a software engineer must understand the basic principles that guide software testing. Following are the main principles for testing:

1. **All Tests should be Traceable to Customer Requirements:** This is in order to uncover any defects that might cause the program or system to fail to meet the client's requirements.
2. **Tests should be Planned Long before Testing Begins:** Soon after requirements model is completed, test planning can begin. Detailed test cases can begin as soon as the design model is designed.
3. **The Pareto Principle Applies to Software Testing:** Stated simply, the Pareto principle implies that 80 percent of all errors uncovered during testing will likely be traceable to 20 percent of all program components. The problem of course, is to isolate these suspect components and to thoroughly test them.
4. **Testing should Begin "in the Small" and Progress Toward Testing "in the Large":** The first tests planned and executed generally focus on individual components. As testing progresses, focus shifts in an attempt to find errors in integrated clusters of components and ultimately in the entire system.
5. **Exhaustive Testing is not Possible:** The number of path permutations for even a moderately sized program is exceptionally large. For this reason, it is impossible to execute every combination of paths during testing. It is possible, however, to adequately cover program logic and to ensure that all conditions in the component-level design have been exercised.
6. **To be Most Effective, Testing should be Conducted by an Independent Third Party:** The software engineer who has created the system is not the best person to conduct all tests for the software. This is shown in Fig. 9.1.

(*a*) Developer

Understands the system
but, will test "gently"
and, is driven by "delivery"

(*b*) Independent tester

Must learn about the system
but, will attempt to break it
and is driven by quality

Fig. 9.1 Who tests the software?

9.5 TEST PLAN

Test plan is a document consisting of different test cases designed for different testing objects and different testing attributes. The plan puts the tests in logical and sequential order as per the strategy chosen, top-down or bottom-up. The test plan is a matrix of test and test cases listed in order of its execution.

Table 9.1 shows the matrix of test and test cases within the test.

Project Name _______ Project ID _______

Project Manager _______ Q.A. Manger _______

Table 9.1 Test plan

Test										
Test ID		Test Name	1	2	3	...	N	Planned Date	
ID	Tester							Completed	Successful

Test ID, test name, test cases are designed well before the development phase and have been designed to those who conduct the tests.

A test plan states:

1. What the items to be tested are?
2. At what level they will be tested?
3. What sequence they are to be tested in?
4. How the test strategy will be applied to the testing of each item and describes the test environment.

9.6 TEST CASE DESIGN

"A test case is a set of instructions designed to discover a particular type of error or defect in the software system by inducing a failure".

The goal of selected test cases is to ensure that there is no error in the program and if it is so then it should be immediately depicted. Ideal test casement should contain all inputs to the program. This is often called exhaustive testing.

There are two criteria for the selection of test case that are:

- Specifying a criterion for evaluating a set of test cases.
- Generating a set of test cases that satisfy a given criterion.

Each test case needs proper documentation, preferably in a fixed format. There are many formats; one format is suggested below:

Test case name	Test Case ID
Purpose of test	Testing object (unit, application or module etc.)
Test attribute	
Tests focus (function, feature, process, interface, validation, verification etc.)	
Test type (alpha, beta, unit, integration, system)	
Test process	Set of instructions for conducting the test-Initial state condition-inputs-specifications-output expected.
Test results	Expected and actual and comparison, error description, post-process state.
Action	Correction, authorization and feedback through retest.
Action to initialize the pre test status	

9.7 TEST ORACLES

To test any program, we need to have a description of its expected behaviour and a method of determining whether the observed behaviour conforms to the expected behaviour. For this we need a test oracle.

A test oracle is a mechanism, different from the program itself, which can be used to check the correctness of the output of the program for the test cases. Conceptually, we can consider testing a process in which the test cases are given to the test oracle and the program under testing. The output of the two is then compared to determine if the program behaved correctly for the test cases, as shown in Fig. 9.2.

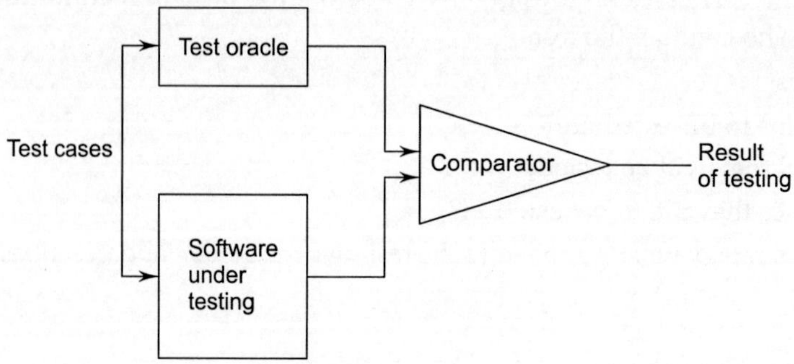

Fig. 9.2 Test oracles

Test oracles are human beings, so they may make mistakes when there is a discrepancy between the oracles and the results of a program, first we have to verify the result produced by the oracle, before declaring that there is a fault is the program, that's why the testing is so cumbersome and expensive.

The human oracles generally use the specifications of the program to decide what the "correct" behaviour of the program should be. To help the oracle to determine the correct behaviour, it is important that the behaviour of the system be unambiguously specified and the specification itself is error free.

9.8 TYPES OF TESTING

9.8.1 White Box Testing/Structural Testing

A complementary approach to functional or black box testing is called ***structural or white box testing***. In this approach, test group must have complete knowledge about the internal structure of the software. We can say structural testing is an approach to testing where the tests are derived from knowledge of the software's structure and implementation. Structural testing is usually applied to relatively small program units such as subroutines, or the operations associated with an object. As the name implies, the tester can analyze the code and use knowledge about the structure of a component to derive test data. The analysis of the code can be used to find how many test cases are needed to guarantee that all of the statements in the program are executed at least once during the testing process. It would not be advisable to release a software which contained untested statements and the consequence of which might be disastrous. This goal seems to be easy but simple objectives of structural testing are harder to achieve than may appear at first glance.

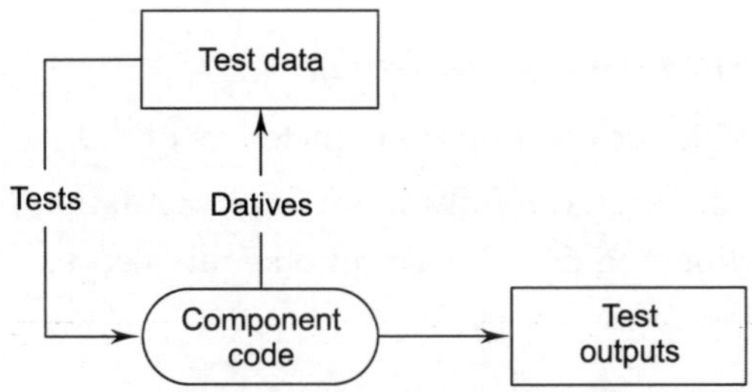

Fig. 9.3 Structural testing

White-box test is also known by other names such as Glass-Box testing, Structural testing, Clear Box testing, Open-box testing, Logic-driven testing, and Path-oriented testing.

In white-box testing, test cases are selected on the basis of examination of the code, rather than the specifications. White-box testing is illustrated in Fig. 9.4.

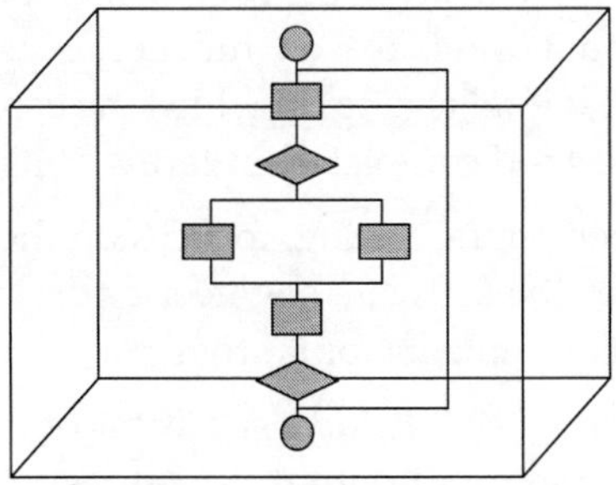

Fig. 9.4 White box testing

Using white box testing methods the software engineer can test cases that:

1. Guarantee that all independent paths within a module have been exercised at least once.
2. Exercise all logical decision on their true and false sides.
3. Exercise all loops at their boundaries.
4. Exercise internal data structures to ensure their validity.

The natures of software defects are:

1. Logical errors and incorrect assumptions are inversely proportional to the probability that a program path will be executed.
2. We often believe that a logical path is not to be executed when, infact it may be executed on a regular basis.
3. Typographical errors are random. When a program is translated into programming language source code, it is likely that some typing errors will occur.

9.8.1.1 Reason Why White Box Testing is Carried Out

White box testing is carried out to test whether.

1. All paths in a process are correctly operational;
2. All logical decisions are executed with true and false conditions;
3. All loops are executed with their limit values tested, and
4. To ascertain whether input data structure specifications are tested and then used for other processing.

9.8.1.2 Advantages of Structural/White-Box Testing

The various advantages of white-box testing are depicted as under:

1. Forces test developer to reason carefully about implementation.
2. Approximates the partitioning done by execution equivalence.
3. Reveals errors in hidden code.

9.8.2 Functional/Black-Box Testing

In functional testing the structure of the program is not considered. Test cases are decided on the basis of the requirements or specification of the program or module and the internals of the module or the program are not considered for selection of test cases.

Functional testing refers to testing, which involves only observation of the output for certain input values, and there is no attempt to analyze the code, which produces the output. The internal structure of the program is ignored. For this reason, functional testing is sometimes referred to as a black box testing (also called behavioral testing) in which the content of a black box is not known and function of black box is understood completely in terms of its inputs and outputs.

Black box testing, also called behavioral testing, focuses on the functional requirements of the software. Black box testing enables the software engineer to derive sets of inputs conditions that will fully exercise all functional requirements for a program.

Other names for Black Box Testing (BBT) include: specifications testing, behavioral testing, data-driven testing, functional testing, and input/output-driven testing.

In black box testing, the tester only knows the inputs that can be given to the system and what output the system should give. In other words, the basis for deciding test cases in functional testing is the requirements or specifications of the system or module. This form of testing is also called functional or behavioral testing.

Black box testing is not an alternative to white-box techniques; rather it is a complementary approach that is likely to uncover a different class of errors than white-box methods.

Black box testing identifies the following kind of errors:

- Incorrect or missing functions.
- Interface missing or erroneous
- Error in data model
- Error in access to external data source.

When these errors are controlled then:

- Function(s) are valid.
- A class of inputs is validated.
- Validity is sensitive to certain input values.
- The software is valid and dependable for certain volume of data or transactions.
- Rare specific combinations are taken care of.

Black box testing tries to answer the following questions:

- How is functional validity tested?
- How are system behavior and performance tested?
- How are the boundaries of a data class isolated?
- How the test cases will make good?
- How the specific combinations of data will effect the system operation?
- What data rates and data volume can the system tolerate?
- Is the system particularly sensitive to certain input values?
- What effect will specific combinations of data have on system operation?

By applying black-box techniques, we derive a set of test cases that satisfy the following criteria:

1. Test cases that reduce, by a count that in greater than one.
2. Test cases that tell us something about the presence or absence of classes of errors.

9.8.2.1 Categories of Black Box Testing

Functional testing falls in two categories:

1. *Positive functional testing:* This testing entails exercising the application's functions with valid input and verifying that the outputs are correct.

   Example: Continuing with the word processing example, a positive test for the printing function might be to print a document containing both text and graphics to a Printer that is online, filled with paper and for which the correct drivers are installed.
2. *Negative functional testing:* This testing involves exercising application functionality using a combination of invalid inputs, unexpected operating conditions and other "out-of-bounds scenarios.

Example:

1. Continuing the word processing example, a negative test for the printing function might be to disconnect the printer from the computer while a document is printing.
2. What probably should happen in this scenario is a plain-English error message appears, informing the user what happened and instructing him/her on how to remedy the problem.
3. What might happen instead is the word processing software simply hangs up or crashes because the "abnormal" loss of communications with the printer is not handled properly.

9.8.2.2 *Example of Black Box Testing*

Figure 9.5 illustrates the model of a system, which is assumed in black box testing. This approach is equally applicable to systems that are organized as functions or as objects. The tester present inputs to the component or the system and examines the corresponding outputs. If the outputs are not those predicted then the test has successfully detected a problem with the software.

The key problem for the defect tester is to select inputs that have a high probability of being members of the set I_e. In many cases, the selection of these test cases is based on the previous experience of test engineers. They use domain knowledge to identify test cases, which are likely to reveal defects. However, the systematic approach to test data selection discussed in the next section may also be used to supplement this heuristic knowledge.

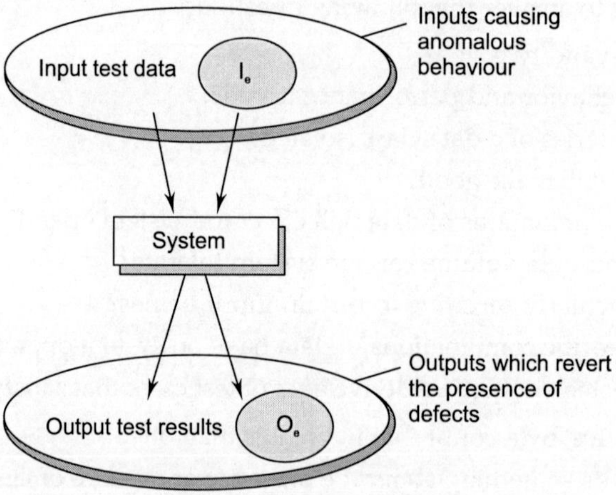

Fig. 9.5 Black box testing

9.8.2.3 *Advantages of Black Box Testing*

The advantages of this type of testing include:

1. The test is unbiased because the designer and the tester are independent of each other.
2. The tester does not need knowledge of any specific programming languages.
3. The test is done from the point of view of the user, not the designer.
4. Test cases can be designed as soon as the specifications are complete.

9.9 LEVELS OF TESTING

There are three levels of testing *i.e.*, individual module to the entire software system.

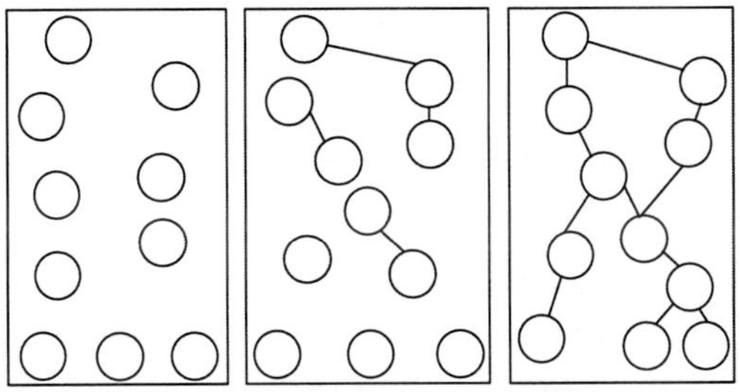

Fig. 9.6 Levels of testing

9.9.1 Unit Testing

In unit testing individual components are tested to ensure that they operate correctly. It focuses on verification effort. On the smallest unit of software design, each component is tested independently without other system components.

There are number of reasons in support of unit testing than testing the entire product:

1. The size of a single module is small enough that we can locate an error fairly easily.
2. The module is small enough that we can attempt to test it in some demonstrably exhaustive fashion.
3. Confusing interactions of multiple errors in widely different parts of the software are eliminated.

9.9.1.1 Unit Test Consideration

The tests that occur as part of unit tests are illustrated schematically in Fig. 9.7. The module interface is tested to ensure that information properly flows into and out of the program unit under test. The local data structure is examined to ensure that data stored temporarily maintains its integrity during all steps in an algorithm's execution. Boundary conditions are tested to ensure that the module operates properly at boundaries established to limit or restrict processing. All independent paths through the control structure are exercised to ensure that all statements in a module have been executed at least once. And finally, all error-handling paths are tested.

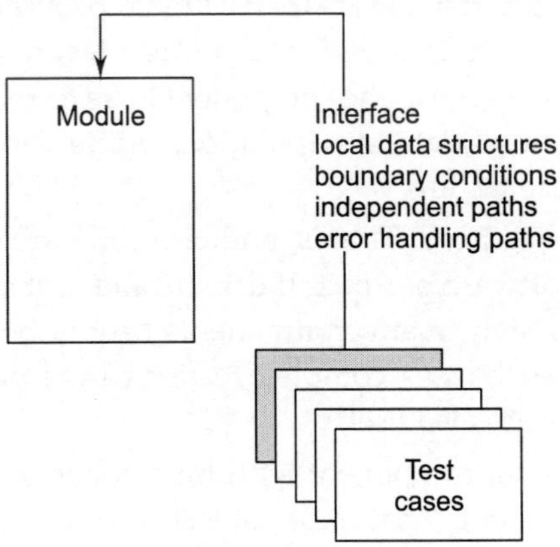

Fig. 9.7 Unit test

Common errors in computation are:

- Incorrect arithmetic precedence.
- Mixed code operations
- Incorrect initialization
- Precision inaccuracy
- Incorrect symbolic representation of an expression.

Test cases in unit testing should uncover errors such as:

- Comparison of different data types.
- Incorrect logical operators or precedence.
- Expectation of equality when precision error makes equality unlikely.
- Incorrect comparison of variables.
- Improper loop termination.
- Failure to exit when divergent iteration is encountered.
- Improperly modified loop variables.

9.9.1.2 Unit Test Procedure

The unit test environment is illustrated in Fig. 9.8.

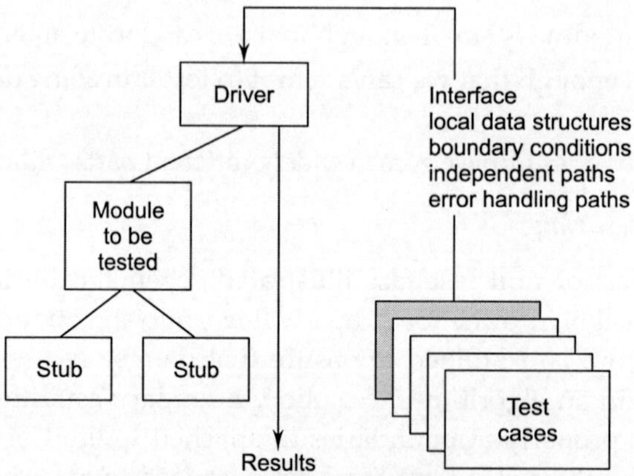

Fig. 9.8 Unit test environment

In most applications a ***driver*** is nothing more than a "main program" that accepts test case data, passes such data to the component (to be tested) and prints relevant results. ***Stubs*** serve to replace modules that are subordinate (called by) to the component to be tested. A stub uses the subordinate module's interface, may do minimal data manipulation, prints verification of entry and returns control to the module undergoing testing.

Drivers and stubs represent overhead. That is, both are software that must be written but that is not delivered with the final software product. If drivers and stubs are kept simple, actual overhead is relatively low. Unfortunately, many components cannot be adequately unit tested with "simple" overhead software. In such cases, complete testing can be postponed until the integration test step (where drivers or stubs are also used).

Unit testing is simplified when a component with high cohesion is designed. When only one function is addressed by a component, the number of test cases is reduced and errors can be more easily predicted and uncovered.

9.9.2 Integration Testing

The second level of testing is called ***integration testing***. Integration testing is a systematic technique for constructing the program structure while at the same time conducting tests to uncover errors is associated with interfacing.

In this testing many units tested modules are combined into sub-systems, which are then tested. The goal here is to see if the modules can be integrated properly.

9.9.2.1 Objective of Integration Testing

The primary objective of integration testing is to test the module interfaces in order to ensure that there are no errors in the parameter passing, when one module invokes another module. During integration testing, different modules of a system are integrated in a planned manner using an integration plan. The integration plan specifies the steps and the order in which modules are combined to realize the full system. After each integration step, the partially integrated system is tested.

9.9.2.2 Approaches to Integration Testing

The various approaches, which are used for the integration testing, are:

1. Incremental Approach
2. Top-down Integration
3. Bottom-up Integration
4. Regression Testing
5. Smoke Testing
6. Sandwich Integration

These various approaches to integration testing are discussed as follows:

1. *Incremental approach:* Incremental approach means first combine only two components together and test it. Remove the errors if it is there else combine another component to it and then again test it and so on until the whole system is developed.

   OR

   In incremental integration the program is constructed and tested in small increments, where errors are easier to isolate and correct.

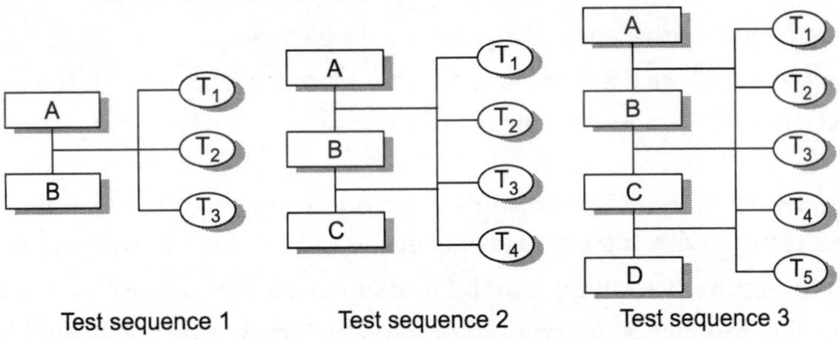

Fig. 9.9 Incremental approach

According to the figure, in test sequence 1 tests T_1, T_2 and T_3 are first run on a system composed of module A and module B. If these are corrected or error free then module C is integrated *i.e.*, test sequence 2 and then tests T_1, T_2 and T_3 are repeated, if problem arises in these tests, then they interact with the new module. The source of the problem is localized, thus simplify defect location and repair. Finally, module D is integrated *i.e.*, test sequence 3 and then tested using existing (T_1 to T_5) and new tests (T_6).

2. *Top-down integration testing:* Top down integration testing is an incremental approach to construction of program structure. Modules are integrated by moving downward through the control hierarchy beginning with the main control module.

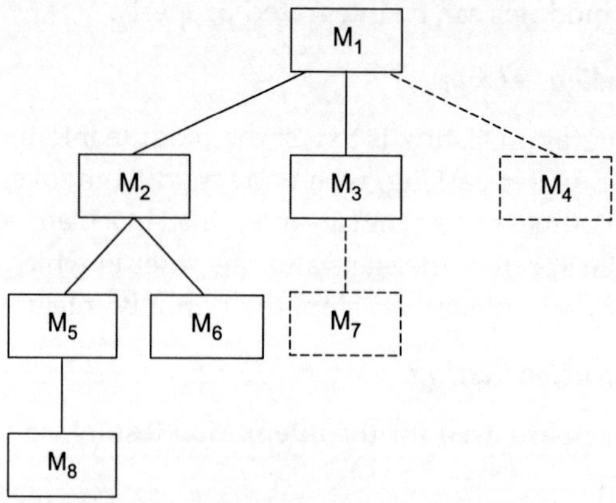

Fig. 9.10 Top-down integration testing

Considering the Fig. 9.10 drawn above:

(*i*) *Depth first integration:* This would integrate all components on a major control path of the structure. For example, selecting the M_1, M_2, and M_5 would be integrated first. Next M_8 or M_6 would be integrated. Then, the central and right-hand control paths are built.

(*ii*) *Breadth-first integration:* This incorporates all components directly subordinate at each level, moving across the structure horizontally. From the Fig. 9.10, components M_2, M_3 and M_4 would be integrated first. The next control level M_5, M_6 and so on, follows.

The integration process is performed in a series of five steps:

1. The main control module is used as a test driver and stubs are substituted for all components directly subordinate to the main control module.
2. Depending on the integration approach selected (*i.e.*, depth or breadth first), subordinate stubs are replaced one at a time with actual components.
3. Tests are conducted as each component is integrated.
4. On completion of each set of tests, another stub is replaced with the real component.
5. Regression testing may be conducted to ensure that new errors have not been introduced.

3. *Bottom-up integration testing:* Bottom-up integration testing, as its name implies begins construction and testing with the components at the lowest level in the program structure.

A bottom-up integration strategy may be implemented with the following steps:

1. Low-level components are combined into clusters (sometimes called builds) that perform specific software sub function.
2. A driver (a control program for testing) is written to coordinate test case input and output.
3. The cluster is tested.
4. Drivers are removed and clusters are combined moving upward in the program structure.

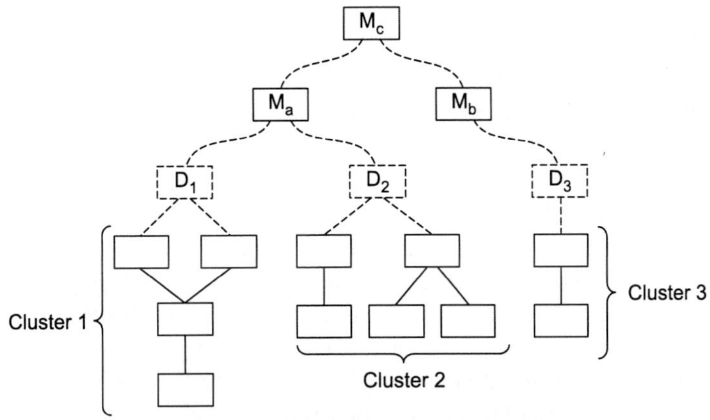

Fig. 9.11 Bottom-up integration testing

Integration follows the pattern illustrated in Fig. 9.11 above. Components are combined to form clusters 1, 2, 3. Each of the clusters is tested using a driver (shown as a dashed block). Components in clusters 1 and 2 are subordinate to M_a. Drivers D_1 and D_2 are removed and the clusters are interfaced directly to M_a. Similarly, driver D_3 for cluster 3 is removed prior to integration with module M_b. Both M_a and M_b will ultimately be integrated with component M_c and so forth.

As integration moves upward, the need for separate test drivers lessens. Infact, if the top two levels of program structure are integrated top down, the number of drivers can be reduced and integration of clusters is greatly simplified.

4. *Regression testing:* Regression testing is the activity that helps to ensure that changes (due to testing or for other reasons) do not introduce unintended behaviour or additional errors.

   Regression test suite contains three different classes of test cases:
   1. Additional tests that focus on software functions
   2. A representative sample of tests that will exercise all software functions.
   3. Test that focus on the software components that have been changed.
5. *Smoke testing:* Smoke testing is an integration testing approach that is commonly used when "shrink-wrapped" software products developed. Smoke testing is characterized as rolling integration approach because the software is rebuilt with new component and testing. Smoke testing encompasses the following activities:
   1. Software components that have been translated into code are integrated into a "build". A build includes all data files, libraries, reusable module and engineered components that are required to implement one or more product functions.
   2. A series of tests is designed to expose errors that will keep the build from properly performing its function.
   3. The build is integrated with other builds and the entire product (in its current form) is smoke tested daily.

   Smoke testing provides a number of benefits when it is applied on complex software engineering projects:
   - Integration risk is minimized.
   - Quality of end product is improved.

- Error diagnosis and correction are simplified.
- Progress is easier to assess.

6. *Sandwich integration testing:* Sandwich integration testing is the combination of both top-down and bottom-up approach. So, it is also called as Mixed Integration testing. In it the whole system is divided into three layers, just like a sandwich: the target is in the middle and one layer is above the target and one is below the target.

   Top-down approach is used in layer that is above the target and bottom-up approach is used in layer that is below the target. Testing coverage on the middle layer, chosen on the basis of structure of component hierarchy and system characteristics. It also combines the advantages of both top-down and bottom up approach. It also requires drivers. Ability to plan and control sequence is hard in it. At beginning the work parallelism is medium. Stubs are also needed. Ability to test particular paths is medium.

9.9.3 System Testing

The sub-systems are integrated to make up the entire system. The testing process is concerned with finding errors that result from unanticipated interactions between sub-systems and system components. It is also concerned with validating that the system needs its functional and non-functional requirements.

There are essentially three main kinds of system testing.

1. Alpha testing
2. Beta testing
3. Acceptance testing

1. **Alpha testing:** ***"Alpha testing refers to the system testing carried out by the test team within the development organization".***

   The alpha test is conducted at the developer's site by the customer under the project team's guidance. In this test, users test the software on the development platform and point out errors for correction. However, the alpha test, because a few users on the development platform conduct it, has limited ability to expose errors and correcting them. Alpha tests are conducted in a controlled environment. It is simulation of real life usage. Once the alpha test is through, the software product is ready for transition to the customer site for implementation and deployment.

2. **Beta testing:** ***"Beta testing is the system testing performed by a selected group of friendly customers."***

   If the system is complex, the software is not taken for implementation directly. It is installed and all users are asked to use the software under testing mode; this is not live usage. This is called the beta test. Beta tests are conducted at customer site in an environment where the software is exposed to a number of users. The developer may or may not be present while the software is in use. So, beta test is a real life software experience without actual implementation. In this test, end users record their observations, mistakes, errors and so on and report them periodically.

   In a beta test, the user may suggest a modification, a major change or deviation. The development has to examine the proposed change and put it into the change management system for a smooth change over from just developed software to a revised, better software. It is standard practice to put all such changes in subsequent version releases.

3. **Acceptance testing:** ***"Acceptance testing is the system testing performed by the customer to determine whether to accept or reject the delivery of the system."***

   When customer software is built for one customer, a series of acceptance tests are conducted to enable the customer to validate all requirements. Conducted by the end-user rather than software engineers, an acceptance test can range from an informal 'test drive' to a planned and systematically executed series of tests. In fact, acceptance testing can be conducted over a period of weeks or months, thereby uncovering cumulative errors that might degrade the system over time.

9.10 TEST STRATEGIES

"Defining a test strategy helps you focus test resources on the right portions of code at the right time". A strategy outlines what to plan, and how to plan it. A successful strategy is your guide through change, and provides a firm foundation for ongoing improvement. Unlike a plan, which is obsolete from the point of creation, a strategy reflects the values of an organization—and remains current and useful.

When an organization tests its products or its tools, it tries to compare them against its expectations and values. By its nature, testing introduces change as problems are identified and resolved. A test strategy is necessary to allow these two impulses to work together. Furthermore, testing can never be said to be 'complete', and a core skill in testing is the justified management of conflicting demands; without a strategy, these judgments will be inconsistent to the point of failure.

Software development is a creative process. A test strategy is a vital enabler to this process-keeping focus on core values and consistent decision-making to help achieve desired goals with best use of resource. A good strategy stands as a clear counter to reactive, counter-productive test approaches.

9.10.1 Definitions

Test strategy decide how we are going to approach the testing in terms of people, tools, procedures and support.

OR

A **test strategy** is an outline that describes the testing portion of the software development cycle. It is created to inform project managers, testers, and developers about some key issues of the testing process. This includes the testing objective, methods of testing new functions, total time and resources required for the project, and the testing environment.

9.10.2 Purpose of Test Strategy

Before we develop test cases and test procedures to test a system, we should define an overall *test* or *test and evaluation* strategy

- To obtain consensus of goals and objectives from stakeholders (*e.g.*, management, developers, testers, customers, users)
- To manage expectations from the beginning
- To be sure we're "headed in the right direction"
- Identifies the types of tests to be conducted at all test levels.

9.10.3 Contents of a Test Strategy

A test strategy provides an overall perspective of testing, and identifies or references:

- Project plans, risks, and requirements
- Relevant regulations, policies, or directives
- Required processes, standards, and templates
- Supporting guidelines
- Stakeholders and their test objectives
- Test resources and estimates
- Test levels and phases
- Test environment
- Completion criteria for each phase
- Required test documentation and review methods.

In the test strategy we describe how the product risks of the stakeholders are mitigated in the test levels, which test types are performed in the test levels, and which entry and exit criteria apply.

The test strategy is created based on development design documents. The system design document is the main one used and occasionally, the conceptual design document can be referred to. The design documents describe the functionalities of the software. For every set of development design, a corresponding test strategy should be created to test the new feature sets.

The test strategy describes the test level to be performed. There are primarily three levels of testing: unit testing, integration testing, and system testing. In most software development organizations, the developers are responsible for unit testing. Individual testers or test teams are responsible for integration and system testing.

9.11 PROGRAM CORRECTNESS

A "correct" program is one that does exactly what its designers and users intend it to do—no more and no less. A "formally correct" program is one whose correctness can be proved mathematically, at least to a point that designers and users are convinced about its relative absence of errors.

For a program to be formally correct, there must be a way to specify precisely (mathematically) what the program is intended to do, for all possible values of its input. We must accept the fact that testing is an integral part of the programming process-and that a program is not really "finished" until we have demonstrated its correctness.

The programmer and user of a program may interpret "correctness" quite differently and hence have different expectations of program performance. Various interpretations/levels of correctness are listed below in order of increasing difficulty of achievement:

1. The program contains no syntax errors that can be detected during translation by the language processor.
2. The program contains no errors, either of syntax or invalid operation, that can be automatically detected during translation or execution of the program.
3. There exists some set of test data for which the program will yield the correct answer.
4. For a typical (reasonable or random) set of test data the program will yield the correct answer.

5. For deliberately difficult sets of test data the program will yield the correct answers.
6. For all possible sets of data that are valid with respect to the problem specification, the program yields the correct answers.
7. For all possible sets of valid test data, and for all likely conditions of erroneous input, the program gives a correct (or at least reasonable) answer.
8. For all possible input, the program gives correct or reasonable answers.

In the early stages of any programming experience you will feel harassed by error messages and feel a sense of relief and accomplishment when none appear. Later you will understand that the real work of testing starts after the error messages have been eliminated. The absence of error messages is only a necessary and not a sufficient condition for reasonable correctness.

Some programmers never mature beyond Level 3 in their attitude toward correctness. Considering, however, the higher levels (say 4, 5 or 6), it is clear that satisfactory performance on any single set of test data is not sufficient grounds for an assertion of correctness. Moreover, failure on a single test is sufficient to demonstrate that the program is not correct. No matter how many tests the program may have passed successfully, just one test on which it fails is enough to show that it is not correct. This is not inherently a democratic process, and a program that works "most of the time" is a dangerous tool.

From the user's point of view a reasonable definition of correctness is certainly not less than level 6. Level 7 is better and Level 8 is what he would really like. The programmer may maintain that a literal interpretation of problem specifications cannot demand more than Level 6, while the user will maintain that certain implied requirements do not have to be explicitly stated. However, the primary responsibility rests with the programmer. A program is incorrect if it does not serve the user's purpose.

In summary, the situation is the following. The user would like to have Level 8 correctness—but this is often unrealistic. Level 7 is a reasonable compromise, which is obviously going to lead to arguments since it leaves critical questions open to varying interpretations. The programmer's dilemma is that Level 5 is the highest that can be achieved by purely empirical means- by running the program on test cases- so he must thoughtfully design test cases that permit a plausible assertion that Level 6 has been achieved. To achieve Level 7 the programmer must know enough about the intended use of the program to estimate what errors are likely to be encountered, and what response is appropriate.

9.12 PROGRAM VERIFICATION AND VALIDATION

Verification and validation (V&V) is the name given to the checking and analysis process that ensure that software conforms to its specification and meets the needs of the customers who are paying for that software. Variation and validation is whole life cycle process. It starts with requirements reviews and continues through design reviews and code inspection to product testing. There should be V&V activities at each stage of the software process. These activities check the results of process activities are as specified.

Verification and validation is not the same thing although they are easily confused. The difference between them is succinctly expressed by Boehm (1979):

- **'Validation**: Are we building the right product?'
- **'Verification**: Are we building the product right?'

These definitions tell us that the role of verification involves checking that the software conforms to its specification. You should check that the system meets its specified functional and non-functional requirements. Validation, however, is a more general process; you should ensure that the software meets the expectations of the customer. It goes beyond checking conformance of the system to its specification to showing that the software does what the customer expects as distinct from what has been specified.

Within the V & V process, *two techniques* of system checking and analysis may be used:

1. **Software Inspections:** Software inspections analyses and check system representations such as the requirements document, design diagrams and the program source code. They may be applied at all stages of the process. Inspections may be supplemented by some automatic analysis of the source text of a system or associated documents. Software inspections and automated analyses are static V & V techniques as they do not require the system to be executed.
2. **Software Testing:** Software testing involves executing an implementation of the software with test data and examining the outputs of the software and its operational behaviour to check that it is performing as required. Testing is a dynamic technique of verification and validation because it works with an executable representation of the system.

9.12.1 Verification

"Verification is the process of determining whether the output of one phase of software development confirms to that of its previous phase."

OR

"Verification involves checking of function and non-functional requirements that the software confirms to its specification."

9.12.2 Validation

"Validation is the process of determining whether a fully developed system confirms to its requirement specifications."

OR

"Validation is an analysis process that is done after checking conformance of the system to its specification."

Thus, the goal of verification and validation process is to establish confidence in customer that the software system is 'fit for customer'. It doesn't mean that the software system is free from error.

9.12.3 Difference between Verification and Validation

Verification is the process of determining whether the output of one phase of software development conforms to that of its previous phase, whereas validation is the process of determining whether a fully developed system conforms to its requirements specification. Thus while verification is concerned with phase containment of errors, the aim of validation is that the final product be error free.

9.13 TEST AUTOMATION AND TESTING TOOLS

Developing software to test the software is called as test automation/automated testing. In simple terms, automated testing is automating the manual testing process. It is used to replace or supplement manual testing with a suite of testing tools. Automated testing tools assist software testers to evaluate the quality of software by automating the mechanical aspects of the software testing task. Automated testing tools vary in their underlying approach, quality and ease of use.

Manual testing is used to document tests, produce test guides based on data queries, provide temporary structures to help run tests and measure the results of the test. Manual testing is considered to be costly and time consuming. Therefore, automated testing is used to cut down time and cost.

Manual Testing: It is defined as developing and executing tests that rely primarily on direct human interaction throughout the entire test case, especially in terms of evaluating correctness and ascertaining test status.

Definitions

Automated testing is the software testing assisted with software tools that require no operator input, analysis, or evaluation.

OR

Automation Testing is defined as developing and executing tests that can run unattended, comparing the actual to expected results and logging status.

OR

"Automated Testing" is automating the manual testing process currently in use.

OR

Test automation is:

"the process of using certain software for the purpose of monitoring and controlling the implementation and execution of tests, comparing the results or outcomes of the same to those which were predicted or foreseen, preparation and set up of the preliminary conditions of the test, the interpretation of the results or outcomes that were derived, and such other functions involving the controlling or handling of the test."

Using the above definition, a test automation tool is actually a piece of software that performs the usual steps that are involved in the implementation and termination of a test in the very same manner that it would be done manually-except that the whole process is automated.

What is test automation?

- Test Automation is the use of software to execute tests without Human intervention. Why test automation?
- Manual validation of application functionality is increasingly inefficient in an environment where developer productivity is increasing as programmers make greater use of higher level APIs and more modern, effective programming interfaces.
- Ever expanding application feature sets are making comprehensive manual testing more tedious and difficult.

Automated testing is expensive in terms of cost. It does not replace the need for manual testing or enable you to "down-size" your testing department. Automated testing is an addition to your testing process.

However, test automation can be cost-effective by following some of the time-tested techniques given below:

- Choose a test tool that best fits the testing requirements of your organization.
- One-time tests are not worth automating. Only automate those tests that are going to be repeated.
- Before starting off with Test Automation, identify the test cases that can be automated.
- Concentrate on automating the majority of your tests, which are fairly straightforward.
- Leave the complex tests for manual testing.
- Never make the mistake of using Record and Playback as a method of automation testing. This method is fraught with problems, and such scripts are very costly to maintain. At best it can be used to perform a Proof of Concept.
- As far as possible use a data-driven automated testing methodology. This allows you to develop automated test scripts that are more "generic", requiring only that the input and expected results be updated. This methodology is ideal for testing systems that are huge, complex and have varied test environments.
- Most importantly, have a set of resources (hardware, software and people) dedicated to test automation. Resources that share their time across manual and automation testing rarely achieve effective test automation.

9.13.1 Myths and Realities of Automated Testing

1. **Myth:** The tool is going to replace the testers.

   Reality: This is hardly the case. One has to remember that it is indeed very difficult to eliminate manual testing. In reality the test tool helps the testers to do their job in a much better manner. They relieve the testers from performing mundane and boring tasks and free up their time so that they can concentrate on the complex tasks.
2. **Myth:** The time span required to train all of the testers to use the tool is too long.

   Reality: If the correct methodology is followed then the learning curve can be reduced to a large extent and the testers can become productive within a short span of time.
3. **Myth:** The tool will be too difficult for testers to use.

   Reality: With adequate training the testers can be easily migrated to any new testing tool.
4. **Myth:** A single tester can easily perform a dual role of manual and automation.

   Reality: This rarely works and usually is one of the biggest blunders an organization makes. Ultimately, the tester gets burned out and both, the manual as well as automation testing suffer. For any test automation project to succeed, it is imperative to have a set of resources dedicated only to test automation.
5. **Myth:** Test Automation is very easy. Just record the scripts at any given point of time and replay them whenever you want to.

   Reality: This kind of attitude is probably most responsible for companies discarding test automation projects and switching back to manual testing. Automation testing requires a lot of planning, preparation and skilled resources.

9.13.2 Advantages of Test Automation

- **Speed:** As manual testing consumes a great deal of time in both the process of software development as well as during the software application testing, automated tools are a faster option as long as the scripts which need to be done are standard and non complex. Test cases generally execute faster when automated. More importantly, different batches of test cases can be executed on multiple computers simultaneously.
- **Reusability:** Assuming automation has been designed and implemented properly, acceptance tests could be run as many times as necessary to test a software release or any future software releases. Over time, this may amount to very significant productivity gains.
- **Accuracy:** Repeating the same tests over and over inevitably lead to boredom-induced complacency that allows bugs that would otherwise be caught, to be overlooked. Oftentimes, this also leads to testing shortcuts which could also have detrimental effects. With automation, test cases are executed with 100% accuracy and repeatability every time.
- **Relentlessness:** Can be run, day and night, 24 hours a day potentially delivering the equivalent of several full-time SQA manual testers.
- **Efficiency:** Automating boring repetitive tasks not only improves employee morale, but also frees up time for staff to pursue other tasks they otherwise could not or would not pursue. Therefore, greater breadth and depth of testing is possible this way.
- **Reliability:** Automation of test script execution eliminates the possibility of human error when the same sequence of actions is repeated again and again. Remember this can be really important as you would be astonished to learn just how many test defects raised are in fact caused by tester error. This particularly happens when the same boring test scripts have to be run over and over again as well as when, at the opposite spectrum, really complex testing has to be done.

9.13.3 Disadvantages of Test Automation

- **Significant investment:** The investment required to implement test automation is expensive but the incremental cost is very cheap. This is often overseen in the rush to complete testing during the initial stages of test automation.
- **Maintenance:** Requires more maintenance than manual testing.
- **Not as robust:** Automated scripts will only check what has been explicitly included for checking.
- **Error detection:** Errors introduced during the automation process are more difficult to detect because once a test has been fully automated and become part of the test regime, Human interaction is minimized and errors will only come to light if the automated test itself includes robust error detection routines or the manual tester is actively monitoring every automated test as they execute.
- **Cannot think:** Cannot detect and intercede when unexpected situations arise.
- **Complexity:** With the increase in the number of requirements (business requirements documentation and software requirements specification) that are to be tested, this leads to more and more complexity which makes the maintenance of test data extremely difficult.

9.13.4 Popular Test Automation Tools

Tool Name	*Company Name*	*Latest Version*
HP QuickTest Professional	HP	10.5
IBM Rational Functional Tester	IBM Rational	8.1.0.3
Rational robot	IBM Rational	2001
Selenium	OpenSource Tool	1.0.1
SilkTest	Microfocus	2009
TestComplete	AutomatedQA	7.52
TestPartner	Micro Focus	6.3
WATIR	OpenSource Tool	1.6.5

Increasing trend of automation in all aspects of personal and work life:

- ATM bank machines, vending machines
- Automated telephone menu systems
- Industrial robots
- Office automation, "paperless office"
- Automobile cruise control.

9.13.5 Advantages and Guidelines of Automated Testing

"Automated Testing" is automating the manual testing process currently in use. This requires that a formalized "manual testing process", currently exists in the company or organization.

Automation is the use of strategies, tools and artifacts that augment or reduce the need of manual or human involvement or interaction in unskilled, repetitive or redundant tasks.

Minimally, such a process includes:

- Detailed test cases, including predictable "expected results", which have been developed from Business Functional Specifications and Design documentation.
- A standalone Test Environment, including a Test Database that is restorable to a known constant, such that the test cases are able to be repeated each time there are modifications made to the application.

The following types of testing can be automated:

- **Functional:** testing that operations perform as expected.
- **Regression:** testing that the behaviour of the system has not changed.
- **Exception or negative:** forcing error conditions in the system.
- **Stress:** determining the absolute capacities of the application and operational infrastructure.
- **Performance:** providing assurance that the performance of the system will be adequate for both batch runs and online transactions in relation to business projections and requirements.
- **Load:** determining the points at which the capacity and performance of the system become degraded to the situation that hardware or software upgrades would be required.

Benefits of Automated Testing

1. **Reliable:** Tests perform precisely the same operations each time they are run, thereby eliminating human error.
2. **Repeatable:** You can test how the software reacts under repeated execution of the same operations.
3. **Programmable:** You can program sophisticated tests that bring out hidden information from the application.
4. **Comprehensive:** You can build a suite of tests that covers every feature in your application.
5. **Reusable:** You can reuse tests on different versions of an application, even if the user-interface changes.
6. **Better quality software:** Because you can run more tests in less time with fewer resources
7. **Fast:** Automated Tools run tests significantly faster than human users.
8. **Cost Reduction:** As the number of resources for regression test are reduced.

Choosing the right tools for the job and targeting the right areas of the organization to deploy them can only realize these benefits. The right areas where the automation fit must be chosen.

The following areas must be automated first:

1. Highly redundant tasks or scenarios.
2. Repetitive tasks that are boring or tend to cause human error.
3. Well-developed and well-understood use cases or scenarios first.
4. Relatively stable areas of the application over volatile ones must be automated.

Guidelines of Automated Testing

Automated testers must follow the following guidelines to get the benefits of automation:

1. **Concise:** As simple as possible and no simpler.
2. **Self-checking:** Test reports its own results; needs no human interpretation.
3. **Repeatable:** Test can be run many times in a row without human intervention.
4. **Robust:** Test produces same result now and forever. Tests are not affected by changes in the external environment.
5. **Sufficient:** Tests verify all the requirements of the software being tested.
6. **Necessary:** Everything in each test contributes to the specification of desired behaviour.
7. **Clear:** Every statement is easy to understand.
8. **Efficient:** Tests run in a reasonable amount of time.
9. **Specific:** Each test failure points to a specific piece of broken functionality; unit test failures provide "defect triangulation".
10. **Independent:** Each test can be run by itself or in a suite with an arbitrary set of other tests in any order.
11. **Maintainable:** Tests should be easy to understand and modify and extend.
12. **Traceable:** To and from the code it tests and to and from the requirements.

10

SOFTWARE QUALITY

10.1 CONCEPT OF SOFTWARE QUALITY

We examine the qualities that are pertinent to software products and software production processes. These qualities will become our goals in the practice of software engineering.

The basic goal of software engineering is to produce quality software. Software quality is a broad and important field of software engineering addressed by several standardization bodies such as ISO, IEEE, and ANSI etc.

10.1.1 Definitions of Software Quality

The definition of the ISO 8204 for quality:

"Totality of characteristics of an entity that bears on its ability to satisfy stated and implied needs."

This means that the software product delivered should be as per the requirements defined.

OR

User Satisfaction = compliant product + good quality + delivery within budget and schedule

– Robert Glass

OR

Software quality is the:

"Conformance to explicit stated functional and performance requirements, explicitly documented development standards, and implicit characteristics that are expected of all professionally developed software".

The above definition emphasize on these three important points:

1. Software requirements are the foundation from which quality is measured. Lack of conformance to requirements is lack of quality.
2. Specified standards define a set of development criteria that guide the manner in which software is engineered. If the criteria are not followed, lack of quality will almost surely in result.

3. There is a set of implicit requirements that often goes unmentioned. If software conforms to its explicit requirements but fails to meet implicit requirements, software quality is suspect.

10.1.2 Classification of Software Qualities

There are many desirable software qualities. Some of these apply both to the product and to the process used to produce the product. The user wants the software products to be reliable, efficient, and easy to use. The producer of the software wants it to be verifiable, maintainable, portable, and extensible. The manager of the software project wants the process of software development to be productive and easy to control.

In this section, we consider two different classifications of software-related qualities: ***internal versus external*** and ***product versus process.***

10.1.2.1 External versus Internal Qualities

We can divide software qualities into external and internal qualities. The external qualities are visible to the users of the system: the internal qualities are those that concern the developers of the system. In general, users of the software only care about the external qualities, but it are the internal qualities-which deal largely with the structure of the software-that help developers achieve the external qualities. For example, the internal quality of verifiability is necessary for achieving the external quality of reliability. In many cases, however, the qualities are related closely and the distinction between internal and external is not sharp.

10.1.2.2 Product and Process Qualities

We use a ***process*** to produce the software product. We can also attribute some qualities to the process, although process qualities often are closely related to product qualities. For example, if the process requires careful planning of system test data before any design and development of the system starts, products reliability will increase. Some qualities, such as efficiency, apply both to the product and to the process.

It is interesting to examine the word ***product*** here. It usually refers to what is delivered to the customer. Even though this is an acceptable definition from the customer's perspective, it is not adequate for the developer who requires a general definition of a software product that encompasses not only the object code and the user manual that are delivered to the customer, but also the requirements, design, source code, test data, etc. In fact, it is possible to deliver different subsets of the same product to different customers.

10.1.3 Software Quality Attributes

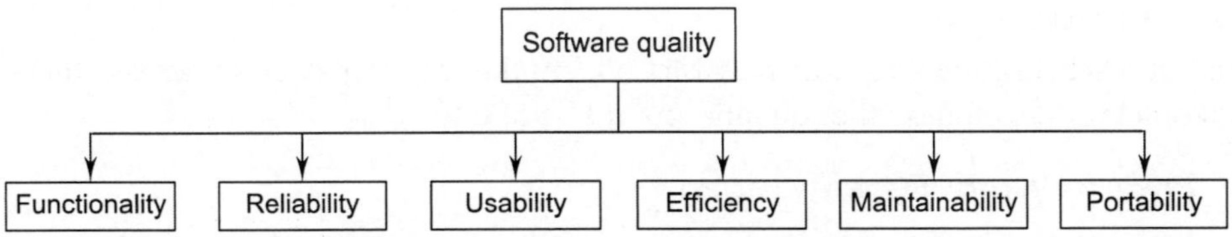

Fig. 10.1 Software quality attributes

Software quality comprises of six main attributes (called characteristics) as shown in Fig. 10.1. These six attributes have detailed characteristics which are considered the basic ones and which can and should be measured using suitable metrics. At the top level, for software products, these attributes can be defined as follows:

1. **Functionality:** The capability to provide functions which meet stated and implied needs when the software is used.
2. **Reliability:** The capability to maintain a specified level of performance.
3. **Usability:** The capability to be understood, learned, and used.
4. **Efficiency:** The capability to provide appropriate performance relative to the amount of resources used.
5. **Maintainability:** The capability to be modified for purposes of making corrections, improvements, or adaptation.
6. **Portability:** The capability to be adapted for different specified environments without applying actions or means other than those provided for this purpose in the product.

10.1.4 McCall's Quality Factors

McCall, Richards, and Walters [MCC77] propose a useful categorization of factors that affect software quality. These software quality factors, shown in Fig. 10.2 focus on three important aspects of a software product: its operational characteristics, its ability to undergo change, and its adaptability to new environments.

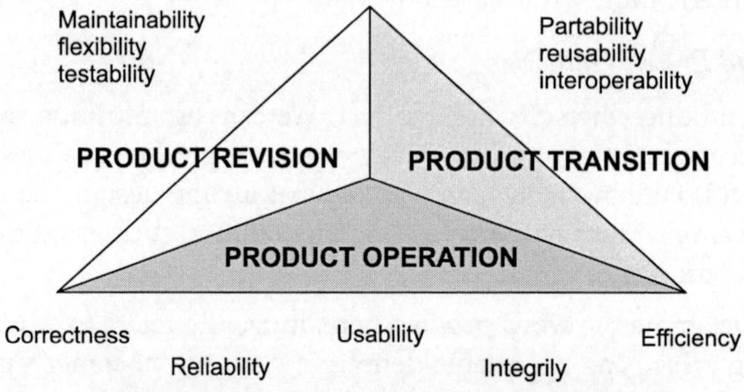

Fig. 10.2 McCall's software quality factors

One attempt to identify specific product qualities that are appropriate to software has been that of James A. McCall. He grouped software qualities into three sets of quality factors:

- Product operation qualities;
- Products revision qualities;
- Product transition qualities.

The definitions below are those given by McCall, but the reader may come across others. These are not all bracing: sometimes other qualities might be of interest.

10.1.4.1 Product Operation Quality Factors

- *Correctness:* The extent to which a program satisfies its specifications and fulfills the user's objectives.
- *Reliability:* The extent to which a program can be expected to perform its intended function with required precision.
- *Efficiency:* The amounts of computer resources required by the software.

- *Integrity*: The extent to which access to software or data by unauthorized persons can be controlled.
- *Usability*: The effort required learning, operating, preparing input and interpreting output.

10.1.4.2 Product Revision Factors

- *Maintainability:* The effort required to locate and fix an error in an operational program.
- *Testability:* The effort required to test a program to ensure it performs its intended function.
- *Flexibility:* The efforts required to modify an operational program.

10.1.4.3 Product Transition Quality Factors

- *Portability:* The effort required transferring a program from one hardware configuration and software system environment to another.
- *Reusability:* The extent to which a program can be used in other applications.
- *Interoperability:* The efforts required to couple one system to another.

10.1.5 Software Quality Criteria

The software quality criteria of various quality factors are depicted in the tabular form below in Table 10.1

Table 10.1 Software quality criteria

Quality Factor	*Software Quality Criteria*
Correctness	Traceability, consistency, completeness
Reliably	Error tolerance, consistency, accuracy, simplicity
Efficiency	Execution efficiency, storage efficiency
Integrity	Access control, access audit.
Usability	Operability, training, communicativeness, input/output volume, input/output area.
Maintainability	Consistency, simplicity, conciseness, modularity, self-descriptiveness.
Testability	Simplicity, modularity, instrumentation, self-descriptiveness
Flexibility	Modularity, generality, expandability, self- descriptiveness.
Portability	Modularity, self-descriptiveness, machine independence, software system independence.
Reusability	Generality, modularity, software system independence, machine independence, self-descriptiveness.
Interoperability	Modularity, communications commonality, data commonalty.

10.1.6 Representative Qualities

In this section, we present the most important qualities of software products and processes.

1. **Correctness:** A program is ***functionally correct*** if it behaves according to the specification of the functions it should provide (called ***functional requirements specifications***). It is common simply to use the term "correct" rather than "functionally correct"; similarly, in this context, the term "specifications" implies "functional requirements specification". We will follow this convention when the context is clear.

The definition of correctness assumes that a specification of the system is available and that it is possible to determine unambiguously whether or not a program meets the specifications. With most current software systems, no such specification exists. If a specification does exist, it is usually written in an informal style using natural language.

2. **Reliability:** Informally, software is reliable if the user can depend on it. The specialized literature on software reliability defines reliability in terms of statistical behavior-the portability that the software will operate as expected over a specified time interval.

   Figure 10.3 illustrates the relationship between reliability and correctness. This figure shows that the set of all reliable programs includes the set of correct programs, but not vice versa.

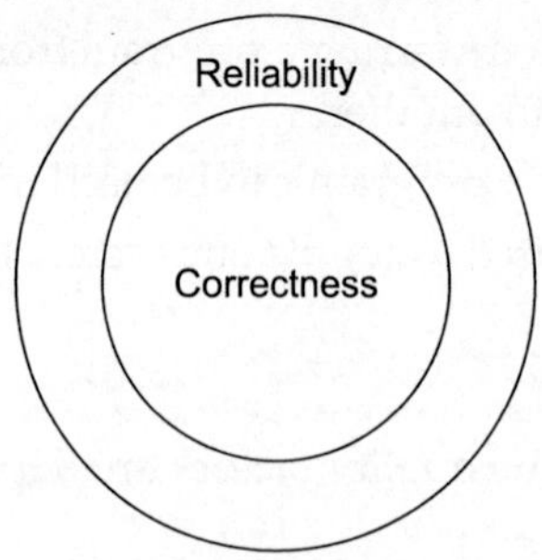

Fig. 10.3 Relationship between correctness and reliability in the ideal case

3. **Robustness:** A program is robust if it behaves "reasonably," even in circumstances that were not anticipated in the requirements specification-for example, when it encounters incorrect input data or some hardware malfunction (say, a, disk crash).

   Obviously, robustness is a difficult-to-define quality; after all, if we could state precisely what we should do to make an application robust, we would be able to specify its "reasonable" behavior completely. The robustness would become equivalent to correctness (or reliability in the sense of Fig. 10.3).

4. **Performance:** Performance is important because it affects the usability of the system. If a software system is too slow, it reduces the productivity of the users, possibly to the point of not meeting their needs. If a software system uses too much disk space, it may be too expensive to run. If a software system uses too much memory, it may affect the other applications that are run on the same system, or it may run slowly while the operating system tries to balance the memory usage of the different applications. Performance is also important because it affects the scalability of a software system.

5. **Verifiability:** A software system is verifiable if its properties can be verified easily. For example, it is important to be able to verify the correctness or the performance of a software system.

   Verifiability is usually an internal quality, although it sometimes becomes an external quality also. For example, in many security- critical applications, the customer requires the verifiability of certain properties. The highest level of the security standard for a trusted computer system requires the verifiability of the operating system kernel.

6. **Repairability:** A software system is repairable if it allows the correction of its defects with a limited amount of work. In many engineering products, repairability is a major design goal. For example, automobile engines are built with the parts that are most likely to fail as the most accessible. In computer hardware engineering, there is a subspecialty called Reparability, Availability, and Serviceability (RAS).

7. **Evolvability:** Like other engineering products, software products are modified over time to provide new functions or to change existing functions. Indeed, the fact that software is so malleable makes modifications extremely easy to apply to an implementation.
8. **Understandability:** Some software systems are easier to understand than others. Of course, some tasks are inherently more complex than others. Given tasks of inherently similar difficulty, we can follow certain guidelines to produce more understandable designs and to write more understandable programs. For example, abstraction and modularity enhance a system's understandability.
9. **Interoperability:** "Interoperability "refers to the ability of a system to coexist and cooperate with other systems.

   With interoperability, a vendor can produce different products and allow the user to combine them if necessary. This makes it easier for the vendor to produce the products, and it gives the user more freedom in exactly what functions to pay for and to combine. Interoperability can be achieved through standardization of interfaces.
10. **Productivity:** Productivity is a quality of the software production process; it measures the efficiency of the process and, as we said before, is the performance quality applied to the process. An efficient process results in faster delivery of the product.

    Productivity offers many trade-offs in the choice of a process. For example, a process that requires specialization of individual team members may lead to productivity in producing a certain product, but not in producing a variety of products. Software reuse is a technique that leads to the overall productivity of an organization that is involved in developing many products, but developing reusable modules is harder than developing modules for one's own use, thus reducing the productivity of the group that is developing reusable modules as part of their product development.
11. **Timeliness:** Timeliness is a process—related quality that refers to the ability to deliver a product on time.

    Timeliness requires careful scheduling, accurate estimation of work, and clearly specified and verifiable milestones.
12. **Visibility:** A software development process is visible if all of its steps and its current status are documented clearly. Another term used to characterize this property is transparency. The idea is that the steps and the status of the project are available and easily accessible for external examination.

10.1.7 Software Quality Indicators

A *software quality indicator* can be calculated to provide an indication of the quality of the system by assessing system characteristics.

Method: Assemble a quality indicator from factor that can be determined automatically with commercial or custom code scanners, such as the following:

- Cyclomatic complexity of code (*e.g.*, McCabe's complexity Measure).
- Unused/unreferenced code segments (these should be eliminated over time).
- Average number of application calls per module (complexity is directly proportional to the number of calls).
- Size of compilation units (reasonable size units have approximately 20 functions (or paragraphs), or about 2000 lines of code; these guidelines will vary greatly by environment).

- Use of structure programming constructs (*e.g.*, elimination of GOTOs, and circular procedure calls).

These measures apply to traditional 3GL environments and are more difficult to determine in environments which are using object-oriented languages, 4GLs, or code generators.

10.1.8 Importance of Software Quality

We would expect quality to be a concern of all producers of goods and services. However, the special characteristics of software, and in particular its intangibility and complexity, make special demands.

1. **Increasing criticality of software:** The final customer or user is naturally anxious about the general quality of software, especially its reliability. This is increasingly the case as organizations become more dependent on their computer systems and software is used more and more in areas which are safety critical, for example to control aircraft.
2. **The intangibility of software:** This makes it difficult to know whether a particular task in a project has been completed satisfactorily. The results of these tasks can be made tangible by demanding that the developers produce 'deliverables' that can be examined for quality.
3. **Accumulating errors during software development:** As computer system development is made up of a number of steps where the output from one step is the input to the next, the errors in the earlier deliverables will be added to those in the later steps leading to an accumulating detrimental effect, an general, the later in a project that an error is found the more expensive is will be to fix. In addition, because the number of errors in the system is unknown the debugging phases of a project are particularly difficult to control.

   For these reasons quality management is an essential of effective overall project management.

10.2 SOFTWARE QUALITY MANAGEMENT

Software Quality Management simply stated comprises of processes that ensure that the Software Project would reach its goals. In other words the Software Project would meet the clients expectations.

The key processes of Software Quality Management fall into the following three categories:

1. **Quality Planning:** In the planning process we determine the standards that are relevant for the Software Product, the organization and the means to achieve them.

   Quality Planning is the most important step in Software Quality Management. Proper planning ensures that the remaining Quality processes make sense and achieve the desired results. The starting point for the Planning process is the standards followed by the organization. This is expressed in the Quality Policy and Documentation defining the organization-wide standards. Sometimes additional industry standards relevant to the Software Project may be referred to as needed. Using these as inputs the Standards for the specific project are decided. The Scope of the effort is also clearly defined.

   Inputs for Quality Planning: The inputs for the Planning are as summarized as follows:

   - Company's quality policy
   - Organization standards

- Relevant industry standards
- Regulations
- Scope of work
- Project requirements.

Using these as inputs the quality planning process creates a plan to ensure that standards agreed upon are met.

Outputs for quality planning: The outputs of the quality planning process are:

- Standards defined for the project
- Quality plan.

Tools and techniques for quality planning: To create these outputs namely the Quality Plan various tools and techniques are used. These tools and techniques are briefly discussed as follows:

1. **Benchmarking:** The proposed product standards can be decided using the existing performance benchmarks of similar products that already exist in the market.
2. **Design of experiments:** Using statistics we determine what factors influence the Quality or features of the end product
3. **Cost of quality:** This includes all the costs needed to achieve the required Quality levels. It includes prevention costs, appraisal costs and failure costs.
4. **Other tools:** There are various other tools used in the Planning process such as Cause and Effect Diagrams, System Flow Charts, Cost Benefit Analysis, etc.

All these help us to create a Quality Management Plan for the project.

2. **Quality Assurance:** Once the standards are defined and we start building the product. It is very important to have processes that evaluate the project performance and aim to assure that the Quality standards are being followed and the final product will be in compliance.

   The Input to the Quality Assurance Processes is the Quality Plan created during Planning.

   Quality Audits and various other techniques are used to evaluate the performance of the project. This helps us to ensure that the Project is following the Quality Management Plan.

   The ***tools and techniques*** used in the Planning Process such as Design of Experiments, Cause and Effect Diagrams may also be used here, as required.

3. **Quality control:** Once the software components are built the results are monitored to determine if they comply with the standards. The data collected helps in measuring the performance trends and as needed help in identifying defective pieces of code.

   Inputs for quality control: Following are the inputs to the quality control process:

   - Quality management plan.
   - Quality standards defined for the project.
   - Actual observations and measurements of the work done or in progress.

   The quality control processes use various tools to study the work done. If the work done is found unsatisfactory it may be sent back to the development team for fixes. Changes to the Development process may be done if necessary.

   If the work done meets the standards defined then the work done is accepted and released to the clients.

10.2.1 Importance of Documentation in Software Quality Management

In all the Quality Management Processes special emphasis is put on documentation. Many software shops fail to document the project at various levels. Consider a scenario where the Requirements of the Software Project are not sufficiently documented. In this case it is quiet possible that the client has a set of expectations and the tester may not know about them. Hence the testing team would not be able test the software developed for these expectations or requirements. This may lead to poor "Software Quality" as the product does not meet the expectations.

Similarly consider a scenario where the development team does not document the installation instructions. If a different person or a team is responsible for future installations they may end up making mistakes during installation, thereby failing to deliver as promised.

Once again consider a scenario where a tester fails to document the test results after executing the test cases. This may lead to confusion later. If there were an error, we would not be sure at what stage the error was introduced in the software at a component level or when integrating it with another component or due to environment on a particular server etc. Hence documentation is the key for future analysis and all Quality Management efforts.

Steps: In a typical Software Development Life Cycle the following steps are necessary for Quality Management:

1. Document the Requirements
2. Define and Document Quality Standards
3. Define and Document the Scope of Work
4. Document the Software Created and dependencies
5. Define and Document the Quality Management Plan
6. Define and Document the Test Strategy
7. Create and Document the Test Cases
8. Execute Test Cases and (log) Document the Results
9. Fix Defects and document the fixes
10. Quality Assurance audits the Documents and Test Logs.

Various Software Tools have been development for Quality Management. These Tools can help us track Requirements and map Test Cases to the Requirements. They also help in Defect Tracking.

10.3 CAPABILITY MATURITY MODEL (SEI-CMM)

SEI-CMM stands for Software Engineering Institute Capability Maturity Model. The CMM was developed by the Software Engineering Institute (SEI) of the Carnegie Mellon University in the USA, which is engaged on a long-term programme of software process improvement, and then came to be known as SEI-CMM.

It is a model, which helps in judging the maturity of software process of an organization. It also helps to identify the main process that will help in increasing maturity of these processes. It has become a standard for assessing and improving software processes.

SEI-CMM can be used in two ways: ***Capability evaluation*** and ***Software process assessment.*** Capability evaluation and software process assessment differ in motivation, objective, and the final use of the result. Capability evaluation provides a way to assess the software process capability of an organization. The results of capability evaluation indicate the likely contractor performance if the contractor is awarded a work. Therefore, the results of software process capability assessment can be used to select a contractor. On the other hand, software process assessment is used by an organization with the objective to improve its process capability. Thus this type of assessment is for purely internal use.

Five levels of process maturing have been proposed for software industry by SEI-CMM, which indicate the sophistication and quality of their software production practices. These levels are defined as follows:

1. **Level 1 (Initial):** The software process is adhoc, and even chaotic at time. The organization whose success depends on individual effort and processes are not defined and documented come under this level.

   Organizations at this level can benefit most by improving project management, quality assurance and change control.

2. **Level 2 (Repeatable):** Here company defines the basic management practices such as tracking cost; schedule and functionality are established but not the procedures of doing it. Here the efforts done previously for success of project may repeat.

   Some of the characteristics of a process at this level are: project commitments are realistic and based on past experience with similar projects, cost and schedule are tracked and problems resolved when they arise, formal configuration control mechanisms are in place, and software project standards are defined and followed.

3. **Level 3 (Defined):** The organization-wide software process includes management and engineering procedures. These procedures are well defined, documented, standardized and integrated. All projects make use of the documented and approved version of the organization process for software development and maintenance. But the process and practices are not analyzed quantitatively. In this process both the development and management processes are formal. ISO 9000 aims at achieving this level.

4. **Level 4 (Managed):** At this level, the focus is on software metrics. Two types of metric are collected. Product metrics measure the characteristics of the product being developed, such as its size, reliability, time complexity, understandability, etc. Process metrics reflect the effectiveness of the process being used, such as the average defect correction time, productivity, the average number of defects found per hour of inspection, the average number of failures detected during testing per LOC, and so forth. The process metrics are used to check if a project performed satisfactorily. Thus, the results of process measurements are used to evaluate project performance rather than to improve the process.

   Software processes and products are quantitatively understood; measured and controlled using detailed procedures.

5. **Level 5 (Optimized):** By using the quantitative feedback from the process in place, exploring new ideas and technologies. At this level, an organization is committed to continuous process improvement. Process improvement is budgeted and planned and is an integral part of the organization's process. The organizations have the means to identify weaknesses and strengthen the process proactively, with the goal of preventing the occurrence of defects. Best software engineering and management practices are used throughout the organization.

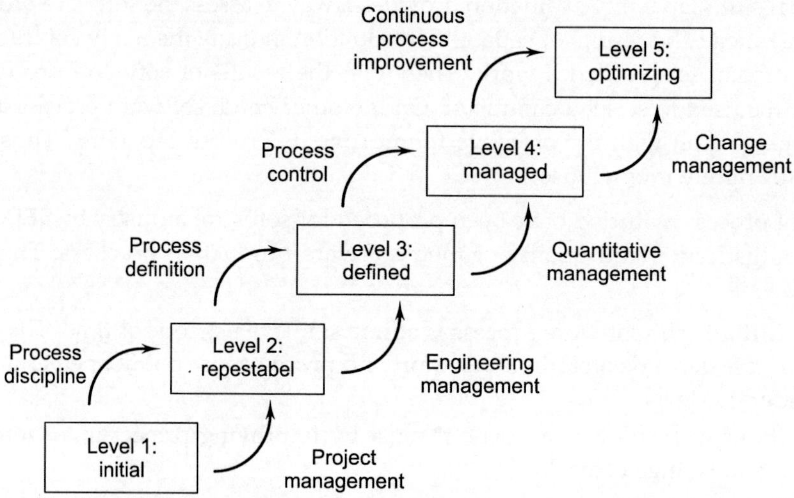

Fig. 10.4 Software engineering institute levels of maturity

Except for level 1, each maturity level is characterized by several Key Process Areas (KPAs) that indicate the areas an organization should focus on, to improve its software process to the next level.

This is shown in the table No. 2 as follows:

MM level	*Characteristics*	*Focus*	*Key Process Areas*
1. (Initial)	Chaotic, unrepeatable, high risk of non- performance.	Competent people	Not applicable
2. (Repeatable)	Methodical in umbrella activities and processes. Performa-nce is repeated but not improved	Project management	Configuration management, quality assurance, sub-contract management, project tracking and oversight, project planning
3. (Defined)	Improved performance in cost, schedule quality and risk management.	Definition of processes	Peer reviews, inter-group coordination, software product engineering, training programme, integrated software management and organization process definition
4. (Managed)	Learns from project experience, and continuous perform-ance improvement in all key areas of the project	Product and process quality	Quality management, process measurement and analysis
5. (Optimizing)	All-round performance, improvement through learning. High performance in all quality attributes and risk management through RMMM.	Continuous process improvement	Process change management, technology innovation, defect preven-tion.

10.4 SOFTWARE QUALITY ASSURANCE

Software quality assurance is an umbrella activity that is applied throughout the software process. The first formal quality assurance and control function was introduced at Bell Labs in 1916 in the manufacturing world. During the 1950s and 1960s, the programmers control their product quality. During the 1970s, quality assurance standards were introduced first in military contract software development.

Software Quality Assurance (SQA) is a formal process for evaluating and documenting the quality of the work products produced during each stage of the software development lifecycle. The primary objective of the SQA process is to ensure the production of high-quality work products according to stated requirements and established standards.

Definitions: "Software Quality Assurance is a set of activities designed to evaluate the process by which software is developed and / or maintained".

OR

Quality assurance is "a planned and systematic pattern of all actions necessary to provide adequate confidence that the item or product conforms to established technical requirements"

(IEEE83)

OR

Software Quality Assurance is

"The function of software quality that assures that the standards, processes, and procedures are appropriate for the project and are correctly implemented" **[Software Definition at NASA]**

The process of software quality assurance:

1. Defines the requirements for software controlled system fault/failure detection, isolation, and recovery;
2. Reviews the software development processes and products for software error prevention and/or controlled change to reduced functionality states; and
3. Defines the process for measuring and analyzing defects as well as reliability and maintainability factors.

10.4.1 Elements of SQA

- Quality management plan
- Effective software engineering technology
- Formal reviews
- Well-conceived testing strategies
- Configuration control and change management
- Enforcement of standards
- Measurement and reporting mechanisms.

10.4.2 SQA Objectives

The various objectives of SQA are as follows:

- Quality management approach
- Measurement and reporting mechanisms
- Effective software engineering technology
- A procedure to assure compliance with software development standards where applicable.

- A multi-testing strategy is drawn
- Formal technical reviews that are applied throughout the software process.

10.4.3 SQA Goals

The major goals of SQA are as follows:

- SQA activities are planned.
- Non-compliance issues that cannot be resolved within the software project are addressed by senior management.
- Adherence of software products and activities to the applicable standards, procedures and requirements is verified objectively.
- Affected groups and individuals are informed of SQA activities and results.

10.4.4 SQA Plan

The SQA Plan defines the activities performed to provide assurance that the software-related items delivered to the customer conform to the established and contracted technical requirements. The SQA Plan also describes how the project will be audited to ensure that the policies, standards, practices, procedures, and processes applicable to the project are followed.

Software Quality Assurance is a plan that defines the quality processes and procedures that should be used. This involves selecting and instantiating standards for products and processes and defining the required quality attributes of the system.

The SQA Plan provides a road map for instituting software quality assurance. Developed by the SQA group (or the software team if a SQA group does not exist), the plan serves as a template for SQA activities that are instituted for each software project.

The quality plan should select those organizational standards that are appropriate to a particular product and development process. New standards may have to be defined if the project uses new methods and tools.

An outline structure for a quality plan includes:

1. **Product introduction:** A description of the product, its intended market and the quality expectations for the product.
2. **Product plans:** The critical release dates and responsibilities for the product along with plans for distribution and product servicing.
3. **Process descriptions:** The development and service processes that should be used for product development and management.
4. **Quality goals:** The quality goals and plans for the product including an identification and justification of critical product quality attributes.
5. **Risks and risk management:** The key risks that might affect product quality and the actions to address these risks.

Preparation of a Software quality Assurance Plan for each software project is a primary responsibility of the software quality assurance group. Topics in a Software Quality Assurance Plan include.

- Purpose-scope of plan;
- List of references to other documents;
- Management, including organization, tasks and responsibilities;

- Documentation to be produced;
- Standards, practices and conventions;
- Reviews and audits;
- Testing;
- Problem reporting and corrective action;
- Tools, techniques and methodologies;
- Code, media and supplier control;
- Records collection, maintenance and retention;
- Training;
- Risk management-the methods of risk management that are to be used.

10.4.5 Organizational Structure of SQA

The SQA organizational structure includes the following major roles; there responsibilities are shown in Table 10.2

- Project manager
- Software technical manager
- Software quality assurance manager.

Table 10.2 Roles and responsibilities

Role	*Responsibilities*
Project Manager	Overall, project co-ordination.
Software Technical Manager	Software Development and Technical Issues/implementation and monitoring of Software and SCM activities.
Software Quality Assurance Manager	Quality issues/implementation and monitoring of SQA activities.

The organizational structure also includes:

- The Technical Teams (one for each task), supervised by the S/W Technical Manager, responsible for product development, transfer and maintenance;
- The Project Secretariat, supervised by the Project Manager, responsible for documentation and records as well as overall administrative support.

10.4.6 SQA Group Activities

Various people who are involved in quality assurance activities are Software engineers, project managers, customers, sale people, and SQA group. The SQA group serves as the customer's in-house representative and assists the software engineering team in achieving high-quality. The main responsibilities of SQA group's are quality assurance planning oversight, record keeping, and analysis and reporting.

The purpose of a software quality assurance group is to provide assurance that the procedures, tools, and techniques used during product development and modification are adequate to provide the desired level of confidence in the work products.

The software quality assurance includes the following activities:

- Prepare SQA plan for the project.
- Participate in the development of the project's software process description.

- Review software engineering activities to verify compliance with the defined software process.
- Audit designated software work products to verify compliance with those defined as part of the software process.
- Ensures that any deviations in software or work products are documented and handled according to a documented procedure.
- Record any evidence of noncompliance and reports them to management.
- Coordinates and controls change.
- Helps collect and analyze metrics.

10.4.7 Formal SQA Approaches

Over the past few years, software engineering community has argued that SQA requires a more formal approach. It can be argued that

- A computer program is a mathematical object.
- Syntax and semantics can be defined for every programming language.
- Formal approaches for software requirements are also available.

If requirement specification and programming language can be represented in a rigorous manner, than it should be possible to apply mathematical proof of correctness to show that a program conforms exactly to its specification—which is SQA.

There are three formal SQA Approaches which are shown in the Fig. 10.5

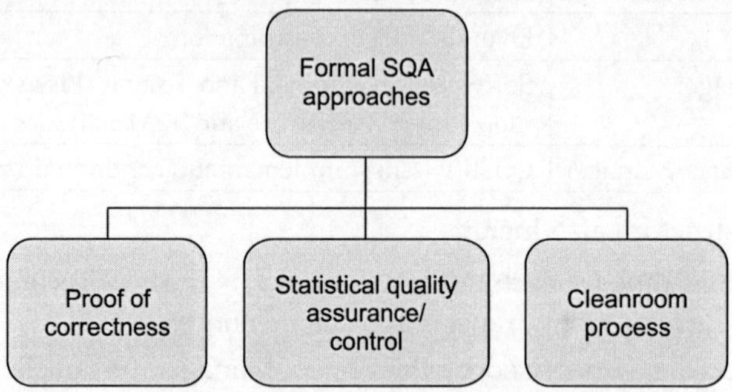

Fig. 10.5 Formal SQA approaches

10.4.7.1 Proof of Correctness

"Proof of correctness is used to demonstrate that a program conforms exactly to its specifications". A proof of correctness is a mathematical proof that a computer program or a part thereof will, when executed, yield correct results *i.e.*, results fulfilling specific requirement. Before proving a program correct, the theorem to be proved must, of course, be formulated.

Hypothesis: The hypothesis of such a correctness theorem is typically a condition that the relevant program variables must satisfy immediately before the program is executed. The condition is called the **"pre-condition".**

Thesis: The thesis of the correctness theorem is typically a condition that the relevant program variables must satisfy immediately after execution of the program. This latter condition is called the **"post-condition".**

So the correctness theorem is stated as below:

"If the condition V, is true before execution of the program S, then the condition, P will be true after execution of S". Where V is pre-condition and P is post-condition.

Notation: Such a correctness theorem is usually written as {V} S {P}, where V, S and P have been explained above.

By 'program variable' we broadly include input and output data, *e.g.*, data entered via a keyboard, displayed on a screen or printed on paper. Any externally observable aspect of the program's execution may be covered by the pre-condition and post-condition.

Howden claims that there is no such thing as an absolute proof of correctness. Instead, he suggests that there are proofs of equivalency *i.e.*, proof that one description of a product is equivalent to another description. Hence, unless a formal specification can be shown to be correct and, indeed, reflects exactly the user's expectations, no claim of product correctness can be made.

10.4.7.2 Statistical Quality Assurance/Control

Statistical quality assurance reflects a growing trend throughout industry to become more quantitative about quality. For software, statistical quality assurance implies the following steps:

- Information about software defects is collected and categorized
- Each defect is traced back to its cause
- Using the Pareto principle (80% of the defects can be traced to 20% of the causes) isolate the "vital few" defect causes
- Move to correct the problems that caused the defects.

By SQC we mean the various statistical methods used for maintenance of quality in a continuous flow of products. It involves two types of controls:

1. *Process control*: Its aim is quickly detect the occurrence of assignable (identifiable) causes of quality variation in the production process so that corrective action may be undertaken before many nonconforming (defects) units are produced. Process control is achieved through the technique of control charts.
2. *Product control*: Its aim is to ensure that lots of manufactured products do not contain large proportion of defective items. Product control is achieved through the technique of acceptance sampling inspection plans.

Steps: Statistical quality assurance implies the following steps:

- Information about software defects is collected and categorized
- An attempt is made to trace each defect to its underlying cause
- Using the pareto principle (80 percent of the defect can be traced to 20 percent and isolate the 20 percent)
- Once the vital few causes have been identified, correct the defects.

Causes of errors: Following are some major causes of errors in SQC:

1. Incomplete or Erroneous Specification (IES)
2. Misinterpretation of Customer Communication (MCC)
3. International Deviation Firm Specification (IDS)
4. Violation of Programming Standard (VPS)
5. Error in Data Representation (EDR)
6. Inconsistent Module Interface (IMI)

7. Error in Design Logic (EDI)
8. Incomplete or Erroneous Testing (IET)
9. Inaccurate or Incomplete Documentation (IID)
10. Error in Programming Language Translation of Design (PLT)
11. Ambiguous or Inconsistent Human-computer Interface (HCI)
12. Miscellaneous(MIS)

Error index: In conjunction with the collection of defect information, software developers can calculate an Error Index (EI) for each major step in the software engineering process.

After analysis, design, coding, testing, and release, the following data are collected:

E_i = the total no. of errors uncovered during the *ith* step in the process.

S_i = the no. of serious errors

M_i = the no. of moderate errors

T_i = the no. of minor errors

PS = the size of the product at the *ith* step.

At each step in the software engineering process, a Phase Index (PII) is computed:

$$PI_i = w_s (S_i/E_i) + w_m(M_i/E_i) + w_t(T_i/E_i)$$

Typical values of weighting factors:

$$w_s = 10, w_m = 3, w_t = 1$$

Error index (EI) can be computed as follows:

$$EI = (PI\,1 + 2\,PI\,2 + 3\,PI\,3 + i\,PI\,I)/PS$$

10.4.7.3 Clean-Room Process

The strategy and tactics of clean-room testing are fundamentally different from conventional testing approaches. Conventional methods derive a set of test cases to uncover design and coding errors. The goal of clean-room testing is to validate software requirements by demonstrating that statistical samples of use-cases have been executed successfully.

Cleanroom process is an approach that stresses correctness of every small bit in every stage of development. With this type of development these are three types of teams:

(i) *Specification team*: This team collects the user requirements and the usage of these requirements in the system.

(ii) *Development team*: This team writes the source code but no testing is done. However, mathematical techniques may be used.

(iii) *Certification team*: This team performs software testing. Until a statistical model shows that the failure intensity has been reduced.

The Cleanroom software development is a process of developing software using formal method. This method is used to build most reliable software. This method was originally developed by Harlan mills at IBM. The name of this method is cleanroom because the term cleanroom is used in electronic industry wherein the introduction of defects was avoided during fabrication of Integrated Circuits (ICs). Similarly using the cleanroom approach the software is built such that rather than identifying the defect, introduction of defects is avoided.

There are five key strategies that are used in cleanroom software development.

1. *Formal specification*: The software to be developed is defined using formal method.
2. *Incremental implementation*: The software has to be development in increments and each increment must be validated separately using cleanroom process. These increments must be supplied with the customer input.
3. *Use of structured programming*: During the program development process the specification is refined in stepwise manner. only limited number of programming constructs is used to transform the specification into the programming code.
4. *Static verification*: Each implemented increment is verified thoroughly. It is attempted to have no defect in the developed software.
5. *Statistical testing*: The integrated incremental software module is then tested to ensure the reliability of the system.

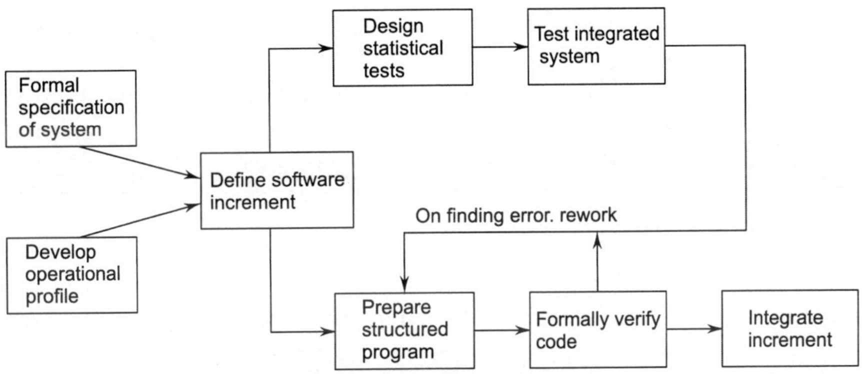

Fig. 10.6 Clean-room process

In the clean-room process of software development, the software is developed in the series of increments. The critical functionalities are added in early increments and less important functionalities are added in the later increments if the requirements problems are discovered then customer gives the feedback to the development team and then these problems are removed by the development team. Sometimes a request for a new release can be made by the customer.

The increments are tested individually as well as these are retested when added with the new increments.

Rigorous program inspection is done in cleanroom process. As per the system specification the state model is produced. It is then refined by adding more and more functionalities and finally an executable program is developed. Each new representation is inspected and mathematically analyzed.

Teams involved in cleanroom software development: When we want to build a large system using cleanroom approach following are the teams that get involved in this process

1. *Specification team*: This team performs the task of preparing and maintaining the system specification. The specification containing the user requirements is created along with the mathematic specification for verification. Sometimes the specification team itself performs development of system.
2. *Development team*: This team performs the task of developing and verifying the software. The Formal structured approach is used while verifying the code. The inspection is carried out for verifying the code.

3. *Certification team*: After developing the code, it has to be tested. The certification team conducts the task of statistical testing. The test cases are used to check the reliability of the system.

Merits of cleanroom engineering:

The merits of Clean-room process are:

1. The zero defect software can be developed using cleanroom approach.
2. The defects are discovered and removed during the development stage. Hence the cost and time of testing is reduced.
3. Cost-effective static verification is carried out in cleanroom process.

Demerits of cleanroom engineering:

The demerits of Cleanroom process are:

1. The formal mathematical proof required to check the correctness of the program. Developing such proofs with respect to specification is very expensive. It also requires the knowledge of mathematics and formal semantic of the program.
2. The cleanroom software development process requires skilled and committed staff.

10.5 INTERNATIONAL STANDARD ORGANIZATION (ISO)

10.5.1 Introduction to ISO

The International Organization for Standardization (ISO) is worldwide federations of national standards bodies form some 100 countries. ISO is a non-governmental organization established in 1947.

The ISO 9000 standard specifies quality assurance elements in generic terms, which can be applied to any business, regards of the product or services being offered. In order to register for one of the quality assurance system models contained in ISO 9000, third party auditors examine an organization's quality system and operations for compliance to the standard and for effective operations. Upon successful audit, the organization receives a certificate from a registered body represented by the auditors. Thereafter, semi-annual audits ensure conformance to the standard.

The ISO 9000 standards view an organization as a set of interrelated processes. In order to pass the criteria for ISO 9000 compliance, the processes must address the identified areas, and document and practice them. When a process is documented, it is better understood, controlled, and improved. However, ISO 9000 does not specify how an organization should implement its quality system. Therefore, the biggest challenge is to design and implement a quality assurance system that meets the standard and gels well with the products/ services of the organization.

ISO 9001 is a quality assurance standard that is specific to software engineering. It specifies 20 standards with which an organization must comply for an effective implementation of the quality assurance system.

ISO 9000 series of standards is as set of documents dealing with quality systems that can be used for quality assurance purpose. IOS-9000 series is not just software standard. It is a series of five related standards that are applicable to a wide variety of industrial activities, including design/ development, production, installation, and servicing.

10.5.2 ISO 9000 Mission

The mission of ISO is to promote the development of standardization and related activities with a view to facilitating the international exchange of goods and services, and to developing cooperation in the spheres of intellectual, scientific, technological and economic activity. ISO published its ISO 9000 standard in 1988. ISO 9000 consists of three standards for external quality assurance. These are ISO 9001, ISO 9002 and ISO 9003.

1. **ISO 9001:** It is an international quality management system. ISO 9001 is mainly related to the software industry. It lay down the standards for designing, developing, servicing, and producing of standard quality of goods. It is also applicable to most software development organizations.
2. **ISO 9002:** ISO 9002 is basically related to the manufacturing only and is silent on designing issues. Examples of this category of industries include steel and car manufacturing industries that buy the product and plant designs from external sources and are involved in only manufacturing those products. Therefore, ISO 9002 is not applicable to software development organizations.
3. **ISO 9003:** ISO 9003 standard applies to service industry. The organizations who are involved in only installation of product, services and testing of product are eligible for ISO 9003 certification.

10.5.3 Why ISO Certification is required by Software Industry?

There are several reasons why a software industry must get an ISO certification. Some of the important reasons are listed below:

1. It is sign of customer confidence. This certification has become a standard for international bidding.
2. It is a motivating factor to the business organizations.
3. It makes the processes more focused, efficient and cost effective.
4. It helps in designing high quality repeatable software products.
5. It highlights weaknesses and suggests corrective measures for improvements.
6. It facilitates the development of optimal process and total quality measurement.
7. It emphasizes the need of proper documentation.

10.5.4 How to Get ISO 9000 Certification?

An organization intending to obtain ISO 9000 certification applies to a ISO 9000 registrar for registration. The ISO 9000 registration process consists of the following stages: -

1. **Application:** Once an organization decides to go for ISO 9000 certification, it applies to a registrar for registration.
2. **Pre-assessment:** During this stage, the registrar makes a rough assessment of the organization.
3. **Document review and adequacy of audit:** During this stage, the registrar reviews the documents submitted by the organization and makes suggestions for possible improvements.
4. **Compliance audit:** During this stage, the registrar checks whether the suggestions made by it during review have been complied with by the organization or not.

5. **Registration:** The registrar awards the ISO 9000 certificate after successful completion of all previous phases.
6. **Continued surveillance:** The registrar continues to monitor the organization, though periodically.

10.5.5 Benefits of ISO 9000 Certification

Benefits from ISO 9000 certification to various organizations can be enumerated as under:

1. **Continuous improvement:** Business ISO 9000 forces an organization to focus on "how they do business". Each procedure and work instruction must be documented and thus, becomes the springboard for continuous Improvement.
2. **Eliminate variation:** Documented processes are the basis for repetition and help eliminate variation within the process. As variation is eliminated, efficiency improves. As efficiency improves, the cost of quality is reduced.
3. **Higher real and perceived quality:**
   (*i*) With the development of solid corrective and preventative measures, permanent, company-wide solutions to quality problems are found.
   (*ii*) This results in higher quality.
4. **Boost employee morale:** Employee morale is increased as they are asked to take control of their processes and document their work processes.
5. **Improved customer satisfaction:** Customer satisfaction, and more importantly customer loyalty, grows as a company transforms from a reactive organization to a pro-active, preventative organization. It becomes a company people want to do business with.
6. **Increased employee participation:** Reduced problems resulting from increased employee participation, involvement, awareness and systematic employee training.
7. **Better product and services:** Better products and services result from continuous improvement processes.
8. **Greater quality assurance:** Fosters the understanding that quality, in and of itself, is not limited to a quality department but is everyone's responsibility.
9. **Improved profit levels:** Improved profit levels result as productivity improves and rework costs are reduced.
10. **Improved communication:** Improved communications both internally and externally which improves quality, efficiency, on time delivery and customer/supplier relations.
11. **Reduced cost:** ISO standards results into a reduced cost of the product.
12. **Competitive edge:** In order to serve to deal with the increased business complexity and for offering higher customer services, ISO 9000 standards adds as competitive edge.

10.5.6 Limitation of ISO 9000 Certification

Limitations of ISO 9000 certification process are the following:

1. ISO 9000 does not provide any guideline for defining an appropriate process.
2. ISO 9000 certification process is not fool proof and no international accrediting agency exists.
3. ISO 9000 does not automatically lead to continuous process improvement, *i.e.,* it does not automatically lead to TQM.

10.5.7 Uses of ISO

ISO certification is used as a reference model for a contract between the external independent parties. It must be remembered that ISO certification does not guarantee a high quality product. It focuses mainly on the processes. ISO is now being used as the standard and basis of evaluation for international bidding. ISO 9000 specifies a set of guidelines for repeatable organizations. A repeatable organization is one where the production process is person independent.

10.5.8 Salient Features of ISO 9001 Requirements

The salient features of ISO 9001 requirements are as follows:

1. All documents concerned with the development of a software product should be properly managed, authorized and controlled.
2. Proper plans should be prepared and then progress against these plans should be monitored.
3. Important documents should be independently checked and reviewed for effectiveness and correctness
4. The product should be tested against its specification.

10.5.9 ISO 9126

Over the years, various lists of software quality characteristics have been put forward such as those of McCall, described above, and of Boehm. A difficulty has been the lack of agreed definitions of the qualities of good software. The term 'Maintainability' has been used, for example, to refer to the ease with which an error can be located and corrected in a piece of software, and also in a wider sense to include the ease of making any changes. For some 'robustness' has meant the software's tolerance of incorrect input, while for others it has meant the ability to change program code without introducing unexpected errors. ISO 9126 standard was published in 1991 to tackle the question of the definition of software quality. This 13 page document was designed as a foundation upon which further, more detailed, standards could be built.

ISO 9126 identifies six software quality characteristics:

- **Functionality:** Which covers the functions that a software product provides to satisfy user needs;
- **Reliability:** Which relates to the capability of the software to maintain its level of performance;
- **Usability:** Which relates to the effort needed to use the software;
- **Efficiency:** Which relates to the physical resources used when the software is executed;
- **Maintainability:** Which relates to the effort needed to the make changes to the software;
- **Portability:** Which relates to the ability of the software to be transferred to a different environment.

ISO 9126 sub-characteristics for each of the primary characteristics. It is indicative of the difficulties of gaining widespread agreement that these sub-characteristics are outside the main standards and are provided for ' information only'. They are useful as they clarify what is meant by the main characteristics.

Characteristic	Sub-characteristics
Functionality	Suitability
	Accuracy
	Interoperability
	Compliance
	Security

Compliance refers to the degree to which the software adheres to application-related standards or legal requirements. Typically these could be auditing requirements.

Interoperability and *security* are good illustrations of the efforts of ISO 9126 to clarify terminology. 'Interoperability' refers to the ability of the software to interact with other systems. The framers of ISO 9126 have chosen this word rather than *compatibility* because the latter cause's confusion with the characteristic referred to by ISO 9126 as 'replace ability' (see below).

Characteristic	Sub-characteristics
Reliability	Maturity
	Fault tolerance
	Recoverability

Maturity refers to the frequency of failure due to faults in a software product, the implication being that the more the software has been used, the more faults will have been uncovered and removed. It is also interesting to note that recoverability has been clearly distinguished from *security* which describes the control of access to a system.

Characteristic	Sub-characteristics
Usability	Understandability
	Learnability
	Operability

Understandability is a pretty clear quality to grasp, although the definitions 'attributes that bear on the users' efforts for recognizing the logical concept and its applicability in our view actually makes it less clear!

Note how *learnability* is distinguished from *operability*. A software tool could be easy to learn but time-consuming to use because, say, it uses a large number of nested menus. This might be fine for a package used intermittently, but not where the system is used for many hours each day. In this case *learnability* has been incorporated at the expense of *operability*.

Characteristic	Sub-characteristic
Efficiency	Time behavior
	Resource behavior
Maintainability	Analyzability
	Changeability
	Stability
	Testability

Analyzability is the quality that McCall called *diagnosability*, the ease with which the cause of a failure can be determined. *Changeability* is the quality that others have called *flexibility*: the latter name is perhaps a better one as *changeability* has a slightly different connotation in plain English- it might implies that the suppliers of the software are always changing it!

Stability, on the other hand, does not mean that the software never changes: It means that there is a low risk of a modification to the software having unexpected effects.

Characteristic	**Sub-characteristics**
Portability	Adaptability
	Installability
	Conformance
	Replaceability

Conformance, as distinguished from *compliance*, relates to those standards that have a bearing on portability. The use of a standard programming language common to many software / hardware environments would be an example of conformance. *Replaceability* refers to the factors that give 'upwards compatibility' between old software components and the new ones. *Downwards compatibility* is specifically excluded form the definition.

ISO 9126 provides guidelines for the use of the quality characteristics. Variation in the importance of different quality characteristics depending on the type of product is stressed. Thus reliability will be of particular concern with safety critical systems while efficiency will be important for some real time systems. For interactive end-user systems, the key quality might be usability. Once the requirements for the software product have been established the following steps are suggested:

1. Quality metrics selection
2. Ratings level definition
3. Assessment criteria definition.

10.5.10 Comparison between ISO 9000 Certification and SEI-CMM

Comparison of some of the key characteristics of ISO 9000 certification and SEI-CMM model are as follows:

1. The emphasis of the SEI-CMM is on continuous process improvement whereas ISO 9000 addresses the minimum criteria for an acceptable quality system.
2. The Capability Maturity Model (CMM) is a five-level framework for measuring software engineering practices, as they relate to process. On the other hand, ISO 9000 defines a minimum level of generic attributes for a quality management program.
3. ISO 9000 is awarded by an international standard body. Therefore, ISO 9000 certification can be quoted by an organization in official documents, in communication with external parties and in tender quotations. However, SEI-CMM assessment is purely for internal use.
4. ISO 9000 standards were basically designed to audit manufacturing/ service organizations whereas CMM was developed specifically for software industry and thus addresses several issues specific to software industry.
5. The SEI-CMM focuses strictly on software, while ISO 9000 has a much wider scope: hardware, software, processed materials and services.

6. SEI-CMM model provides a list of Key Process Areas (KPAs) on which on organization at any maturity level needs to concentrate to take it from one maturity level to the next. Thus, it provides a way for achieving gradual quality improvement.
7. SEI-CMM aims for achieving Total Quality Management (TQM), which is beyond quality assurance, whereas ISO 9000 aims at Level 3 (Defined Level) of SEI-CMM model.
8. ISO 9000 requires that procedures for handling, storage, packaging, and delivery be established and maintained, while replication, delivery and installation are not covered in the SEI-CMM.
9. ISO 9000 requires that the product be identified and traceable during all stages of production, delivery, and installation while SEI-CMM covers this clause primarily in Software Configuration Management.

11

Software Configuration Management

11.1 SOFTWARE CONFIGURATION MANAGEMENT

Software configuration management deals with effectively tracking and controlling the configuration of a software product during its life cycle.

Before we discuss configuration management, we must be clear about what exactly is meant by a ***version*** and a ***revision of a software product***. A new ***version*** of software is created when there is significant change in functionality, technology, or the hardware it runs on, etc. On the other hand, a new ***release*** is created if there is only a bug fix, minor enhancements to the functionality, usability, etc.

The configuration management team is responsible for assuring that each version or release is correct and stable before it is released for use, and that changes are made accurately and promptly. ***Accuracy*** is critical, because we want to avoid generating new faults while correcting existing ones. Similarly, ***promptness*** is important, because fault detection and correction are proceeding at the same time that the test team searches for additional faults. Thus, those who are trying to repair system faults should work with components and documentation that reflect the current state of the system.

Thus ***"Configuration management is the art of identifying, organizing and controlling modifications to the software being built by a programming team. The goal is to maximize productivity by minimizing mistakes."***

OR

Software Configuration Management (SCM) is a set of activities designed to control change by identifying the work products that are likely to change, establishing relationships among them, defining mechanisms different versions of these work products, controlling the changes imposed and auditing and reporting on the changes made.

Configuration management procedures define how to record and process proposed system changes, how to relate these to system components and the methods used to identify different versions of the system. Configuration management tools are used to store versions of system components, build systems from these components and track the release of system versions to customers.

The IEEE defines SCM as "the process of identifying and defining the items in the system, controlling the change of these items throughout their life cycle, recording and reporting the status of items and change requests, and verifying the completeness and correctness of items.

Figure 11.1 shows a simple configuration management based rebuilding and deployment process

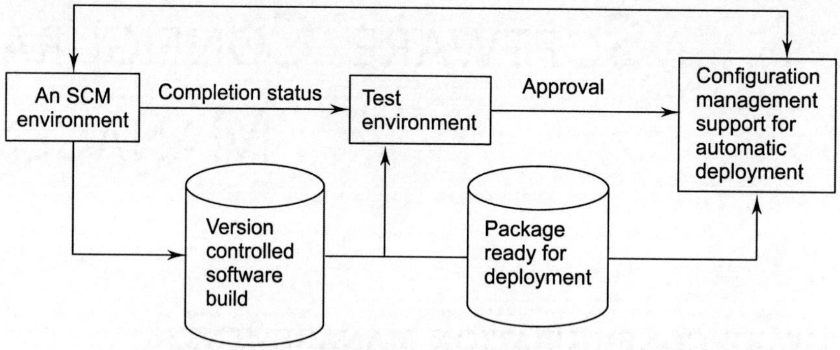

Fig. 11.1 Simple configuration management environment

11.1.1 Software Configuration Management Activities

Configuration management is carried out through three principal activities:

1. Configuration identification,
2. Configuration control,
3. Configuration accounting.

Briefly these three activities can be described as:

Configuration identification: Which parts of the system must be kept track of?

Configuration control: Ensures that changes to a component happen smoothly.

Configuration accounting: Keeps track of what has been changed, when, and why.

1. **Configuration identification:** The project manager normally classifies the object associated with a software development into three main categories: *controlled, pre-controlled, and uncontrolled.* Controlled objects are those, which are already put under configuration control. You must follow some formal procedures to change them. Pre controlled objects are not yet under configuration control, but will eventually be under configuration control. Uncontrolled objects are not and will not be subject to configuration control. Controllable objects include both controlled and pre controlled object. Typical controllable objects include:
   - Requirements specification document
   - Designing documents
   - Tools used to build the system, such as compliers, linkers, lexical analyzers, parsers, etc.
   - Source code for each module
   - Test cases
   - Problem reports.

   Configuration management plan written during the project-planning phase lists all controlled objects.

2. **Configuration control:** Configuration control is the process of managing changes to controlled objects. The configuration control system prevents unauthorized changes to any controlled object. In order to change a controlled object such a module, a developer can get a private copy of the module by a reserve operation (see Fig. 11.2). Configuration management tools allow only one person to reserve a module at any time. Once an object is reserved it does not allow anyone else to reserve this module until the reserved module is restored. Thus, by preventing more than one engineer to simultaneously reserve a module, the problems associated with concurrent access are solved.

   The CCB is a group of people responsible for configuration management. The CCB evaluates the request based on its effect on the project, and the benefit due to change.

   An important reason for configuration control is people need a stable environment to develop a software product.

   Suppose you are trying to integrate module A, with the modules B and C, you cannot make progress if developer of module C keeps changing it; this is especially frustrating if a change to module C forces you to recompile A.

   As soon as a document under configuration control is updated, the updated version is frozen and is called a baseline, as shown in Fig. 11.2.

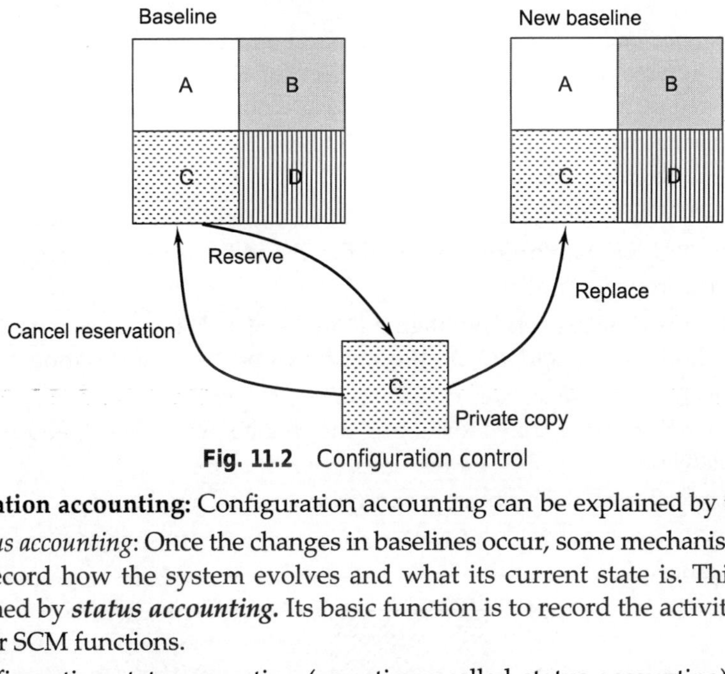

Fig. 11.2 Configuration control

3. **Configuration accounting:** Configuration accounting can be explained by two concepts:
   (*i*) *Status accounting*: Once the changes in baselines occur, some mechanisms must be used to record how the system evolves and what its current state is. This task is accomplished by ***status accounting.*** Its basic function is to record the activities related to the other SCM functions.

   Configuration status reporting (sometimes called status accounting) is an SCM task that answers the following questions:
   - What happened?
   - Who did it?
   - When did it happen?
   - What else will be affected?

   The flow of information for Configuration Status Reporting (CSR) is illustrated in figure of change control process above. Each time an SCI is assigned new or updated identification, a CSR entry is made. Each time a change is approved by the CCA (*i.e.*, an ECO is issued), a CSR entry is made. Each time a configuration audit is conducted, the results are reported as part of the CSR task. The key elements under status accounting are shown in Fig. 11.3.

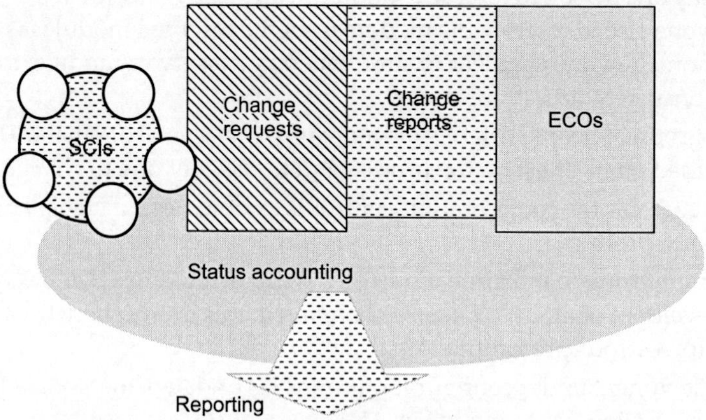

Fig. 11.3 Status accounting

(*ii*) *Configuration audit*: A software configuration audit complements the formal technical review by assessing a configuration object for characteristics that are generally not considered during review. The audit asks and answers the following questions:

- Has the change specified in the ECO been made? Have any additional modifications been incorporated?
- Has a formal technical review been conducted to assess technical correctness?
- Has the software process been followed and have software engineering standard been properly applied?
- Has the change been "highlighted" in the SCI? Have the change date and change author been specified? Do the attributes of the configuration object reflect the change?
- Have SCM procedures for noting the change, recording it, and reporting it been followed?
- Have all related SCIs been properly updated?

SCM Audit revolves around the software configuration items, change requests and software quality assurance plan.

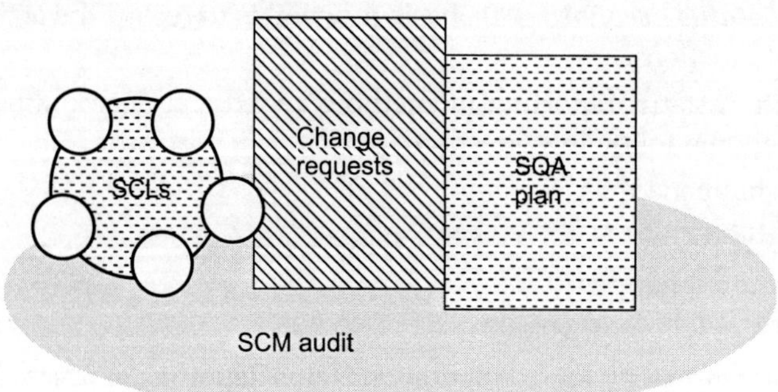

Fig. 11.4 Configuration accounting

11.2 SCM ROLES

Software Configuration Management plays the following vital roles in different areas:

11.2.1 Baseline

In the context of software engineering, a baseline is a milestone in the development of software. A baseline is marked by the delivery of one or more software configuration items that have been approved as a technical review. For example, the elements of a design model have been documented and reviewed errors are found and corrected. Once all parts of the model have reviewed, corrected and then approved, the design model becomes a baseline. Further changes to the program architecture (documented in the design model) can be made only after each has been evaluated and approved although baselines can be defined at any level of detail.

A baseline is a fixed schedule which represents the standard that is used to measure the performance of the project. Everytime a change to the scope of the project is approved, the schedule should be adjusted and a new revision of the baseline should be used instead. Many project management software packages have a feature which allows the project manager to maintain a baseline schedule and track revisions to it. Thus Baseline

- Is a tested and certified version of a software system representing milestones:
  - Only approved items are accepted into baseline
  - Baseline may have certain build-sequences associated with it.
- Is designated at any agreed time from which the product changes require justification?
  - Baseline + approved changes = current configuration.
- Is modified only through well-controlled procedures?
- Also serves as the basis for further development.
- Are normally established at the end of a successful milestone review?
- Are also connected to milestone during integration?

Baselines are typically agreed on between developers, customers, and managers, and are controlled and maintained by a software configuration management board. Before a software configuration item becomes a baseline, changes may be made quickly and informally. However, once a baseline is established, changes can be made, but a specific, formal procedure must be applied to evaluate and verify each change. The baselines provide a development and test environment for the new software components undergoing development and integration.

Baseline commonly used by the department of defense are functional, allocated, and product baselines. Baselines are frequent deliverables and often provide the basis for further work.

11.2.1.1 Definitions

Baseline refers to a set of configuration items which together depict a project milestone (or a product version), *e.g.*, a particular version of MS-Excel, MS-Word, MS-PowerPoint, etc., may together constitute MS-office.

OR

A baseline is an agreed on technical configuration at some point in the software project.

OR

A baseline is a work product that has been formally reviewed and agreed upon and that can be changed only through formal change control procedures.

OR

The **IEEE (IEEE Std. no 612.12-1990)** defines a baseline as.

"A specification or product that has been formally reviewed and agreed to by responsible management, that there after serves as the basis for further development, and can be changed only through formal change control procedures."

OR

A baseline is a software configuration management concept that helps you to control change without seriously impeding justifiable change.

11.2.1.2 When to do Baselining?

Whenever there is a major change in requirements that require the entire life cycle to be repeated, the baseline is changed. Typical application development baselines are:

- Initial baseline
- SRS baseline
- Design baseline
- Integration baseline
- Acceptance baseline.

Typical conversion project baselines are:

- Initial source baseline
- Filtered source baseline
- Converted baseline
- Release baseline.

Typical maintenance baseline:

- Release baseline.

11.2.1.3 Baseline Control

In many environments, baselines are controlled such that certain subsequent activities against work product in that baseline are either prohibited or permitted. These activities are carefully selected and controlled, and again, depending upon the configuration management system, are also monitored. Consequently, baselines are ordinarily subjected to configuration management's audits. Audits may include an examination of specific action performed against the baseline, identification of individuals involved in any action, an evaluation of change within the baseline, certification for approval, accounting, and metric collection, comparison to another baseline, or all of these.

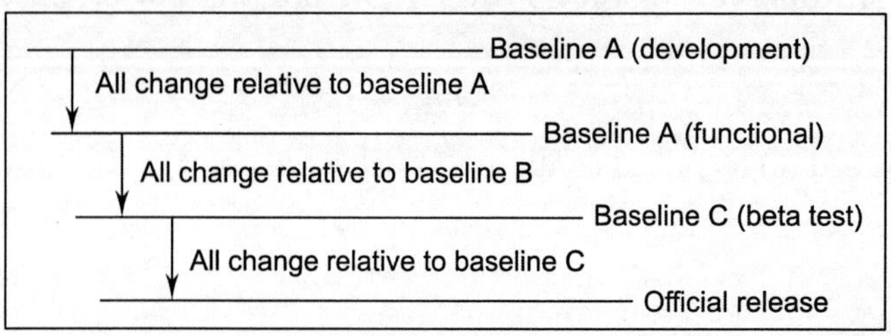

11.2.1.4 Baseline Schematic Diagram

The pictorial view of a baseline is shown in the Fig. 11.5.

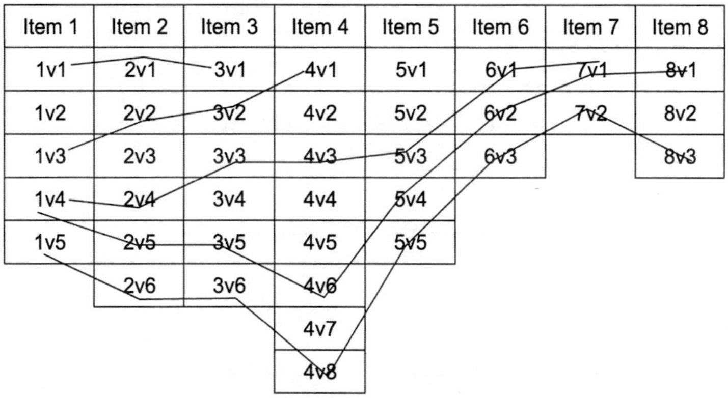

Fig. 11.5 Baseline schematic diagram

11.2.1.5 Problem in a Baseline

Figure 11.6 shows the Problem which occur in baseline

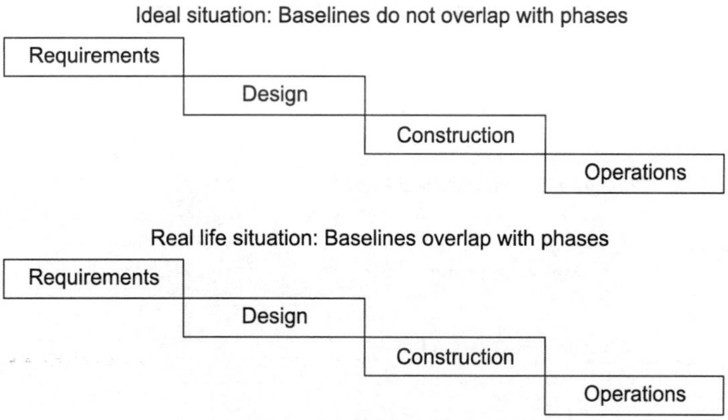

Fig. 11.6 Problem in a baseline

11.2.2 Change Control Process

At any moment, the configuration management team must know the state of any component or document in the system. Consequently, configuration management should emphasize communication among those whose actions affect the system. Cashman and Holt (1980) suggest that we always know the answers to the following questions:

- **Synchronization:** When was the change made?
- **Identification:** Who made the change?
- **Naming:** What components of the system were changed?
- **Authentication:** Was the change made correctly?
- **Authorization:** Who authorized that the change be made?
- **Routing:** Who was notified of the change?
- **Cancellation:** Who can cancel the request for change?

- **Delegation:** Who is responsible for the change?
- **Valuation:** What is the priority of the change?

Notice that these questions are management questions, not technical ones. We must use procedures to manage change carefully.

Change control combines human procedures and automated tools to provide a mechanism for the control of change. The change control process is illustrated schematically in Fig. 11.7.

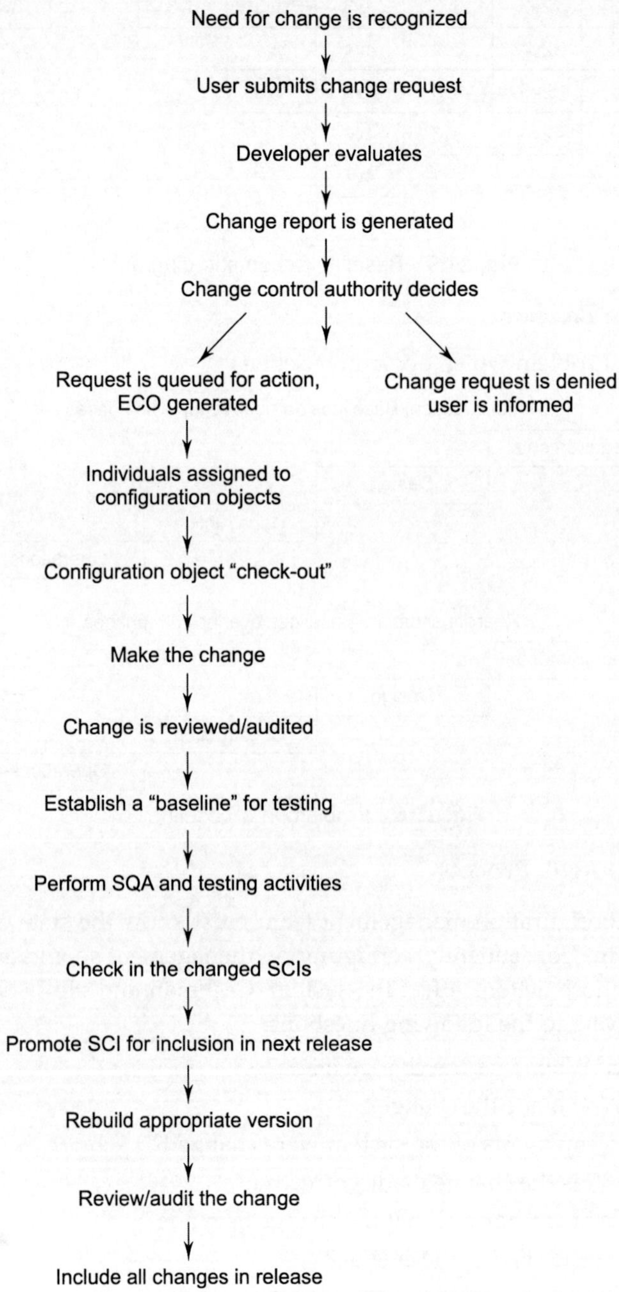

Fig. 11.7 Change control process

11.2.3 Change Request Management (CRM)

We need to manage the change request that is initiated by the customer. This handling of request is known as change management or CRM.

In case of a complex system with high reliability, the change request has many pages of request and thus need to be approved by several managers and takes more time. Whereas in case of a simple tool, informal communication may be sufficient. In both the causes, the change process involves the following steps:

Step 1. The change is requested. This can be done by a user or a developer.

Step 2. The request is then assessed against the projects goals. In large projects, this is done by control broad whereas in smaller projects, this is done by the Project Manager [PM]. This may be done by using Cost Benefit Analysis (CBA) or by finding out the impact of change on the rest of the product.

Step 3. It is then decided whether to accept or reject this change request.

Step 4. If accepted then the changes is planned and prioritized. It is then implemented by the developer.

Step 5. This implemented changes is then audited. This is done by quality control team.

11.2.4 Software Version Control

A configuration for a particular system is sometimes called a ***version***. Thus, the initial delivery of a software package may consist of several versions, one for each platform or situation in which the software will be used. For example, aircraft software may be built so that version 1 runs on Navy planes, version 2 runs on Air Force planes, and version 3 runs on commercial airliners.

A new ***release*** of the software is an improved system intended to replace the old one. Often, software systems are described as version n, release m, or as version n.m, where the number reflects the system's position as it grows and matures. Version n is sometimes intended to replace version n-1, and release m supersedes m-1.

11.2.4.1 Version and Release Management

Version and release management are the processes of identifying and keeping track of different versions and releases of a system. New system version should always be created by the CM team rather than the system developers, even when they are not intended for external release. This makes it easier to maintain consistency in the configuration database as only the CM team can change version information.

A ***system version*** is an instance of a system that differs, in some way, from other instances. New versions of the system may have different functionality, performance or may repair system faults. Some versions may be functionally equivalent but designed for different hardware or software configurations. If there are only small differences between versions, one of these is sometimes called a variant of the other.

A ***system release*** is a version that is distributed to customers. Each system release should either include new functionality or be intended for a different hardware platform. There are always many more versions of a system than releases as version are created within an organization for internal development or testing that are never released to customers.

11.2.4.2 Version Control

During the process of software evolution, many objects are produced, for example files, electronic documents, paper documents, source code, executable code and bitmap graphics. A version control tool is the first stage towards being able to manage multiple versions. Once it is in place, a detailed record of every version of the software must be kept. This comprises the:

- Name of each source code component, including the variations and revisions,
- The versions of the various compliers and linkers used,
- The name of the software staff who constructed the component,
- The date and the time at which it was constructed.

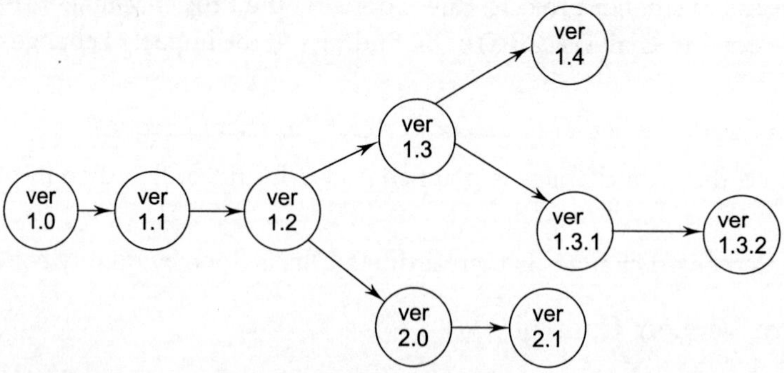

Fig. 11.8 An evolutionary graph for a different version of an item

The above evolutionary graph (Fig. 11.8) depicts the evolution of a configuration item during the development life cycle. The initial version of the item is given version number Ver 1.0. Subsequent changes to the item which could be mostly fixing bugs or adding minor functionality is given as Ver 1.1 and Ver 1.2. After that, a major modification to Ver 1.2 is given a number Ver 2.0 at the same time; a parallel version of the same item without the major modification is maintained and given a version number 1.3.

Commercial tools are available for version control, which perform one or more of following tasks:

- Source code control
- Revision control
- Concurrent version control.

There are many commercial tools like Rational Clear Case, Microsoft Visual Source Safe and a number of other commercial tools to help version control.

12

SOFTWARE RISK MANAGEMENT

Risk analysis and management are a series of steps that help a software team to understand and manage uncertainty. Many problems can plague a software project. A risk is a potential problem-it might happen, it might not. But, regardless of the outcome, it's a really good idea to identify it, assess its probability of occurrence, estimate its impact, and establish a contingency plan should the problem actually occur.

12.1 RISK

Risk is defined as an exposure to the chance of injury or loss. That is risk implies that there is a possibility that something negative may happen. In the context of software projects, negative implies that there is an adverse effect on cost, quality, or schedule.

12.1.1 Definitions

Risk: An uncertain event or condition that, if it occurs, has a positive or negative effect on a project's objectives.

OR

Risk can be defined as the combination of the probability of an event and its consequences. **(ISO/IEC Guide 73)**

OR

Risk can be defined as any event that is likely to adversely affect a project's ability to achieve the defined objectives.

OR

A risk is any possible situation that is not planned for but that, if it occurs, is likely to divert the project from its planned result.

OR

Risk is defined as "the possibility of suffering harm or loss; danger."

OR

Risk is "the chance of exposure to the adverse consequences of future events".

OR

Risk is "the uncertainty or lack of complete knowledge of set of all possible future events".

OR

The basic dictionary definition says that risk is" the possibility of loss or injury."

OR

In software engineering risk is a measure of the inability to achieve overall program objectives within defined cost, schedule, and technical constraints.

OR

Risk is, thus an unexpected event that produces an adverse effect during SDLC. It is the combination of constraints and uncertainties. Consider the graph of Fig. 12.1.

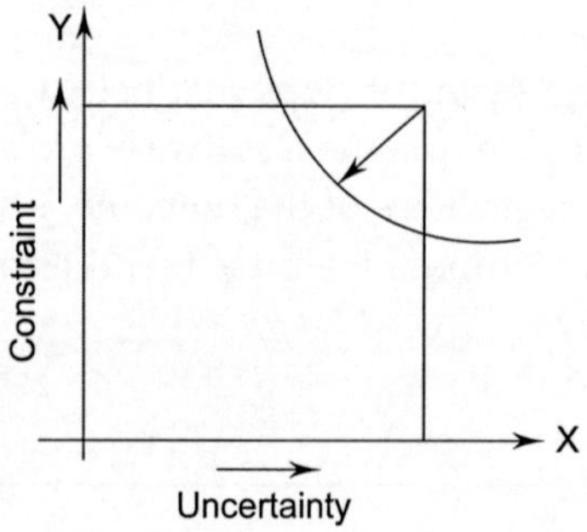

Fig. 12.1 Risk

12.1.2 Types of Risks

There are three types of risks, which are discussed as follows:

1. **Product risks:** Product risks are risks, which affect the quality or performance of the software being developed. This originates from the conditions such as unstable requirement specifications, not being able to meet the design specifications affecting software performance and uncertain test specifications. In view of the software product risk, there is a risk of losing the business and facing strained customer relations. For example CASE tools under performance.
2. **Business risks:** Business risks are risks, which affect the organization developing or procuring the software. For example, technology change and product competition. The top five business risks are:
   - Building on excellent product or system that no one really wants (market risks).
   - Building a product that no longer fits into the overall business strategy for the company (strategic risk).
   - Building a product that the sales force doesn't understand how to sell.
   - Losing the support of senior management due to a change in focus or a change in people (management risk).
   - Losing budgetary or personnel commitment (budget risks).

3. **Project risks:** Project risks are risks, which affect the project schedule or resources.

   This risk occurs due to conditions and constraints about resources, relationship with vendors and contractors, unreliable vendors and lack of organizational support. Funding is the significant project risk the management has to face. It occurs due to initial budgeting constraints and unreliable customer payments. For example Staff turnover, management change, hardware uninvertibility.

12.1.3 Sources of Risks

There are two major sources of risk, which are as follows:

1. **Generic risks:** Generic risks are the risks, which are common to all s/w projects. For example, Requirement misunderstanding, allowing insufficient time for testing, is losing key personnel etc.
2. **Project-specific risks:** A vendor may be promising to deliver particular software by a particular date, but he is unable to do it.

12.1.4 Risk Reducing Ways

In general there are four main ways to reducing risks:

1. **Risk avoidance:** don't do something which might be risky. This is an obvious way to reduce risk, but it also reduces possibility of gains.
2. **Risk reduction:** put measures in place to act against the risk. For example, install a burglar alarm to reduce the risk of robbery in a building.
3. **Risk retention:** accept the consequences of a particular risk. Normally only suitable for low-level risks, it can be more cost-effective than insuring against them. For example, accepting an excess charge on a typical car insurance.
4. **Risk transfer:** getting somebody else to take the risk. The most obvious example is taking out insurance, but you may also be able to arrange risk transfer by writing it into a contract with, for instance, a subcontractor.

12.1.5 Components of Risk

Risk has two main components:

- The probability of failing to achieve a particular outcome and.
- The consequences of failing to achieve that outcome.

For example, a common risk for many software projects is that they fail to deliver acceptable systems within schedule and budget.

12.1.6 Characteristics of Project Risks

Project risk is characterized by the following:

- Uncertainty is involved in projects.
- A loss is associated with it (life, money, property, reputation and so forth.)
- It is manageable in the sense that human action can be applied to change its form and degree.

12.1.7 Nature of Risk

Table 12.1 gives broadly the types of risk that are common in software development scenarios. The nature of risk and its class are, however, fixed, and they are stated below:

- **Technology risks:** These risks fall in the domain of hardware, software and network communication technology, which are subject to continuous improvement and may lead to obsolescence.
- **People risk:** These risks are associated with persons in the teams and risk concerns availability, capability, skills, maturity and so on.
- **Organizational risks:** These are in the area of development organization and customer organization. The environment in both the organizations is a matter of concern.
- **Requirement risks:** This is about clarity, completeness and confirmation of the requirement by the end users and customer. It is about the volatility of the requirement.
- **Estimation risks:** Not being able to judge in precise terms the component of the software, reusability and system characteristic affecting the size, effort and schedule.

Table 12.1 Risk and risk types

Risk	*Risk Type*	*Explanation*
Manpower	Project	Sudden turnover, internal transfers not materialized
Capability	Product	Not sure of capability and maturity of the team
Requirement Specifications	Product, and Process	Customer and end users not sure about the requirement or problem, affecting the design, performance and quality.
Problem	Project	Not sure about the development platform or deployment platform, and its configuration.
Requirements Change	Product and Process	Number of changes more than expected at a very late stage in the development cycle.
Size	Project	Size (loc or FPC) not estimated correctly.
Technology	Project and Process	New technology affecting the application.
Delays	Project	Delays in delivery of tools ,software products, customer confirmations etc.

The risks discussed can be categorized into three categories, namely, known risks, predictable risks and unpredictable risks.

Known risks are the ones that are present in some degree in all cases. The examples are estimation, requirement and people risks. With proper analysis, they can be identified, assessed and mitigated.

Predictable risks are the ones that can be identified based on past experience in development. The examples are people, organizational and technology risks.

The unpredictable risks are the ones that appear suddenly and out of the blue. They are technology, obsolescence, business and management change.

12.1.8 Examples of Risks

1. Improper use of technology
2. Repetition of errors.
3. Cascading of errors.
4. Illogical processing.
5. Incorrect entry of data.
6. Inability to control technology.
7. Inability to react quickly.
8. Concentration of responsibilities.
9. Uncontrolled system access.
10. Program errors.
11. Lack of IT personnel.
12. Unrealistic schedules and budget.
13. Gold plating—scrubbing requirements, designing to cost.
14. Rapid technological changes.
15. Inexperienced staff and so on.

12.2 RISK BREAKDOWN STRUCTURE

As a project unfolds, the project management team and or the project management team leader will find themselves in positions in which they realize that a particular component as to the project and or a particular facet of that project does in fact come with a set or series of inherent risk. When attempting to organize any and all risks for the purposes of attempting to determine what the best strategy in dealing with them may be, it is often helpful to utilize this tool that is known as the ***risk breakdown structure***.

The risk breakdown structure is specifically a tool that represents an organized description of any known project risks that are arranged by a number of categories and characteristics. It will display all of the risks as well as some of their possible causes. This tool, when utilized by the project management team and or the project management team leader, is often broken down and tailored by project type.

Risks are then prioritized according to their potential implications for affecting the Project's success. Other things to take into account are stakeholder's risk tolerance levels, reporting formats and how you will track the risks. The next step in the process will be Risk Identification.

Risk Breakdown Structures will vary between projects. One benefit of doing one is to remind those people engaged in the Risk Identification process of areas to think about. It will also be an input to Qualitative Risk Analysis where probabilities and impacts are assigned. The impacts can be numerical or High, Medium, Low. Instead of going through big spreadsheet with hundreds of verbose entries about risks, RBS provides-a pictorial representation of related items through tree structure as an excellent way of getting the whole picture in a single place for effective communication, management and governance.

By using the RBS, you can also identify risk dependencies, understand the risk exposure to a project, and determine the root cause of risks. The RBS is a very useful tool for project managers.

12.2.1 Definitions

David Hillson defines Risk Breakdown Structure (RBS) as:

"A source-oriented grouping of project risks that organizes and defines the total risk exposure of the project. Each descending level represents an increasingly detailed definition of sources of risk to the project."

OR

Risk Breakdown Structure (RBS) is a hierarchically organized depiction of the identified project risks arranged by category.

OR

RBS is a tool through which we can group project risks and organize them in categories. Each category is then broken down into levels. Every level details out the source of risks to the project.

12.2.2 Advantages of RBS

RBS has lot of advantages—here are few:

1. RBS give structured approach to risk identification through which all risk areas are explored without fail.
2. Grouping risks by common root causes can lead to developing effective risk responses.
3. RBS helps in risk assessment by interviewing or meetings with participants selected for their familiarity with a specific risk category.
4. RBS give greater ability monitor and control risks identified classified under the same area or root.

12.2.3 Example of RBS

Risk breakdown structure is a hierarchical list of risks. It helps to identify and manage project risks. In Risky Project you can define different risk breakdown structures at the project level and for each separate task or resource. Each risk is defined by its chance of occurrence, outcome (increase duration, cost, cancel task, etc.) and time of occurrence.

Risk breakdown structure is implemented with Global Risks view as well as Local Risks. Risky Projects also has a number of risk templates. Risks templates are standard risk breakdown structures that allow you to quickly and simplify add risks to tasks and projects. In addition, it is easy to create your own templates, which you can use for your own projects.

12.2.3.1 Generic Example of a Risk Breakdown Structure (RBS)

The following Table 12.2 shows an RBS that can be used for any project:

Notice how each risk area is systematically broken down into levels. This is the reason why it is easier to identify, analyze and communicate risks impacting your project. As you go deeper into each level, you can identify potential risk triggers. In turn, this helps you to respond to risks effectively. In addition, the total risk exposure to the project is easier to understand and hence easier to plan for.

Note: There is no such thing as a one-fits-all project RBS. You will need to customize the generic RBS as per your industry, organization, and type of project.

Table 12.2 RBS for generic project (Hall and Hulett,2002)

Level 0	*Level 1*	*Level 2*	*Level 3*
Project risk	Management	Corporate	History/experience/culture
			Organisational stability
			Financial
			...etc...
		Customer & stakeholder	History/experience/culture
			Contractual
			Requirements definition & stability
			...etc...
	External	Natural environment	Physical environment
			Facilities/site
			Local services
			...etc...
		Cultural	Political
			Legal/regulatory
			Interest groups
			...etc...
		Economic	Labour market
			Labour conditions
			Financial market
			...etc...
	Technology	Requirements	Scope unvertainty
			Conditions of use
			Complexity
			...etc...
		Performance	Technology maturity
			Technology limits
			...etc...
		Application	Organisational experience
			Personnel skill sets & experience
			Physical resources
			...etc...

12.2.3.2 Software Development Example of RBS

The following Table 12.3 shows the Risk Breakdown Structures for Software Development for a Risky Project:

Table 12.3 RBS for software development

S.No	*Categories of Risk*	*Sub-Categories*
1.	Risks affecting whole company/division	Budgetary Risks Environmental Risks Legal Risks
2.	Resource Risks	Lack of knowledge of the specific area Lack of knowledge of tools Staff turnover Risks related to the competence of the management
3.	Requirement/Client Relationship	New or updated requirement Risks related to interpretation of requirements Results are not accepted by the client Risks related to communication with the client
4.	Risks related to hardware or IT infrastructure	Hardware performance or other parameters are not suitable for the project Risks related to communication infrastructure
5.	Problems with development tools	Selected software tools are not suitable for particular task Selected third party are not suitable for particular task
6.	Other Risks	Critical bugs are discovered Configuration management issues Chosen software architecture is not suitable

12.3 RISK MANAGEMENT

Risk management is the area that tries to ensure that the impact of risks on cost, quality, and schedule is minimal.

Risk Management is a scientific process based on the application of game theory, decision theory, probability theory and utility theory. The Software Engineering Institute (SEI) classifies the risk hierarchy as shown in Fig. 12.2

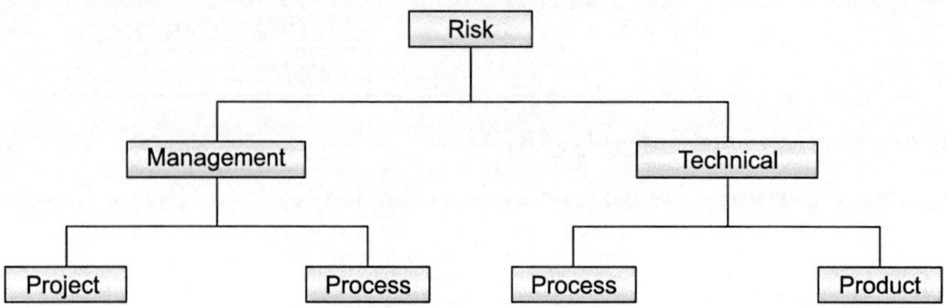

Fig. 12.2 Risk hierarchy

Risk scenarios may emerge out of management challenges and technical challenges in achieving specific goals and objectives.

Risk Management must be performed regularly throughout the achievement life cycle. Risks are dynamic, as they change over time. Risk Management should not be regarded as an activity integral to the main process of achieving specific goals and objectives. Risk and its management should not be treated as an activity outside the main process of achievement. Risk is managed best when Risk Management is implemented as a mainstream function in the software development and goal achievement process. Different perspectives of various authors and organizations about Risk Management are

Capers Jones's (1998) Perspective: "Large software projects will never be without some risk, but if risks can be brought down to acceptable levels, that will be a good beginning"

Peter's Kulik (1996) Perspective: "Tomorrow's problem are today's risks-Software risk management is becoming more and more widely implemented because of its proven results to identify and eliminate risks before they become problems"

The National Aeronautics and Space Administration (NASA), 1999 Perspective:

"Software risk management is important because it helps avoid disasters, rework and overkill, but more importantly because it stimulates win-win situation".

12.3.1 Definitions

Risk management is the identification, assessment, and prioritization of risks followed by coordinated and economical application of resources to minimize, monitor, and control the probability and/or impact of unfortunate events or to maximize the realization of opportunities.

OR

Project risk management is the art and science of identifying, assigning and responding to the project risks throughout the life of a project with the best interest of meeting project objectives.

OR

Risk Management is an organized means of identifying risk factors (risk identification), developing and selecting risk handing options (risk analysis), and mitigating risk when they become problems (risk handling).

OR

Risk management is the process of identifying, assessing, evaluating risk exposure, prioritizing the risk incidences, and developing risk monitoring, management and mitigation plan.

OR

Project risk management is the systematic process of identifying, analyzing, controlling and responding to risk through a project.

OR

Risk management is the process of identifying, addressing and mitigating the risks before they damage our project.

OR

Risk management is scientific process based on the application of game theory, decision theory, probability theory and utility theory.

OR

Software Risk management is a proactive approach for minimizing the uncertainty and potential loss associated with a project.

12.3.2 Risk Management Objectives

The objective of risk management is:

- To ensure that the risks facing the business are appropriately managed. This gives stakeholders confidence to deal with or invest in the business.
- To identifying and respond to potential problems with sufficient lead time to avoid a crisis.
- To provide insights to support decision-making.
- Increase the probability and impact of positive events, and
- Decrease the probability and impact of adverse events.
- To identify and prioritize potential risk events.
- To help in developing risk management strategies and risk management plans.
- Use established risk management methods, tools and techniques to assist in the analysis and reporting of identified risk events.
- Find ways to identify and evaluate risks.

12.3.3 Risk Management Principles

The International Organization for Standardization identifies the following principles of risk management:

Risk management should:

- create value.
- be an integral part of organizational processes.
- be part of decision-making.
- explicitly address uncertainty.
- be systematic and structured.
- be based on the best available information.
- be tailored.
- take into account human factors.
- be transparent and inclusive.
- be dynamic, iterative and responsive to change.
- be capable of continual improvement and enhancement.

12.3.4 Risk Management Activities as Applied to Project Management

In project management, risk management includes the following activities:

- Planning how risk will be managed in the particular project. Plan should include risk management tasks, responsibilities, activities and budget.

- Assigning a risk officer—a team member other than a project manager who is responsible for foreseeing potential project problems. Typical characteristic of risk officer is a healthy skepticism.
- Maintaining live project risk database. Each risk should have the following attributes: opening date, title, short description, probability and importance. Optionally a risk may have an assigned person responsible for its resolution and a date by which the risk must be resolved.
- Creating anonymous risk reporting channel. Each team member should have possibility to report risk that he/she foresees in the project.
- Preparing mitigation plans for risks that are chosen to be mitigated. The purpose of the mitigation plan is to describe how this particular risk will be handled—what, when, by who and how will it be done to avoid it or minimize consequences if it becomes a liability.
- Summarizing planned and faced risks, effectiveness of mitigation activities, and effort spent for the risk management.

12.3.5 Risk Management Categories

Risk management plays an important role in ensuring that the software product is error free. Firstly, risk management takes care that the risk is avoided, and if it is not avoidable, then the risk is detected, controlled and finally recover.

A priority is given to risk and the highest priority risk is handled first. Various factors of the risk are who are the involved team members, what hardware and software items are needed, where, when and why are resolved during risk management. The risk manager does scheduling of risks. Risk management can be further categorized as follows:

1. **Risk avoidance**
    - Risk anticipation
    - Risk tools.
2. **Risk detection**
    - Risk analysis
    - Risk category
    - Risk prioritization.
3. **Risk control**
    - Risk pending
    - Risk resolution
    - Risk not solvable.
4. **Risk recovery**
    - Full
    - Partial
    - Extra/alternate feature.

Figure 12.3 depicts a risk manager tool.

From the Fig. 12.3, it is clear that the first phase is to avoid risk by anticipating and using tools from previous project history. In case there is no risk, risk manager halts. In case there is risk, detection is done using various risk analysis techniques and further prioritizing risks. In the next phase, risk is controlled by pending risks, resolving risks and in the worst case, (if risk is not solved) lowering the priority. Lastly, risk recovery is done fully, partially or an alternate solution is found.

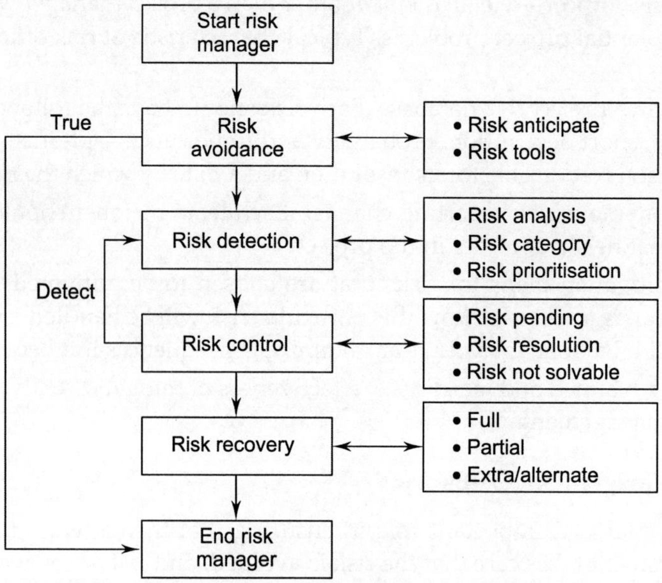

Fig. 12.3 Risk manager tool

1. **Risk avoidance:**
   - **Risk anticipation:** Various risk anticipation rules are listed according to standards from previous projects, experience, and also as mentioned by the project manager.
   - **Risk tools:** Risk tools are used to test whether the software is risk free. The tools have built-in-data base of available risk areas and can be updated depending upon the type of project.
2. **Risk detection:** The risk detection algorithm detects a risk and it can be categorically stated as:
   - **Risk analysis:** In this phase, the risk is analyzed with various hardware and software parameters as probabilistic occurrence (pr), weight factor (wf) (hardware resources, lines of code, persons), risk exposure (pr * wf). Table 12.4 depicts a risk analysis table

Table 12.4 Risk analysis table

S.No.	*Risk Name*	*Probability of Occurrence (pr)*	*Weight Factor (wf)*	*Risk Exposure (pr*wf)*
1.	Stack overflow	5	15	75
2.	No password forgot option	7	20	140
......	......	......	......	......

Maximum value of risk exposure indicates that the problem has to be solved as soon as possible and be given high priority. A risk analysis table is maintained as shown above.

   - **Risk category:** Risk identification can be from various factors like persons involved in the team, management issues, customer specification and feedback, environment, commercial, technology, etc. Once proper category is identified, priority is given depending upon the urgency of the product.

- **Risk prioritization:** Depending upon the entries of the risk analysis table, the maximum risk exposure is given high priority and has to be solved first.

3. **Risk control:** Once the prioritization is done, the next step is to control various risks as follows:
    - **Risk pending:** According to the priority, low priority risks are pushed at the end of the queue with a view of various resources (hardware, man power, software) and in case it takes more time their priority is made higher.
    - **Risk resolution:** Risk manager makes a strong resolve how to solve the risk.
    - **Risk elimination:** This action leads to serious error in software.
    - **Risk transfer:** If the risk is transferred to some part of the module, then risk analysis table entries get modified. Thereby again risk manager will control high priority risk.
    - **Disclosures:** Announce the risk of less priority to the customer or display message box as a warning. And thereby the risk is left out to the user, such that he should take proper steps during data entry, etc.
    - **Risk not solvable:** If a risk takes more time and more resources, then it is dealt in its totality in the business aspects of the organization and thereby it is notified to the customer, and the team member proposes an alternate solution. There is a slight variation in the customer specification after consultation.
4. **Risk Recovery**
    - **Full:** The risk analysis table is scanned and if the risk is fully solved, then corresponding entry is deleted from the table.
    - **Partial:** The risk analysis table is scanned and due to partially solved risks, the entries in the table are updated and thereby priorities are also updated.
    - **Extra/alternate features:** Sometimes it is difficult to remove some risks, and in that case, we can add a few extra features, which solve the problem. Therefore, a bit of coding is done to get away from the risk. This is later documented or notified to the customer.

12.3.6 The Structure and Administration of Risk Management

12.3.6.1 Role of the Risk Management Function

Depending on the size of the organization the risk management function may range from a single risk champion, a part-time risk manager, to a full-scale risk management department. The role of the Risk Management function should include the following:

- setting policy and strategy for risk management
- primary champion of risk management at strategic and operational level
- building a risk aware culture within the organization including appropriate education
- establishing internal risk policy and structures for business units
- designing and reviewing processes for risk management
- co-coordinating the various functional activities which advise on risk management issues within the organization
- developing risk response processes, including contingency and business continuity programmes
- preparing reports on risk for the board and the stakeholders.

12.3.6.2 Role of Internal Audit

The role of Internal Audit is likely to differ from one organization to another. In practice, Internal Audit's role may include some or all of the following:

- focusing the internal audit work on the significant risks, as identified by management, and auditing the risk management processes across an organization.
- providing assurance on the management of risk
- providing active support and involvement in the risk management process
- facilitating risk identification/assessment and educating line staff in risk management and internal control
- coordinating risk reporting to the board, audit committee, etc.

In determining the most appropriate role for a particular organization, Internal Audit should ensure that the professional requirements for independence and objectivity are not breached.

12.3.6.3 Resources and Implementation

The resources required to implement the organization's risk management policy should be clearly established at each level of management and within each business unit.

In addition to other operational functions they may have, those involved in risk management should have their roles in coordinating risk management policy/strategy clearly defined. The same clear definition is also required for those involved in the audit and review of internal controls and facilitating the risk management process.

Risk management should be embedded within the organization through the strategy and budget processes. It should be highlighted in induction and all other training and development as well as within operational processes *e.g.*, product/service development projects.

12.4 RISK MANAGEMENT PROCESS

Risk Management (RM) is a process made up of the following steps: risk identification, risk analysis, risk assessment, risk planning, risk monitoring and risk mitigation. Risk management resolves the risk scenario through these steps as shown in Fig. 12.4.

Fig. 12.4 Risk management process

12.4.1 Risk Identification

The first step in risk management is identification of project risk factors. Risks cannot be analyzed or handled until they are identified and described in an understandable way. In this phase all possible risks are anticipated and a list of potential risks is prepared. The risk identification process not only identifies the risk but also determines attributes and communicates further to people in the team.

12.4.1.1 Definitions

Risk identification is an iterative process, involving the project team, management team, stakeholders and subject matter experts (if required).

OR

Identifying risks is the process of gaining an understanding of what potential unsatisfactory outcomes are associated with a particular project.

OR

Risk identification is a process to identify project, product and business risks.

OR

Risk identification is an organized, thorough approach to seeking out the real risks associated with a program.

OR

Risk identification is a systematic attempt to specify threats to the project plan (estimates, schedule, resource loading, etc).

12.4.1.2 Methods for Risk Identification

There are many methods for identifying risk. Any source of information that allows recognition of a potential problem can be used for risk identification. These include the following:

- Lifecycle cost and schedule analysis
- Requirements documents
- Prototyping and simulation models
- Lessons-learned files
- Trade studies and analyses
- Work breakdown structure (WBSs)
- Schedule networks

The identified risk can be categorized in the following categories.

1. *Technical risk*: This risk is related to the hardware or software technology used to develop the system.
2. *People risk*: It is related to the people who are developing the system.
3. *Tools*: Risks concerned with the CASE tools and other supporting tools,
4. *Requirement risk*: The risks related to change in environment leads to certain risks in the project.
5. *Organizational risk*: Related with the organizational environment
6. *Estimation risk*: This risk is associated with the estimation of the project and required resources.

12.4.2 Risk Analysis

Risk Analysis is also known as ***Risk Quantification***. Risk Quantification or risk analysis is the process of evaluating risks to assess the range of possible project outcomes. In other words we can define Risk Analysis (RA) as a process that defines activities and methods to estimate and evaluate risk.

The risk analysis process begins with list of risks obtained from the earlier process of risk identification. Each risk from this list is taken for estimation and evaluation. To act on this stem, the organization needs an evaluation criteria and the risk database.

First, the probability and consequence is estimated and then the Risk Exposure (RE) determined.

Risk exposure = probability × loss

It helps determine which opportunities and risks to respond to, which to accept, and which to ignore. The process of Risk Quantification involves determining an estimate of each risk's probability of occurrence, an estimate of its impact to the project, and potential strategies for reducing each risk. By being able to quantify a risk, project managers can prioritize risks and establish thresholds to determine which risks deserve the greatest attention. Techniques for quantifying risks include expected monetary value analysis, calculation of risk factors, PERT estimations, simulations, and expert judgement.

12.4.2.1 Purpose of Risk Analysis

The purpose of risk analysis is to discover the causes, effects, and magnitude of identified risks, and to develop and examine alternative options for managing the identified risks. Many tools, such as schedule network models and lifecycle cost models, can aid the analysis.

12.4.3 Risk Planning

Risk planning is the identification and scheduling of actions needed to reduce the level of risk within a project. In risk planning, a plan or a strategy is decided about handling of the risk. Risk planning differs depending on whether the risks are negative or positive.

There are four basic strategies for dealing with negative risk:

1. **Risk avoidance:** Some activities may be avoided altogether. If you are worried about crocodiles then do not go into the water. For example, given all the problems with developing software solutions from scratch, managers might decide to retain existing clerical methods, or to buy an off-the-shelf solution.
2. **Risk scceptance:** A Project team can accept the consequence of a possible risk.
3. **Risk transference:** Risk can be transferred to a third party. In this process, the risk is transferred to another person or organization. For example, you might expect the supplier to quote a higher figure to cover the risk that the project takes longer than the "average" expected time.

   On the other hand, a well established external organization might have productivity advantages as its developers are experienced in the type of development to be carried out. The need to compete with other software development specialists would also tend to drive prices down. For example, insurance can be purchase, or an outside supplier can be utilized to transfer risk, etc.

   Another example: Outsourcing some software development task to an outside agency.
4. **Risk mitigation:** It is also known as ***Risk Contingency***, which deals with the risk only if it occurs. For example, Staff absence due to illness is a risk that needs a contingency plan. A project manager might put another member of staff to complete that work. Another example could be like identifying alternative sources of funding if the financial backers stop supporting the project work

Similarly, there are four basic strategies for dealing with positive risk:

1. **Risk exploitation:** Investing project resources to increase the chances that an opportunity will occur

2. **Risk sharing:** Increasing the likelihood that an opportunity will occur by partnering, sharing any positive outcomes
3. **Risk enhancement:** Changing the size of the opportunity by maximizing the risk drivers
4. **Risk acceptance:** It is a passive acceptance of possible opportunity without investing any project resources.

12.4.4 Risk Monitoring

The Risk Monitoring is a process in which the identified risk is analyzed, its probability of occurrence is judged. It is then observed whether the effects of the risk can be changed or not. The risk monitoring is a continuous process and each risk must be discussed separately.

Following Table 12.5 shows the factors that must be considered while monitoring the risk:

Table 12.5 Risk types and their monitoring factors

Risk Type	*Monitoring Factors*
Technological Risks	• Required support technology may not be available
Organizational	• Reluctance from the senior management for necessary action • Organizational politics
People	• Poor relationship among the team members • Lack of required skill set • Lack of appreciation for the staff from senior authority
Requirement Risks	• Change in requirements • Customer complaints
Tools	• How to handle the tool is not known to the staff • Inefficient tool • Complaint about the CASE tool
Estimation	• Fail to meet the deadlines • Failure to clear the reported bugs or defects

12.4.5 Cost Benefit Analysis

Cost Benefit Analysis is defined as the process of comparison of alternative courses of action or alternative technical solutions for the purpose of determining which of the alternative would realize the greatest cost benefit. Cost Benefit Analysis (CBA) is the weighting-scale approach for decision-making. The benefits of a project include four types:

1. **Cost savings benefits:** Cost savings benefits lead to reductions in administrative and operational costs. For example, reduction in the size of the clerical staff used in the support of an administrative activity.
2. **Cost avoidance benefits:** Cost avoidance benefits are those which eliminate future administrative and operational costs. For example, no need to hire additional staff in future to handle an administrative activity.
3. **Improved service level benefits:** Improved service level benefits are those where the performance of a system is improved by a new computer based method. For example, registering a student in fifteen minutes rather than an hour.
4. **Improved information benefits:** Improved service level benefits are where computer based methods are used and one should use better information for decision-making. For example, a

system that reports the most improved fifty customers, as measured by an increase in sales is an improved information. This information makes it easier to provide better service to major customers.

12.4.5.1 *Applications of CBA*

1. Individual software engineers may use this technique to make their day to day decisions.
2. It is widely being taught in management courses also

12.4.6 Resolve Risk

Risk resolution process is defined where risk action plan forms the basis for resolving the risk using resolution tools and techniques and risk database. The objective of the process is to reduce the risk to level of acceptable risk. The output of the risk resolution process is list of acceptable Risk, Reduced rework and corrective actions.

Risk resolution activities are

- Act on the trigger.
- Execute the risk action plan
- Monitor the action plan and assess the new risk scenario.
- Control the risk exposure through action, and/or action on deviation.

The skills required to resolve risk are creativity and collaboration.

Effective implementation of risk action plan calls for generation of new and innovative ideas. This calls for creativity in the project team. Further, the risk action plan implementation is not straight linear action process by an individual.

It is a collaborative process, and not a process implementation in isolation. The fundamental risk resolution strategy is to reduce uncertainty, gain additional knowledge and draw upon the experience of others from internal and external sources.

Resolution of risk is not a structured method but a process where creativity and collaboration of team members are key success factors. Table 12.6 gives summary of the steps in the Risk Resolution Process (RRP).

Table 12.6 Steps in the Risk Resolution Process (RRP)

Process Steps	*Inputs*	*Outputs*
Identify Risk	Uncertainty, lack of knowledge, concerns, issues, risk database	List of Risk by category class, type and context
Analyze Risk and Assess	List of risks, risk database	Risk list with probability, loss, exposure, severity and prioritized risk list
Plan Risk for Resolution	Prioritized risk list determining resolution strategies, and its implementations	Risk actions plan *i.e.*, conversion of strategy into concrete steps for action
Track Risk	Risk status through MIS, risk thresholds.	Emergence of threshold deviation, triggers to act measures and metrics on to update risk database
Resolve Risk	Risk action plan and use of tools and techniques	Changing risk scenarios into acceptable risk and reduce risk exposure.

Thus, Effective risk management demands that the project manager and risk manager fully understand the project risks. A successful risk management process would also require a good knowledge and understanding of the business objectives of the project. During risk identification, a large volume of risks can be identified. Simply listing these risks or putting them in a spreadsheet or database does not provide the in-depth understanding of the identified risks necessary to allow a solid risk response planning task. The RBS provides the tool necessary to assist in identifying risks, analyzing risk, creating a successful risk response plan, and it provides a vehicle for "deep-dives" into the complexity of the risk. Using a hierarchical RBS, similar in its design to the WBS, allows the project and risk managers the opportunity to carefully align the risks in proper categories, using as deep an analysis as time and resources would permit.

13

Computer Aided Software Engineering

13.1 CASE AND ITS SCOPE

CASE stands for Computer Aided Software Engineering.

"CASE is a tool which aids a software engineer to maintain & develop software". The workshop for software engineering is called an Integrated Project Support Environment (IPSE) and the tool set that fills the workshop is called CASE.

CASE is a computer aided software engineering technology CASE is an automated support tool for the software engineers in any software engineering process.

Software engineering mainly includes the following processes:

(*i*) Translation of user needs into software requirements
(*ii*) Transaction of software requirements into design specification
(*iii*) Implementation of design into code
(*iv*) Testing of the code
(*v*) Documentation.

CASE technology provides software process support by automating some process activities and by providing information about the software, which is being developed. Examples of activities, which can be automated using CASE, include:

1. The development of graphical system models as part of the requirements specification or the software design.
2. Understanding a design using a data dictionary, which holds information about the entities and relations in a design.
3. The generation of user interfaces from a graphical interface description, which is created interactively by the user.
4. Program debugging through the provision of information about an executing program.
5. The automated translation of programs from an old version of a programming language such as COBOL to a more recent version.

13.2 LEVELS OF CASE

There are three different levels of CASE technology:

1. **Production Process Support Technology:** This includes support for process activities such as specification, design, implementation, testing and so on.
2. **Process Management and Technology:** This include tool to support process modeling and process management. These tools are used for specific support activities.
3. **Meta-CASE Technology:** Meta-CASE tools are generators, which are used to create production process management support tools.

13.3 ARCHITECTURE OF CASE ENVIRONMENT

The architecture of CASE environment is illustrated in the Fig. 13.1.

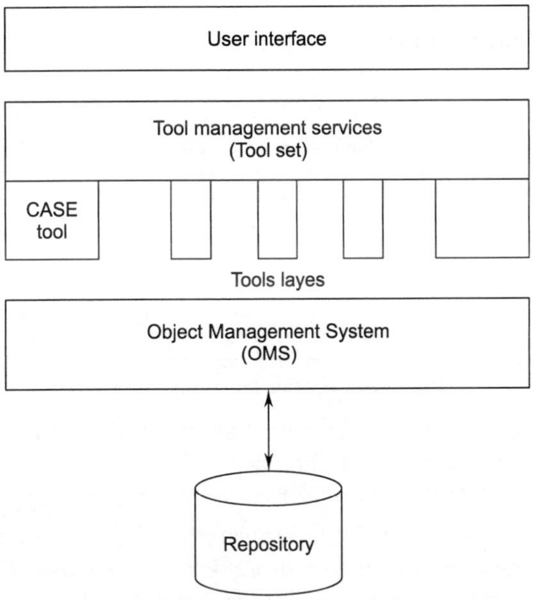

Fig. 13.1 Architecture of case environment

The important components of a modern CASE environment are the user interface, the Tools Management System (Tools set), the Object Management System (OMS) and the repository. These various components are discussed as under:

1. **User Interface:** It provides a consistent framework for accessing different tools; thus making it easier for the user to interact with different tools and reduces learning time of how the different tools are used.
2. **Tools Management Services (Tools Set):** The tools set section holds the different types of improved quality tools. The tools layer incorporates a set of tools management services with the CASE tool themselves. Tools Management Service (TMS) control the behavior of tools within the environment. If multitasking is used during the execution of one or more tools, TMS performs multitask synchronization and communication, coordinates the flow of information from the repository and object management system into the tools, accomplishes security and auditing functions, and collects metrics on tool usage.

3. **Object Management System (OMS):** The object management system maps these (specification design, text data, project plan etc.) logical entities into the underlying storage management system *i.e.*, repository.

   Working in conjunction with the CASE repository, the OML provides integration services a set of standard modules that couple tools with the repository. In addition, the OML provides configuration management services by enabling the identification of all configuration objects performing version control, and providing support for change control, audits and status accounting.
4. **Repository:** It is the CASE database and the access control functions that enable the OMS to interact with the database. The word CASE repository is referred in different ways such as project database, IPSE database, data dictionary, CASE database and so on.

13.4 BUILDING BLOCKS FOR CASE

The building blocks for CASE are illustrated in Fig. 13.2:

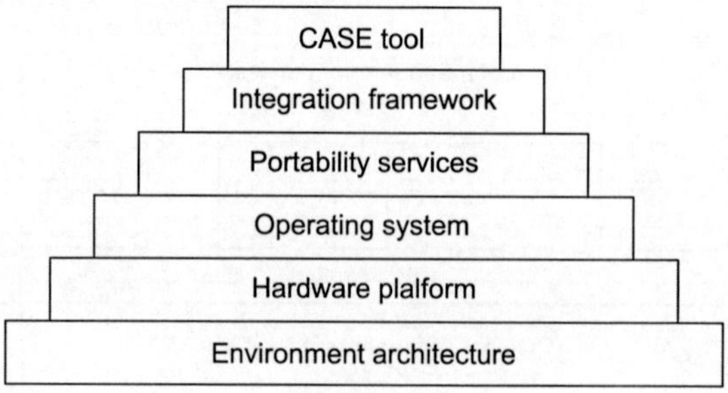

Fig. 13.2 CASE building blocks

1. **Environment Architecture:** The environment architecture, composed of the hardware platform & operating system support including networking and database management software, lays the groundwork for CASE but the CASE environment itself demands other building blocks.
2. **Portability Services:** A set of portability service provides a bridge between CASE tools and their integration framework and the environment architecture. These portability services allow the CASE tools and their integration framework to migrate across different hardware platforms and operating systems without significant adaptive maintenance.
3. **Integration Framework:** It is a collection of specialized programs that enables individual CASE tools to communicate with one another, to create a project database.
4. **CASE Tools:** CASE Tools are used to assist software engineering activities (like analysis modeling, code generation etc.) either communicating with other tools, project database (integrated CASE environment) or as point solutions.

13.5 CASE SUPPORT IN SOFTWARE LIFE CYCLE

There are various types of support that CASE provides during the different phases of a software life cycle which are discussed as follows:

1. **Prototyping Support:** The prototyping is useful to understand the requirements of complex software products, to market new ideas and so on. The prototyping CASE tools requirements are as follows:

(i) Define user interaction

(ii) Define the system control flow

(iii) Store and retrieve data required by the system

(iv) Incorporate some processing logic.

Few features, which are supported by prototyping tools, are:

1. Main use of prototyping CASE tool is developing Graphical User Interface (GUI) development. The user should be allowed to define all data entry forms, menus and control.
2. Integrate well with the data dictionary of a CASE environment.
3. It should be able to integrate with the external user-defined modules written in high-level languages.
4. The user should be able to define the sequence of states through which a created prototype can run.
5. The prototype should support mock up run of the actual system and management of the input and output data.

2. **Structured Analysis and Design:** A CASE tool should support one or more of the structured analysis and design techniques. It should also support making of the fairly complex diagrams and preferably through a hierarchy of levels. The tool must also check the incompleteness, inconsis-tencies and anomalies across the design and analysis through all levels of analysis hierarchy.

   Analysis and design tools enable a software engineer to create models of the system to be built. The models contain a representation of data, function, and behavior (at the analysis level) and characterizations of data, architectural, component level, and interface design. By performing consistency and validity checking on the models, analysis and design tools provide a software engineer with some degree of insight into the analysis representation and help to eliminate errors before they propagate into the design, or worse, into implementation itself.

3. **Code Generation:** A support expected from a CASE tool during the code generation phase comprises the following:

   (i) The CASE tool should support generation of module skeletons or templates in one or more popular programming languages.

   (ii) The tool should generate records, structures, class definitions automatically from the contents of the data dictionary in one or more popular programming languages.

   (iii) It should be able to generate database tables for relational database mgmt system.

   (iv) The tools should generate code for user interface from prototype definitions for X-Windows and MS Window based applications.

4. **Test CASE Generator:** The CASE tool for test case generator should have following features:
   - It should support both design and requirement testing.
   - It should generate test set reports in ASCII format, which can be directly imported into the test plan document.

Under testing phase, Test management tools are used to control and coordinate software testing for each of the major testing steps. Testing tools manage and coordinate regression testing, perform comparisons that ascertain differences between actual and expected output, and conduct batch testing of programs with interactive human/computer interfaces. In addition to the functions noted, many test management tools also serve as generic test drivers. A test driver reads one or more test cases from a testing file, formats the test data to conform to the needs of the software under test, and then invokes the software to be tested.

13.6 OBJECTIVE OF CASE

1. **Improve Productivity:** Most organizations use CASE to increase the speeds with which systems are designed and developed. Imagine the difficulties; the carpenters would face without hammers and saws. Tools increase the analysts' productivity by reducing the time needed to document, analyze, and construct information system.
2. **Improve Information System Quality:** When tools improve processes, they usually improve the results as well.
   - Ease and improve the testing process through the use of automated checking.
   - Improve the integration of development activities via common methodologies.
   - Improve the quality and completeness of documentation.
   - Help standardize the development process
   - Improve the management of the project
   - Simplify program maintenance
   - Promote reversibility of modules and documentation
   - Shortens the overall construction process
   - Improve software portability across environments
   - Through reverse engineering and re-engineering, CASE products extend the file of existing systems.

   Despite the various driving forces (objectives) for the adoption of CASE, there are many resisting forces also that preclude many organizations from making investment in CASE.
3. **Improve Effectiveness:** Effectiveness means doing the right task (*i.e.*, deciding the best task to perform to achieve the desired result). Tools can suggest procedures (the right way) to approach a task. Identifying user requirements, stating them in an understandable form, and communicating them to all interested parties can be an effective development process compared to moving quickly into coding.
4. **Organizations Reject CASE Because**
   - The start-up cost of purchasing and using CASE
   - The high cost of training personnel
   - The big benefits of using CASE come in the late stages of the SDLC
   - CASE often lengthens the duration of early stage of the project
   - CASE tools cannot easily share information between tools
   - Lack of methodology standards within organizations, CASE products forces analysts to follow a specific methodology for system development
   - Lack of confidence in CASE products
   - IS personnel view CASE as a threat to their job security.

Despite these issues, in long-term, CASE is very good. The functionality of CASE tools is increasing and the costs are coming down. During the next several years, CASE technologies and the market for CASE will begin to mature.

13.7 CASE REPOSITORY

A CASE repository is a system developer database. Synonyms include dictionary and encyclopedia. It is a place where developers can store system models, detailed descriptions and specifications, and other products of system development.

Analysts use CASE repositories for five important reasons:

- To manage the details in large systems
- To communicate a common meaning for all system elements
- To document the features of the system
- To facilitate analysis of the details in order to evaluate characteristics and determine where system changes should be made.
- To locate errors and omissions in the system

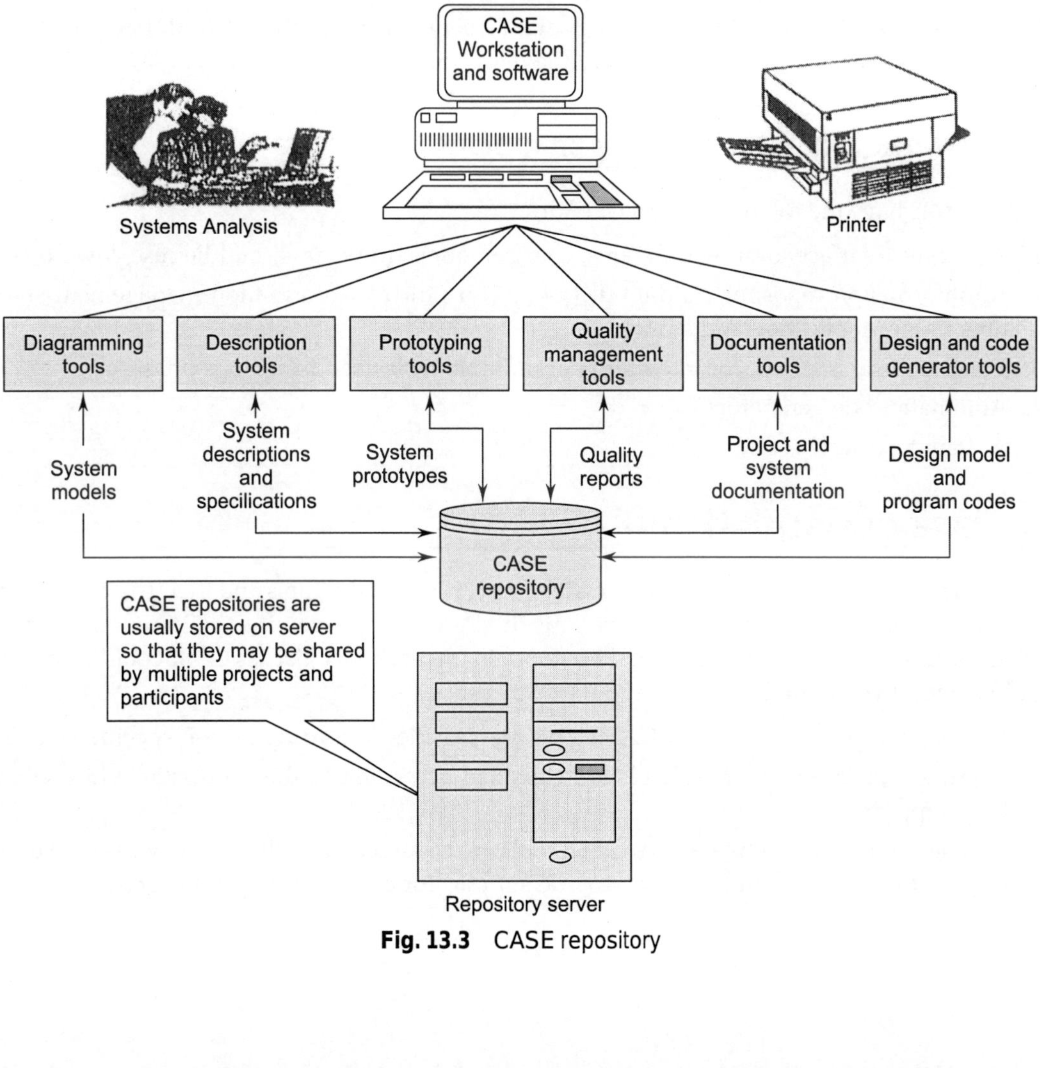

Fig. 13.3 CASE repository

To limit the amount of narrative needed to describe relationships between data items and at the same time to show the structural relationship clearly, analysts often use formal notation in data dictionary, a component of CASE repository.

Data dictionary can be developed manually or using automated systems. Automated systems offer the advantage of automatically producing data element, data structure, and process listings; they also perform cross-reference checking and error detection. The data dictionary is a repository of all data definitions for all organizational applications and is used to manage and control access to the information repository, another component of CASE repository. Information repository provides automated tools used to manage and control access to business information and application portfolio.

CASE repository is an idea central to I-CASE. Integrated-CASE tools rely on common terminology, notations and methods for systems development across all tools. Within an I-CASE environment, all diagrams, forms, reports and programs can be automatically updated by the single change to the data-dictionary definition. **Besides specific tool integration, there are two additional advantages of using a comprehensive CASE repository that relate to project management and reusability.** The CASE repository provides a wealth of information to the project manager and allows the manger to exert an appropriate amount of control on the project. If all organizational systems were created using CASE technology with a common repository, it would be possible to reuse significant portions of prior systems in the development of new ones.

13.8 CHARACTERISTICS OF CASE TOOLS

All CASE tools have the following characteristics:

1. A graphic interface to draw diagrams, charts, models (uppercase, middle case, lowercase)
2. An information repository, a data dictionary for efficient information management selection, usage, application and storage
3. Common user interface for integration of multiple tools used in various phase
4. Automatic code generators
5. Automatic testing tools.

13.9 CASE CLASSIFICATION

CASE classifications help us understand the different types of CASE tools and their role in supporting software process activities. There are various different ways of classifying CASE tools, each of which gives us a different perspective on these tools. In this section, I discuss CASE tools from three of these perspectives, namely:

1. A functional perspective where CASE tools are classified according to their specific function.
2. A process perspective where tools are classified according to the process activities which they support.
3. An integration perspective where CASE tools are classified according to how they are organized into integrated units which provide support for one or more process activities.

13.9.1 List of Case Tools

Application	*Case Tool*	*Purpose of Tool*
1. Planning	Excel spreadsheet, MS-Project, PERT/CPM Network, Estimation tools	Functional Application: Planning, scheduling, control
2. Editing	Diagram editors, Text editors, Word Processors	Speed and Efficiency
3. Testing	Test Data Generators, File Comparators	Speed and Efficiency
4. Prototyping	High level Modeling language , User Interface Generators	Confirmation and Certification of RDD and SRS
5. Documentation	Report Generators, Publishing imaging, PPT presentation	Faster structural documentation with quality of presentation
6. Programming and Language Processing Integration	Program Generators, Code Generators, Compilers, Interpreters Interface, connectivity	Programming of high quality with no errors, System Integration
7. Templates	----------------	Guided Systematic development
8. Re-engineering tools	Cross reference systems, program re-structuring systems	Reverse-engineering to find structure, design and design information
9. Program analysis tool	Cross reference generators Static analyzers, dynamic analyzers	Analyses risks, functions, features

13.10 CATEGORIES OF CASE TOOLS

The schematic diagram of CASE tools is drawn below in Fig. 13.4:

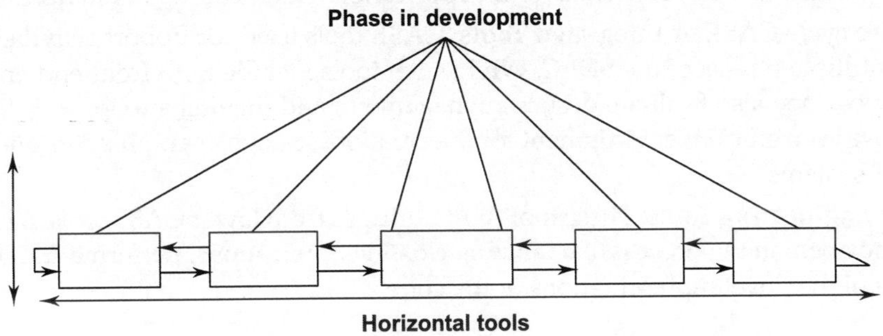

Fig. 13.4 Categories of CASE tools

Smith and Oman have defined CASE tools which are divided into the following two categories.

1. Vertical CASE tools
2. Horizontal CASE tools

1. **Vertical Case Tools:** Vertical CASE tools provide support for certain activities within a single phase of the software life cycle.

   There are two subcategories of vertical CASE tools

   (*i*) **First category:** It is the set of tools that are within one phase of life cycle. These tools are important so that development in each phase can be as quick as possible.

(*ii*) **Second category:** It is a tool that is used in more than one phase, but does not support moving from one phase to the next. These tools ensure that the developer does move on the next phase as appropriate.

2. **Horizontal CASE Tools:** These tools support automated transfer of information between the phases of a life cycle. These tools include project management, configuration management tools and integration services.

The above two categories of CASE tools can further be broken down into the following:

1. **Upper CASE Tools/Front-end CASE Tools:** CASE tools designed to support the analysis and design phases of SDLC. All the analysis, design and specification tools are front-end tools. These tools also include computer-aided diagramming tools oriented towards a particular programming design methodology, more recently including object-oriented design.

   The general types of upper CASE tools are listed below:
   - **Diagramming tools:** Diagramming tools enable system process, data and control structures to be represented graphically. They strongly support analysis and documentation of application requirements.
   - **Form and report generator tools:** They support the creation of system forms and reports in order to show how systems will "look and feel" to users.
   - **Analysis tools:** Analysis tools enable automatic checking for incomplete, inconsistent, or incorrect specifications in diagrams, forms and reports.
2. **Lower CASE or Back-End Tools:** CASE tools designed to support the implementation and maintenance phases of SDLC. All the generator, translation and testing tools are back-end tools.

   The general types of Lower CASE tools are:
   - **Code generators:** Code generators automate the preparation of computer software. Code generation is not yet perfect. Thus, the best generator will produce approximately 75 percent of the source code for an application. Hand coding is still necessary.
3. **Cross life cycle CASE or Integrated Tools:** CASE tools used to support activities that occur across multiple phases of the SDLC. While such tools include both front-end and back-end capabilities, they also facilitate design, management, and maintenance of code. In addition, they provide an efficient environment for the creation, storage, manipulation, and documentation of systems.
4. **Reverse Engineering Tools:** These tools build bridges from lower CASE tools to upper CASE tools. They help in the process of analyzing existing applications, performa & database code to create higher level representations of the code.

13.11 ADVANTAGES OF CASE

The major benefits of using CASE tools include the following:

1. Improved productivity
2. Better documentation
3. Improved accuracy
4. Intangible benefits
5. Improved quality
6. Reduced lifetime maintenance
7. Opportunity to non-programmers

8. Reduced cost of software
9. Produce high quality and consistent documents
10. Impact on the style of a working of company
11. Reduce the drudgery in a software engineer's work
12. Increase speed of processing
13. Easy to program software
14. Improved co-ordination among staff members who are working on a large software project
15. An increase in project control through better planning, monitoring and communication.

13.12 DISADVANTAGES OF CASE

1. Purchasing of case tools is not an easy task. Its cost is very high. Due to this reason small software development firm do not invest in case tools.
2. **Learning Curve:** In general cases programmer productivity may fall in initial phase of implementation as user need time to learn this technology.
3. **Tool Mix:** It is important to make proper selection of case tools to get maximum benefit from the case tools, so wrong selection may lead to wrong result.

INDEX

T

U

V

W